DR FRANZ HILDEBRANDT

Mr Valiant-for-Truth

Then said Mr Valiant-for-Truth:

I am going to my fathers, and though with great difficulty I am got
hither, yet now I do not regret me of all the trouble I have been at
to arrive where I am. My sword I give to him that shall succeed me
in my pilgrimage and my courage and skill to him that shall get it.
My marks and scars I carry with me to be a witness for me that I
have fought His battles who now will be my Rewarder.

John Bunyan
The Pilgrim's Progress

To Nancy Hildebrandt

Professor Dr Eberhard Bethge writes:

I am very happy that finally there is a biography about Franz Hildebrandt. Without the existence of this spirited, upright and constant friend of Bonhoeffer in these especially important years one cannot have and know Dietrich Bonhoeffer ...

All this last half century I have felt that actually one of us would fulfil the task of writing this biography, but somehow this did not happen. So I am relieved that friends from the Anglo-American side, under the eyes of Nancy Hildebrandt, have undertaken and finished the work.

DR FRANZ HILDEBRANDT

Mr Valiant-for-Truth

Amos S. Cresswell
and Maxwell G. Tow

First published in 2000
by

Gracewing
2 Southern Avenue
Leominster
Herefordshire
HR6 0QF

UK ISBN 0 85244 322 6

Typeset by Action Publishing Technology Ltd,
Gloucester GL1 1SP

Printed in England by
MPG Books Ltd,
Bodmin PL31 1EG

CONTENTS

ACKNOWLEDGEMENTS

To Nancy Hildebrandt for her enthusiasm, encouragement and warm hospitality whenever we were in Edinburgh; to her children David, Ruth and Esther for helpful conversations – and to them all for the invitation to take up this task.

To Nancy's unpublished account of her life with Franz *No Winter* – our starting point.

To the National Library of Scotland, the Cambridge Records Office, *The Times* and the *Methodist Recorder*, to Dr Michael Ryan and Dr Kenneth Rowe of Drew University, and Dr Robert Simpson of the United Methodist Archives; all gave help readily. To the Electoral Reform Society for a photocopy of a 1932 voting paper.

To the Revd Professor C. Kingsley Barrett of Durham for many conversations and valuable suggestions drawn from his close friendship with Franz, for reading through the whole manuscript and for writing the Foreword, a sign of his personal friendship.

To the many, many friends who have shared memories in conversation, letters and telephone calls, especially (in the UK) Ella Wardrop, the Revd Dr Oliver Beckerlegge, the Revd Tom Hall, the Revd Roy Manson and the Revd Dr Henry Sefton; and (in the USA) the numerous Drew alumni including John Goodell, Max Case, Bill Lewis, Skip Smith, Stanley Long and John Painter.

To Dr Holger Roggelin for putting his thesis at our disposal so willingly, and to Judge Jan Niemoeller, Professor Eberhard Bethge and Marianne Leibholtz for their help and encouragement; and to other German friends who shared their experiences.

To the Revd William Benson for help so freely given. To Geri Tow for making sense of and typing almost illegible handwriting;

to Stephen Cresswell for putting his office and home facilities at our service and giving so much time to correcting, re-arranging the manuscript and putting it on disc (and to son David who stood in when his father was not well 'to help you out, Grandad!); to Evelyn Cresswell who has driven the car so many miles in the UK and Germany, has given constant help and has also compiled the index of names.

Without these the book could not have been written.

Amos S. Cresswell
Maxwell G. Tow

FOREWORD

Franz Hildebrandt was a great and good man. To tell the story of his life, bringing out the theological convictions that gave it both its direction and its strength, was a demanding task, and we must be grateful to Amos Cresswell and Max Tow for undertaking it.

My own acquaintance with Franz began about 60 years ago when he lectured at Wesley House, Cambridge, on the Lutheran inheritance in English Christianity, and especially in Methodism. They were fascinating lectures, an early sketch, I think, of the book *From Luther to Wesley*, the most accessible of his books, and one I should like to see in the hands of every Methodist preacher – and indeed of all preachers. As the title suggests, it is an implicit autobiography. It was in Luther first that Franz discovered the foundations of Christianity: grace, faith, Scripture, all focused upon the incarnate Word; and it was in Wesley that he rediscovered them. What distinguished him from many was the recognition that these principles are the determinative criteria not only of Christian belief but of everything else, of our ethics, including our politics, of church order and of liturgy.

From its early beginnings our friendship developed through the years. In one sense, I suppose, we moved in opposite directions: he moved on from Luther to Wesley, I moved back from Wesley to Luther. There was difference enough to add savour to every conversation, but a profound unity. For Franz's friendship, and for all that I learned from him, I am deeply grateful; and I hope this book will lead many to share my indebtedness.

The Revd Professor Dr C. K. Barrett MA., DD., FBA.
Emeritus Professor of Theology
University of Durham

CHAPTER 1

MEETING THE MAN

Then said Mr. *Great-heart*, What art thou? The man made answer, saying, I am one whose name is *Valiant-for-Truth*. I am a Pilgrim, and I am going to the Celestial City.

John Bunyan, *The Pilgrim's Progress*

At the end of September 1950, after a precollegiate year serving as a minister in the Clitheroe circuit (N. Lancs.) I went to Wesley House, Cambridge, to read theology in the University as part of my ministerial training. In Cambridge, I soon heard of the German-born, one time refugee from Hitler, now a Methodist minister, the Revd Dr Franz Hildebrandt. He was not minister of 'Wesley', the church nearest our college, which students usually attended, but, from time to time, as happens in UK circuits, he conducted worship and preached there. We had many good preachers in Cambridge then and, as we were students for whom preaching was a vital tool, we went to hear them to learn from them. We were listening to preaching style, theological argument, sermon construction, presentation and use of illustration.

It was the second Sunday in Advent, the evening service, December 1950, a Sunday when I was not out on a preaching appointment as we students often were, and so with some other 'free souls' I went to Wesley. The preacher was Franz Hildebrandt, a slight, slim figure with greying hair. The traces of German background in his voice, traces which never left him, added fascination as he spoke. He preached a sermon full of good sound Reformation theology, on the coming of Christ. All of it came up to my expectations. Then, I remember, he concluded by quoting from Charles Wesley. The quotation was so apt and so well delivered that I felt something like an electric shock go through my body. It was majestic. I had loved Wesley's hymns for years. I possessed my great grandfather's copy. I had read both Bernard Manning and Henry Bett and my mind was receptive to their beauty.

Now I was hearing one who was a Methodist because of Charles Wesley's hymns, one to whom they were so dear that he was to become a world expert on them. He was showing us as he quoted, just how theology should be preached:

> Knees and hearts to him we bow
> Of our flesh and of our bone
> Jesus is our brother now
> And God (here he paused) ... is all our own.

On that evening I did not know that in the years to come Franz Hildebrandt would become a beloved friend from whom I should learn so much. All I know is that if in any of my sermons at any time I have done for anyone what Franz Hildebrandt did for me that night, then I am very thankful.

In the 1960s, particularly after the 1963 Methodist Conference at Preston, Methodism and the Church of England were discussing the 'Conversations' report, the scheme for uniting the churches. I had been unhappy about the 'Interim' report which had been published a few years earlier. The final report in no way allayed my unease and I saw that this unease was captured and expounded by much of what was said in the 'Dissentient' report, written and signed by four of the team of twelve Methodist representatives. Their scholarship and integrity assured me that my unease was neither folly nor ill-founded. Opinion was divided in the church. Men and women of great scholarship and integrity supported each side.

Franz Hildebrandt was at that time a professor at Drew University in the United States. He regularly returned to the UK, where he had a home in Edinburgh. He soon became involved in these discussions. He too looked carefully and critically at the text of the document. To him the main question was ordination. The so-called Service of Reconciliation was clearly an ordination of Methodist ministers into the Church of England and thus challenged the validity of his own ordination.

A group of us who were 'dissentients' began to meet, feeling that the leaders and organization of our church were pressing for acceptance of the report. We tried to present clear arguments against acceptance and when in the UK, Franz joined us. It was through these meetings that I as a young minister came to know him and to correspond with him – and I learned so much from him. In 1965 at the Plymouth Conference, Methodism gave provisional acceptance to the report – to be confirmed or not after a further report.

In 1968 Franz resigned from the Methodist ministry. We who knew him well were sad. Later I was shown, confidentially, his letter of resignation. A particular incident had brought things to a head. He felt his stance on the 'Conversations' sparked it off.* He felt let down by the Church he loved.

In 1983 I became President of the Methodist Conference of the UK. The Sunday morning service of the conference was broadcast nationwide on radio. By the next available mailing I had a lovely letter from Franz. He had listened and his letter was full of encouragement and praise. I was thrilled. The letter came at the right time. I replied, telling him I would be in Edinburgh in September. He said he would try to be there.

When I was in Edinburgh, in Leith, on a Monday evening, I preached on Luther's Catechism, *Iron Rations in a Dark Age*. After the service I went to the door to meet the people and almost first out of the church was Franz. He held out his arms and hugged me – a very emotional act for a dour German and an adopted Scot:

> I said, 'Franz, I must have been crazy.'
> He asked, 'Why?'
> I continued, 'Fancy preaching on Luther with you a Luther expert in my congregation.'
> 'It was a good sermon,' he replied. 'You must preach it again.' And I have done.[†]

⊕

In 1953 Franz Hildebrandt accepted a teaching appointment at Drew University Theological School in Madison, New Jersey. For

---

*See ch. 16 for a detailed discussion of the Conversations.
[†]In these first paragraphs, Amos Cresswell recalls his earliest memories of Franz Hildebrandt. (The sermon is now published in *I've Told You Twice*.)

several generations of Drew students he was a challenging teacher and a unique model for ministry. His distinctly European appearance and manner were enough to inflict a newly arrived seminarian with a sense of wonderment. It was further reported that he had been a friend of Dietrich Bonhoeffer, an assistant to Martin Niemoeller and an early and unrelenting foe of Adolf Hitler. Of more direct concern to us first year students was his reputation as a rigorously organized lecturer, who had little patience with those who didn't know their Bibles and dared to admit their ignorance of Charles Wesley's hymns. It was even reported that he began his classes on the theology of the Wesleys by sitting down at the piano and leading the students in one of his favourite Wesley hymns.

Simply to encounter him walking across campus could be a daunting experience. He was tall, of medium build, walked with a measured gait, slightly bent, slightly rumpled, his clerical collar looking just a bit too large for his neck. His face bore an inscrutable expression, leaving one to surmise he was deeply engaged in unravelling some knotty theological problem. If one mustered the courage to greet him, he would respond with a smile and a 'Hello' that revealed genuine warmth and humanity.

For some students, myself included, Franz Hildebrandt became a mentor, friend and father in God. My encounter with the venerable Drew professor was the beginning of a lifelong friendship, due, in part, to a single circumstance. While still a student, I accepted a ministerial appointment to Christ Methodist Church, Paterson, New Jersey, in the former Newark Conference. I became the first non-German speaking pastor to serve the small German and Swiss immigrant congregation in Paterson's crumbling Northside. I needed all the help I could get and Dr Hildebrandt (it would not have occurred to me to address him any other way) was kind enough to record on tape for me to practice the liturgy, prayers and scripture passages which I must read in the services – albeit without always understanding what I was so diligently trying to pronounce correctly.

More importantly, on Sundays when he was free, he was willingly prevailed upon to preach at the German service and sometimes at the later English service as well. After services he always insisted on accompanying me on hospital visits where his ability to empathize with a person's suffering and fear was abundantly clear. He read from the Psalms and his heartfelt prayers unfailingly brought hope and comfort. When his family was in Edinburgh, he would gladly come to the parsonage for Sunday dinner , delighting in my wife Geri's good cooking and company, and frolicking with our children. The afternoon often ended with the two of us in opposing chairs in front of the fire, our eyes closing and our chins gradually drooping into our respective sections of the *New York Times.*

Following his resignation from Drew in the autumn of 1967, he preached for the last time in the US at Christ Church, Paterson on 10 December. Although we exchanged letters occasionally, we didn't see each other again for ten years, until Geri and I visited Edinburgh in 1977. In 1981, when I was pastor of Morrow Memorial United Methodist Church in Maplewood, New Jersey, I tried mightily to get Franz to come over for a week to be our Theologian-in-Residence during Lent. He clearly wanted to do it, but in the end, concern for his health, in what he described as his 'post-geriatric condition,' kept him from coming. I was not to see him again. In January 1986, I flew to Edinburgh and participated in his memorial service. Characteristically, he wanted no eulogies – only scripture and his beloved Charles Wesley hymns.*

For Franz Hildebrandt, faithful ministry began, continued and ended with the Word of God. Without that Word there was no credible witness, no faithful church and no lasting Christian impact on the world. This is his story. It is not written as a classi-cal biography, although great care has been taken to check the records. It is an account written by two men who knew him first in awe and then in friendship and love. It is a story about a friend who gave out warmth, about one who fought for what he saw was right before God. We came to love him for what he was because of what he was. Many stories about him appear in this book. Through them and often through his own words we aim to let the reader meet him and come to know, as we knew, one who fought the Lord's battles who now is his Redeemer. We can only say it is the story of Mr Valiant-for-Truth.

*Maxwell Tow recalls his early memories of Franz Hildebrandt.

CHAPTER 2

GERMANY – A CONFIDENT AND TROUBLED NATION

Germany, when Franz Hildebrandt was born, was a powerful nation, vastly different from today, still living in the aura of the great 'Iron Chancellor', Otto von Bismarck.

Since then there have been two world wars. Germany could be said to have been the cause of both. In both wars Germany was defeated and had to struggle to recover. In 1909 Kaiser Wilhelm II was head of state. He was an autocrat. In 1888 at the age of 29 he became Emperor. In 1890 he dismissed the ageing Bismarck: 'Germany can only have one ruler and I am he.' He used the position built up by Bismarck to develop alliances. With his own appointees in office to support his ideas, he built up the naval and land strength of the military. The German people were stimulated into believing that they were invincible. The Kaiser had big ideas. His father had once commented to Bismarck that there was a danger in allowing his son to be too involved with foreign affairs. There was, however, no one prepared to restrain him.

He had always kept a fond relationship with his grandmother Victoria, Queen of England. Indeed during her reign, in 1889, he had been made a British admiral and enjoyed wearing his admiral's uniform. He was allowed to run up his flag as a British admiral on the British battleship, *Dreadnought*, when he visited his cousin, later George V, in 1906. He had an uneasy relationship with his uncle, King Edward VII, and therefore saw little reason for holding Great Britain in high esteem.

The Boer War in South Africa at the turn of the century

reminded all European countries that, much as they might be sympathetic to the cause of the Boers, without naval power to match that of Great Britain, they were powerless. So, when his own appointed counsellors advised him to build up his navy, the Kaiser was happy. A large navy, comparable in size and weight of fire-power with the British Navy, would put Germany, already possessed of the strongest army in Europe, clearly at the head in Europe.

In 1906 Wilhelm had been impressed with the *Dreadnought* and wanted some battleships like it. This attitude pleased Admiral Tirpitz who approved of his warlike stance but the Kaiser did not appear to be aware that in building up his navy he was giving a direct challenge to Great Britain. The disenchantment which his grandmother had felt with him in her later years was paralleled by a watchfulness in Britain and in other nations towards all he was doing. A series of alliances (Austria 1879, Italy 1882 and an 'on-off relationship' with Russia) had strengthened the influence of Germany and the Austria-Hungary empire, which dominated central Europe. France and Great Britain, however, were alert and had an understanding, the Entente Cordiale. Other nations began to look for alliances with their weather eye on Germany.

In the realm of scholarship Germany was also progressing. Under Bismarck German universities had become the best known for scholarship and research. They had produced scholars outstanding in the arts (history, philosophy, theology), music and the sciences. It has been said that no people in Europe read more seriously or more widely. It was in the time of the Kaiser that the great Professor Adolf von Harnack rose to his peak in theology and began to influence a whole generation. In every area of life Germany was looking to be the leader, either consciously or subconsciously. Yet in spite of all the philosophy and learning, Germany was not a democratic nation. Bismarck had not been a lover of democracy, neither was Kaiser Wilhelm II. But the German people seemed content.

Scholarship in any field began to look to Germany for a lead. (In one sense this has not changed. In the post-1945 period there was a joke that the reason the USA was ahead of Russia in the nuclear arms race was that the USA had captured better German scientists than had the Russians!) At home and abroad Germans with academic gifts happily pursued their scholarship.

Historians make the point that this new developing Germany was very conscious of its strength and, believing it was so strong, saw no dangers. There were, however, politicians in different countries who did see danger and sensed that war was near. It is recorded that when Lord Haldane, the British Secretary of State for War, dropped a hint that Britain would be unhappy with a repeat of the Franco-Prussian War, the Kaiser was angry and stated that no one would ever tell him what he should do. This gave a clear message.

There was a ferment in Germany in some places against totalitarian ideas. Rosa Luxemburg (1870–1919) was a stirring speaker within the socialist movement and was working and speaking in Germany from 1898. She was frequently in prison. Add to this the fact that the Kaiser was strongly anti-Semitic; that he was full of violent ideas of ways to handle strikers or dissension and a picture emerges within which there were several fuses to explosive material which were awaiting a match to be struck.

It seems strange that, with the vast background of scholarship especially in philosophy and the classics of Greek and Roman thought, no one pointed out to Kaiser Wilhelm II the point made by the Greek philosopher Plato (*Republic*, Book I) that the unjust man always overreaches himself. Bismarck seemed to have sensed this and he had halted his advance.

It was into this Germany that, in 1909, Franz Hildebrandt was born. Before he was ten years old Germany had risen higher and then fallen very low. Terrible chaos resulted from the defeat in 1918. The Kaiser fled to Holland for refuge in a neutral country. The socialists, Rosa Luxemburg and Karl Liebknecht, always Marxist, constituted themselves as the German Communist Party but later in 1919 both these leaders were murdered. The 'stab in the back' theory of why Germany lost the war, namely that the soldiers at the front were let down by those in power at home, was fostered by some leaders and ex-soldiers. Various groups of fanatics were raising opposition to the young Republic.

The Weimar Republic did not receive the help it needed to survive. A defeated Germany needed support but the attempt to create a democracy gave openings and opportunities to enemies of democracy. The country also had severe economic problems with inflation galloping away. Ordinary folk who had worked hard to build up some small savings lost everything. Following

A five thousand German marks banknote, 1922.
Present day value to collectors £1.50.

A one million German marks banknote, 1923.
Present day value to collectors £1.50.

President Friedrich Ebert, Field Marshal Paul von Hindenburg tried to hold the democratic line – to the surprise of some who saw him as a natural right-winger. However, right-wing parties like the National Socialists were causing trouble for the infant democracy. This was also true of the groups on the left.

Adolf Hitler, an ex-soldier, had joined the National Socialist German Workers Party on the suggestion of the leader of the band of the *Freikorps*, the auxiliary soldiers of the Weimar Republic to which he belonged. Before long he began to give lectures on the Versailles treaty and the 'stab in the back' and he soon became a leader. He wrote pamphlets and, while imprisoned in 1924, he began to write *Mein Kampf*. Here his policy was laid down, though few at home and fewer abroad investigated him seriously. Those who did listen were swept away by his blandishments. The world should have listened and read and remembered. In some ways he was an echo of the Kaiser with his emphasis on power, strength and autocracy. His anti-Semitism, much stronger and more violently expressed, followed the Kaiser too. He too desired a large and powerful German Empire. In an official Nazi party commentary in 1920 he said: 'We demand a union of all Germans to form a Great Germany' – and he listed Sudetenland, Alsace-Lorraine, Poland and Austria as places where Germans were living who could and should belong together:

'There is no such thing as coming to an understanding with the Jews.' (*Mein Kampf*)

'We are not on principle a parliamentary party. That would be a contradiction of our whole outlook. We are a parliamentary party by compulsion, under constraint and that compulsion is the constitution.' (speech, 1930)

The troubled times were a fertile breeding ground for one who would readily make promises to gain votes. Hitler had clearly marked out his path.

The ideas of Bismarck and Kaiser Wilhelm II which lived in Hitler's speeches prompted some of his lackeys to describe him as 'greater than Bismarck.' The Communists on the other side of the political spectrum were also flexing their muscles. The nation of

Germany was looking for a way of salvation and rehabilitation. To whom could they turn?

The events surrounding the Beer Hall Putsch in Munich in November 1923 were often regarded by some of the Nazis as *the* crucial time for their party. The Nazis made an attempt to take control of the city but the police gained the upper hand. Hitler and others were arrested and in 1924 brought to trial. At his trial he attacked those who were not with him: 'There is no such thing as high treason against the traitors of 1918 ...' 'I consider myself not a traitor but a German who wanted the best for the German people.' He was sentenced to five years imprisonment. Field Marshal von Ludendorff, who had marched with him, was acquitted. This made the headlines. The party received a great boost and to some it was a turning point, for Hitler now decided that the ballot box was the way forward. He was released from prison under an amnesty in December 1924 and from that point concentrated on using his great gifts as an orator and a demagogue.

While in prison he completed the first part of *Mein Kampf*. Here he stated his philosophy and the ambitions for a country ruled by the Nazi party. Baron Fritz von Thyssen, the son and heir of an ageing industrialist, gave some money to the Nazis, probably via von Ludendorff, and also helped Hitler to speak to groups of industrialists. Hitler needed contributions to help his party finances, and they were a good source of appeal.

Later, in January 1932, Goebbels expressed anxiety that the party needed money and it was difficult to obtain. In February 1932 he was much happier because on 27 January Hitler had spoken to and won over the members of the Industry Club at the Park Hotel in Duesseldorf. He realized that businessmen tended to mistrust him and he appeared to be offering them new opportunities. The speech, which is sometimes described as one of the best he ever made, won him, in the words of Alan Bullock his biographer, 'an important victory'. At the event, organized by von Thyssen, Hitler spoke for two and a half hours. It was a speech well shaped and, no doubt, well rehearsed. He told of the struggle he had had in the beginning, of the need to create a 'new' party. He said his organization would not hold back because of criticism and he could call on 400,000 men to go on the streets. (The number had grown since the 1920s). He spoke of the rediscovery of the road which leads upwards; of the responsibility which lay on the whole German people for the country's collapse and the obligation which now lay on them to complete the regeneration of the German body politic. All must join in a common effort.

Cleverly, he stated that he was not asking for votes, nor for support for his party, but wanted to expound his point of view, which was the only starting point for a German recovery. He wanted to give them ideals, otherwise they would be purely materialistic. He spoke of the riots on the streets caused by the National Socialists claiming they were for the protection of the public, indeed those on the streets were men who served and sacrificed for an ideal. If the whole nation had the same ideals Germany would stand in the world in a different position. Germany needed either more living space and the development of a great internal market or the protection of German economic life against the world without using all German strength to do it. He wanted a Germany intolerant of all who would harm her and willing to live at peace with anyone who desired peace and friendship.

The threat of violence was a thread running through his whole speech. 'An indomitable aggressive spirit' which reacts to 'provocation' from opponents says 'We fight today! We fight tomorrow! If this meeting is provocation we will hold another tomorrow'. His ideals, however, were vaguely expressed. Here *Mein Kampf* is the textbook. Germany will be rebuilt as Adolf Hitler wishes! The industrialists were swayed by suggestions of ideals, business opportunities, development and peace. They did not hear or did not care to hear the sounding knell of the bell signifying ruthless power.

After such speeches those seeking openings grasped the hand of one offering opportunities of development; those who were hungry reached out to the hand offering bread; the unemployed looked to one who offered work; those who had lost all followed one who offered economic stability; and all tried to take the hand of one who offered recognition, national pride and an ideal. But the hand was clad in an iron glove and it would lead them into servitude as they trusted, and then into a perverted nationalism, selfish, greedy and oppressive. They did not see that Hitler was using democracy to destroy democracy.

There were some who in the 1920s saw a hope in the Nazis. Wilhelm and Martin Niemoeller, later committed opponents, belonged to the Nazi party in its early days. But they were soon disillusioned and were seen amongst the leaders of the church opposition. Martin Niemoeller was a hero from the Great War and his defection was a great loss of face to the Nazis, for which they eventually demanded a price. Niemoeller, to the end of his life in 1984, confessed his sad error of judgement even though his subsequent life and testimony showed where he really stood. Hitler felt forced to put him in a concentration camp and, but for the rapid advance of the American forces to Dachau, he would have been executed. One version has it that the order for his execution was on the commandant's desk but the commandant had fled.

Hitler gradually established the practice which became routine when he took on power in the state. He eliminated rivals *within his own party*. There were no obituaries in the press and media for those eliminated. Hitler's cold, icy words have echoed:

> 'If anyone reproaches me and asks why I did not resort to the regular courts of justice for the conviction of offenders, then all that I can say to him is this: in this hour I was responsible for the fate of the German people and thereby *I became the supreme justice* of the German people'.

When Martin Niemoeller headed the church opposition to Adolf Hitler he was aided by two young pastors whose lives had been lived entirely in the 20th century and who had grown up through these troubled years. They were half a generation younger than he, though in talking with them he often referred to 'our generation'. They were Dietrich Bonhoeffer, born 1906, and Franz Hildebrandt born 1909 – Lutheran pastors, firm friends, deeply committed Christians.

CHAPTER 3

EARLY YEARS

Franz Hildebrandt was born on 20 February 1909 in Berlin. His father was Edmund (1872–1939); his mother was Ottilie (1872–1952) whose maiden name was Schlesinger. Franz was an only child. Ottilie belonged to an important Jewish merchant family in Berlin. Her brother George (1874–1949) was a professor in the Technical College in Berlin, one of the first German professors in the time of the Kaiser who came from 'the faith of Moses'. He was an internationally renowned pioneer in machine construction. He survived the Holocaust only because he fled in time. Little is known of other members of the Schlesinger family though it is highly probable that Marie Schlesinger, Franz's aunt, died in 1944 in the concentration camp at Theresienstadt.

Franz described his mother as a Jewess 'by race and profession' but he could not remember any occasion when she attended a synagogue. His maternal grandmother, however, was a practising Jewess. He said she brought her own distinctive gifts into the family circle and heritage. His father was the son of Georg Franz Hildebrandt who was born in Berlin in 1843 and died in the same city in 1910. He was an official of the law court. His father's mother Theone Wolkoff was a Berliner (1839–1901). She was the daughter of Theobald Wolkoff, a writer and translator from Prussia.

Franz's grandfather married again after the death of his grandmother Theone and his step-grandmother lived some years after his grandfather died. Franz recalls that she was a practising Christian and a wonderful influence on all who met her. He used to tell how, when his grandfather married for the second time, his father and his aunts (his father's sisters) left home in protest, but their new stepmother was such a lovely gracious person that they 'returned spontaneously' to the parental house.

His father, Edmund, claimed to be a pantheist. He was a man who fought against dogmatism of any kind and admired greatly Leonardo da Vinci and Goethe.

Franz had a mixed religious pedigree! It is not altogether surprising, therefore, that when Edmund and Ottilie married in 1907, the marriage ceremony took place in a registrar's office. They did not attend a church for any part of the ceremony.

Franz was baptized on 30 December 1909 in the Auenkirche of Deutsch-Wilmersdorf, then just outside the Berlin city boundaries. He was named Wolfgang Ernst Erich Heinrich Franz. His godparents were his grandfather, Georg *Franz* Hildebrandt, and two elderly maiden ladies, friends of the family, from Naumburg, Emma and Maria Becker. They were always regarded by Franz as adoptive aunts and he loved to visit them in vacation times as he grew older. The baptismal ceremony was conducted by Pastor Kriebitz.

He remembered being told that the doctor coming to attend his mother at his birth came on a sleigh drawn by horses. He also confessed that he never knew or understood why he had been through the ceremony of Christian Baptism. He thought it might have been because it was 'the done thing', though he sometimes admitted that there may have been pressure within the family from those who had a vital Christian faith. Later in his life his two 'adoptive aunts' were to play an important part, as 'agents', when they encouraged him to go with them to church.

His father, Edmund Hildebrandt was, initially, a lecturer in the history of art in Berlin. He wrote a dissertation on Friedrich Tiech, a work which established him in his position, a post which he held until 1917. From 1921 he was a professor in the University of Berlin. He wrote many books on art and was a specialist on the history of art in the Renaissance period and also on eighteenth-century art. His mother, Ottilie, was a qualified teacher. She, therefore, took charge of his early education.

When Franz was very young his parents moved from the apartment where he was born (in Berlin) to a house in Charlottenburg. From his fifth to his twenty-second year, this was his home base. Here he lived through his school and university years. He used to tell of this apartment on the top floor of the house, an apartment with two balconies which, he said, had 'a lovely view into the countryside'. It is surprising that he made such a comment for in later life Franz used to profess that he could not appreciate nature's beauty. Once when on a vacation in the fjords of Norway, his wife Nancy tells that 'on the deck one day I asked if he couldn't appreciate the beauty he saw because it was part of God's world and he replied "It's a fallen world!"' But in the intervening years many things had happened.

His mother, in taking charge of his education in the early years, taught him along with half a dozen other children. They met together twice a week during the forenoon. They were all given homework, but the rest of their time was free. There was a garden where they could all play. In her 'schooling' his mother taught the children to read. She also taught them some French, arithmetic and some religion. This consisted mainly of stories from the Old Testament which came naturally from her Jewish background. She also tried to give them a wider interest in other matters than the simple curriculum. Her teaching was so good that Franz, with his home generated education, was able to take an examination for a higher school. He won a place with results which showed him to be qualified for a year higher than normally expected for his age.

When young Franz was five years old, events were moving which were to lead to the upheaval of the First World War (1914–18). Some of the leading Germans, not uninfluenced by Kaiser Wilhelm II, were becoming more and more hostile in their attitude to Great Britain. The driving motive was their aim to become the most powerful nation in Europe. On 28 June 1914 a bullet was fired in Sarajevo. Archduke Francis Ferdinand of Austria-Hungary was assassinated. It has been argued that it was part of a deliberate plot orchestrated by the major powers. Whatever the truth in that, a series of alliances began to work and on 4 August 1914 Great Britain and Germany were at war with one another.

Contrary to what this mighty and powerful nation expected, the course of the war brought much suffering to the German people. Helmut Thielicke in his autobiography, *Notes from a Wayfarer*, tells of the times in 1917 when they, like the Hildebrandts, a middle class family with a father in the forces, were very hungry. His mother collapsed in weakness from hunger because she gave what food she had to her children. Thielicke was a year older than Franz. The effect of the war on the Hildebrandt family produced two very powerful and influential memories in the young boy.

The first was the memory of the food he had to eat as the war ran its course. He used to tell how at the age of nine in 1918 at his school he and others who appeared to be especially thin were given extra rations by the Quakers. He was fed, he remembered, on a diet which, to the young Franz, seemed to be basically turnip which came in various disguises: 'turnip soup; turnip steak; turnip as a vegetable; turnip as dessert; turnip as jam; turnip tart'. When he was about six or seven years old, he said he told his mother that he loved her 'as much as a potato', for at that time a potato was indeed an almost unobtainable luxury. He also remembered having 'to queue up for everything'. His beloved aunt Lisel obtained a pound of butter one day. To keep it cool she put it on the floor of the greenhouse, which they called the 'Winter Garden'. When she went to collect it, she saw the dog licking his lips; a small wartime tragedy!

His second memory influenced the rest of his life. In 1917 when his father was forty-four, he was taken from his teaching position, drafted into the army and directed to serve as a reservist on the land. He was in a garrison in Karlsruhe and given the task of cleaning stables until a doctor saw how this work was causing damage to his health. He was then moved to an office and a clerical post. Here he served in the Press Relations section of the Foreign Office.

This whole time had such a terrible effect on his father's health that he could not later fulfil to his own satisfaction his duties as professor . At first he paid an extra assistant who helped him run the History of Art seminar and then in 1930 he sought early retirement. Indeed in 1930–31 he took two terms interval to recuperate in a sanatorium in Dresden-Leschwitz. He suffered from severe depression and also agoraphobia, which made it difficult for him to spend time in the city or to participate in the life of the community. Sadly he became more and more withdrawn, staying mainly at home until his death in January 1939.

All this time Ottilie cared for her husband with all the compassion and energy she possessed. They had a good friend, Edward Spraenger, whose loyalty over many years bound him closely to them. To him she turned and with him she shared her grief at her husband's plight. She asked him if he would look after Franz 'if he needs you'. Her own family gave her help and support as well. Looking back, Franz believed that the permanent damage to his father's health, which had been caused by bureaucratic obtuseness, was an early influence in his opposition to war, to any form of military life, to nationalistic flag-waving and all kindred ideas.

When the young Franz moved from his mother's 'school' to his secondary education he was not happy. Reflecting in later years, he believed that although the atmosphere in the school was pleasant, he did not remember the skills of the teachers as being particularly good. He was taught the Greek and Latin classics, but he never wished to return to them (and never did), although he used both his Greek and his Latin later in his theological and Luther studies and writings. Indeed some of his books (e.g. *Melancthon*) demand a knowledge of both from the reader. He quotes Latin but does not always translate his quotations. This can make life difficult for the ordinary reader. Fortunately when writing on the Wesleys he is kinder. His father maintained that the teaching had the wrong emphasis. He said that too much time was spent on linguistics and grammar. This, he believed, caused one to miss out on the joy of coming to know literature as literature.

When the time came for Franz to go to university he was glad to leave behind subjects in which he had little interest. Indeed when he left at age seventeen his happiest memory, he recalled later, was of the journey to and from school in which he had to change trains.

This necessary inconvenience meant that he was allowed to arrive at school a few minutes after 8 a.m. when school began. The station officials came to know the young boy. They chatted with him and from time to time allowed him to change the direction boards which announced the destination of the incoming trains. For a boy, a taste of bliss!

He described the 'religious education' given at school as 'completely useless'. He was certainly not stimulated by it. It was taught last thing in the morning after the other lessons were completed. He remembered it to be Protestant in emphasis albeit his class included a large number of Jews and a smaller number of Catholics. He also remembers repeating books of the Old

Testament with little note or comment – very different from the way his mother had taught.

In after years he met the master concerned and the matter was discussed. Franz discovered that his former teacher had a genuine interest in religion but, as far as he was concerned as a pupil, none of this interest was passed on. Indeed had it been left to the teaching of religious instruction at school, this boy from a 'practising non-Christian' home would never have been captured by Jesus Christ and the Christian faith. However, in the economy of God other influences were at work in the life of young Franz Hildebrandt. His godparents, Emma and Maria Becker, single, elderly ladies who lived in the city of Naumburg, cared for him. They loved him very much. Frequently in autumn he would go to stay with them on vacation and when he was twelve years old, he went on a regular basis. They were gracious ladies who, as often happens with caring folk of an older generation, had more understanding of Franz than he realized. They invited him to go to their church with them. His normal practice on Sundays was to go to the cinema. He admitted to being 'over fond' of it. He knew, however, that he could see the film, which was showing in Naumburg, at a later date in Berlin. Because he believed it would please his beloved 'aunts' if he went to church with them, because it was a special kind of service and because there was a promise of no sermon, he went.

He could not remember ever having been to church before. His attitude towards the Christian church and Christian faith up to this moment especially in view of his school experience was 'anti' rather than 'pro', so running in parallel with his home and family background; but during the service he 'discovered there and then that this is where I really belonged'. From this point there was no turning back. The date was 5 October 1921. The church was St Othmar's church in Naumburg. Afterwards, especially in his later years, he used to say that he was captured by the beauty of the Lutheran liturgy just as later in England he was captured by the hymns of Charles Wesley. If that service in Naumburg had been a modernized liturgy or a Bible in modern speech he thought it would have passed him by. He was in fact caught by 'the beauty of God's holiness'.

His parents were surprised that their young son should have been captured by an experience which they in their own lives had

scorned, as seen by their non-church marriage. Franz, nevertheless, spoke proudly of them and of the way they never put any
obstacle in his way. Indeed they showed the integrity of their
character by giving him positive support even from their own
position and point of view. Thus they underlined to the young
boy the right, God-given right as Franz saw it, to follow the way
one is led with both heart and mind. Here we can see planted the
seeds of that integrity in Franz Hildebrandt which was so much a
part of his later thinking and believing. His debt to his parents
was great.

Following this experience Franz knew that the next step was to
attend confirmation classes and, subsequently to be confirmed.
The Naumburg experience had gone very deep. He wrote later 'I
was already determined to pursue theological studies before I
found my way to my confirmation by Pastor D. Albert Freitag of
Trinity'. During a later vacation he met D. Albert Freitag, entered
his classes and, at the age of fifteen, was confirmed. Later in his
life, looking back, Franz described Freitag as 'a Lutheran scholar;
a typical, colourless liberal in theology and preaching'. In 1933
Freitag became the Head of the Press Office of the German
Christians and 'an outright convinced Nazi'.

It was in the church where Freitag was pastor that the young
Franz Hildebrandt began to teach the Christian faith – in the
Kinder Gottesdienst or Sunday School. Here also he first began to
preach. It was from this time that he began his methodical and
meticulous register of every church service or lesson he prepared
and in which he was involved or which he conducted, noting
briefly in his diary the scripture text for the day, sometimes the
theme and usually the hymns selected. He now began to train his
memory by remembering the sermons which he heard. He would
listen to a preacher and within a day or so would write down the
main points of the sermon. This tended to make him something of
a 'sermon taster', for with friends he would go to the church to
which a good preacher was appointed. These visits created a
problem as he was committed to serving all the children's
services at his own church. Loyalty and duty were always a part
of his make-up. However as the *Kinder Gottesdienst* began at 11.30
a.m., (the main service in most churches began at 10 a.m.) with
careful planning all could be arranged – just!

His parents arranged for him early in his life to take music lessons. His father loved music and strangely, though he did not follow his father in appreciation of fine art and visual images, the piano touched a great talent which continued to develop. He took lessons until he was ordained and became an excellent pianist. Both father and son loved the piano. For his confirmation on 14 March 1924 his parents gave him a Bluethner-Fluegel grand piano which greatly encouraged him. This link was important to his father, who always claimed that Franz was 'completely blind' to the beauties of the visual arts.

It is possible that school teaching did not help much in this area. His father was critical not only of their teaching of the classics but also of their teaching of art and music. The young boy was expected to play a piece of music for the class, such as a movement from Beethoven's *Pathetique* sonata. Then the members of the class were expected to set down on paper their impression of the music. Edmund Hildebrandt thought this was a terrible method, for it forced the pupils to pretend they had seen something or gained some particular impression when, if they were like Franz, they had not. Franz used to produce something formless, covered with black ink. (One wonders what Edmund Hildebrandt would have made of Disney's treatment of the *Toccata and Fugue in D. Minor* for organ by J.S. Bach in the film *Fantasia*.)

Franz also played the piano with a young violinist who was in a class higher than himself. On the occasion when he broke his leg in a cycling accident he took to playing the harmonium since treading the pedals helped to strengthen the muscles of his damaged leg.

Edmund gave up playing the piano before he was fifty years old 'because', said Franz, 'he was a perfectionist. He didn't like to try things he didn't know and he didn't like to spoil things he did know'. Fortunately his son did not follow in father's footsteps. Franz found his music constantly helpful and a great source of joy. He later moved to the church organ and when he became a pastor in Berlin recorded in his diary that he must prepare himself by practising on the church organ for a soloist. Presumably she had come at the senior pastor's invitation to sing during the service. He never spoke much of his playing the organ in church. He was very modest about his accomplishments. (Not even Nancy, his wife, knew of playing the organ until she was shown the entry in his diary. His son David has taken up from his father this interest in the church organ and plays regularly). Later in life his musical knowledge and sensitivity appear again; in *From Luther to Wesley*, he recommends tunes for hymns which will help the singers to appreciate the meaning of the words and also tunes which do not. His views, as always, are emphatically stated!

During his teens there was one other special event which had a lasting effect on his life. While his broken leg was healing and in plaster, the family obtained a cat. Eventually, because his father feared for its life (it used to try to walk along the edge of the balcony of the Hildebrandt's top floor flat) it was taken to friends in the country. But the feline magnetism held Franz, as all who have ever visited the Hildebrandt home will testify. The family loves cats. So much is this true that Franz used to say that when he died, he would ask to be put in charge of the cat department in heaven. He never doubted that cats would be there.

So the young Franz Hildebrandt grew. He finished school and was ready to further his studies at university. He was a young man whose gifts and accomplishments were maturing, for whom the Christian faith (theology, pastoral care and church worship) were very much the main purpose in his life.

CHAPTER 4

PREPARATION FOR THE TASK

Franz gained his 'Abitur' examination on 25 February 1926, and was therefore qualified to enter the university. A university student in Germany is part of an educational system which seems both freer and more complicated than the pattern in either the United Kingdom or the United States. The German method of training for the ministry of the church differs also.

In the UK a student applies for a place on a course of study and, depending on examination and interviews at the university to which application has been made, a place will be offered. A course of study is prescribed lasting three or four years and then an examination is taken and if the candidate is successful a degree of Bachelor of Arts or Science is awarded. All this occurs in the university where the course is begun. The candidate offering for the ministry of any denomination offers to the church to which he or she belongs and is subjected to the selection method of that church. The methods differ but always there are examination panels which have searching questions and only after selection by them can the appropriate preparation for ministry begin. Sometimes the candidate may have already studied theology. Often the candidate has studied other subjects or, in some cases, has no academic qualifications. The particular denomination always submits the accepted candidate to a specially designed course of study. This may involve a degree course, or a further degree, or, simply, a concentrated preparation for pastoral or preaching work.

In the US, following the bachelor's degree from college or university, the candidate enrols in a seminary or a graduate school of theology for a three or four year course leading to a

Master of Divinity degree. During this postgraduate course the candidate enters the process leading to ordination by the church. In Germany the student finds a place to study under a professor of a particular subject having decided on his general line of study. He or she could study, for example, at Bonn for Old Testament; at Goettingen for New Testament; at Heidelberg for Church History, thereby selecting to hear the professor whom he or she favours. A minimum number of courses must be completed. The courses attended and completed are recorded on a career card or register along with other Pro-Seminars and Seminars which are satisfactorily attended and favourably completed. In a course on theology the biblical languages must be learned at the beginning. Towards the end of the study the student is examined by the body in charge of the subject after he or she has completed a dissertation on a given theme. Thus the student is able to study at different universities if so desired and to move around listening to different professors. Universities gather their reputations according to the professors on their staff and lecturers, from junior to senior, build up reputations as students go to hear them. Their reputation improves as they write books or publish lectures and papers in their subjects. Franz naturally followed this way of study.

After his decision at the age of twelve in Naumburg that theology and the Christian pastorate was to be the way of life to which he was dedicated, he spent the years in going to church and helping in the Sunday School and Children's Worship. His diaries for this time reveal how meticulously he prepared and how wideranging was his approach to the Bible. Each subject is recorded with the apposite Bible reading under the date in question. He also records his great debt for the help given him by the pastor of the Sunday School to which he had been recommended by his own pastor.

The pattern of Children's Worship followed a routine: a liturgical introduction conducted by the pastor, a period of instruction by the helper for members of the group to which each had been appointed, and then a final period summing up the teaching and with questions and catechesis. This last period was conducted by the pastor. Franz believed that the time so spent was important, for after their confirmation many of the children lost their links with the church. This was an opportunity to give them something on which they could draw later in life. He also maintained that his own preparation for this service, combined with listening to the pastor, had given him an excellent preparation for his later study of theology.

Pastor Freitag saw Franz through his confirmation and remained a good friend who directed him in the footsteps of Luther. Yet he turned more and more to Pastor Alexander Frederking who became a most vital mentor and partner in discussion, a true 'father in God'. He later confessed that he had learned more theology from him than from many professors.

In the Foreword of his doctoral thesis in Berlin (*Licentiate Arbeit*) he gives thanks to 'the two people who determined my way from the earliest times: Pastors D. Albert Freitag and Alexander Frederking in Charlottenburg. What binds me to them in reverence and friendship over the generations may be said in the words which today is the Sunday Epistle and at the same time the Introduction to the text of the Lord's Supper.' Then followed 1 Cor. 10.1a, 4: 'Moreover, brethren I would not that you should be ignorant how that all our fathers were under the cloud ... and did all drink the same spiritual drink: for they drank of that spiritual rock that followed them: and that rock was Christ.'

Franz's comment is apt. His church work and his studies belonged to one another from that day in Naumburg when Luther's liturgy grasped his heart. Although they did not share his faith and practice, his parents gave him great support in his calling. Indeed, in 1925 his mother had arranged for him to meet the great Professor Dr Adolf von Harnack and so he visited the Harnack home in Berlin. He told how Harnack spoke of the 'discipline of theology' which is much more about the present and the future than the past ... 'he stands before me still as I knew him, the whole person who is inspiring us often in the words I use in a specially deep agreement.'

Harnack was one of the outstanding thinkers of the century whose works had influenced many scholars. His best remembered work, *What is Christianity?* the English translation of *Das Wesen des Christentums*, was published in 1900 and remains a great piece of theological writing. In 1925 he was an old man and Franz was one of the last generation to study under his guidance. He always remembered this fact with pride. The influence of Harnack on his thinking was great. It is worth remembering that though Harnack died before Hitler reached his peak, his son, Ernst von Harnack, died in March 1945 as a Christian martyr who dared oppose Nazism.

From the time of his Abitur until 1930 he was a theological student mainly in the University of Berlin. He spent just two summer semesters in other universities: his first year in Tuebingen and his third in Marburg. He came to like Tuebingen very much. He had not thought of going there at first and claimed that he 'was dragged there by the fact that four or five of my class-mates who had matriculated with me (i.e. passed their Abitur exam) had gone there'. They had either medical or missionary contacts (or both) and so he ended up staying with them in a hostel known as the Institute of Medical Missions.

It was in Tuebingen that he heard the renowned Professor Dr Adolf Schlatter who had come out of retirement to lecture follow-ing the death of the professor who had succeeded him. Schlatter's knowledge was vast but Franz said he didn't find him easy to listen to. Schlatter came from the south and had a heavy accent. He used a language which Franz described as a mixture of German and Swiss. He used a lot of idiomatic phrases too, and the students used to refer to his language as 'Schlatterisch.' This did not help the concentration particularly when the subject was not one which captivated him. At one time Schlatter had been a professor in Berlin alongside Harnack. The idea, Franz records, was to counterbalance Harnack as both were scholars of monu-mental importance. They were also good friends. However, in due course, Schlatter left Berlin and went to Tuebingen. Franz did not claim to have attended enough lectures by Schlatter to give a critical appreciation of him. Schlatter's commentaries on New Testament books show his great learning and still reward the reader with many perceptive comments.

While he was in Tuebingen Franz attended a course of lectures on church history held in the Roman Catholic college which he found very interesting. It was also in Tuebingen that with great joy he met a nephew of Harnack. Harnack was for Franz the measure by which things were judged. He also attended some good and popular lectures by Professor Heilman.

Franz was not particularly happy in Marburg. He found Rudolf Bultmann, perhaps the best known of the Marburg professors, to be both a 'cynic' and a 'skeptic.' Another time he described

Bultmann as a 'nihilist.' He found it difficult to imagine how, with the ideas he claimed to profess, Bultmann could preach the Christian gospel. Certainly Bultmann had a group of followers but Franz was not among their number. He loved Harnack whom he would only criticize when he was in conflict with Martin Luther, but Bultmannn and his followers he found 'off-putting' and described their conversation as 'agnostic/atheistic'. Indeed he says, he 'fled' from the lectures of Bultmann to those of von Soden. Von Soden was in fact a friend and colleague of Bultmann, but Franz told how, in his lectures, von Soden took Bultmann to pieces. It is interesting to note that von Soden was one of the first professors to be dismissed by the Nazis when they came to power. Bultmann, as far as Franz remembered, joined the Confessing Church, but was, in fact, allowed by the Nazis to stay in office. Tuebingen and Marburg each produced an interesting pointer regarding the future life of the young Franz Hildebrandt. The Catholic College in Tuebingen, where he had heard the lectures on Church History, which attracted him so much, was a 'college of rebellious Catholics under a cloud' with their hierarchy. The streak of rebellion in Franz responded. There was always a note of 'dissent' with him, given good reasons.

The other interesting fact occurred in Marburg, where one of the professors was a convert from Roman Catholicism. He did not take to this professor's lectures and, later in his life described him 'in outlook really an Anglican'. Humorously he would comment 'my aversion to Anglicanism probably dates as far back as that'. Apart from these two semesters he studied at the University of Berlin for the remainder of his four years study course.

As he had studied the classical languages for theology (Hebrew, Greek and Latin) before leaving school, he had a good start. He now had to prepare for his 'First Examination' to be taken at the end of the four years. While the student makes all his decisions about the courses to attend he consults professors and pastors and builds up his preparation. The 'First Examination' was the point where the church took over. It was conducted on church premises by professors and pastors, some known to the candidates and some not. All the work accomplished, courses attended, dissertations presented, seminars completed would come for review and examination. After this the candidate would serve as a 'curate' probably in two situations and also attend a

Prediger Seminar to develop pastoral and preaching skills.

While he was a student in Berlin one of the greatest and most memorable moments in his life took place. On 16 December 1927, he met Dietrich Bonhoeffer. It was the beginning of a deep friendship which may possibly have affected the church and its theology more than has been realized. On occasion Franz loved to tell the story to his friends.

It was the evening before Dietrich's oral examination for his Licentiate in Theology (the old 'Doktorat' Franz used to describe it.) They were waiting for the seminar conducted by Professor Reinhold Seeberg. 'Within five minutes we were in an argument with each other – and we never stopped arguing from that day until we were separated by exile and war.' Then he would usually add, sadly, thinking of April 1945, 'After Dietrich, having an argument has never been the same'.

This oral examination was the time when the candidate, Dietrich, had to defend his *doktorat* thesis. He had to defend one or two statements about which he had given notice 'on the blackboard', as Martin Luther had nailed his theses to the Castle Church door in Wittenberg.

One of his statements was 'Every evangelical Christian is a dogmatist.' The initial argument between the friends centred on the early Christian heretic, Marcion, who would have dispensed with the Old Testament. Franz had read Harnack's book on Marcion and, greatly influenced by it, maintained Harnack's point of view. Dietrich loved the Old Testament. He found great strength in it, especially the Psalms which he called 'the Prayer Book of the Bible.' He therefore supported strongly the place of the Old Testament in worship and theology. One of the debating points was the 'Psalms of vengeance'.

From that first meeting on, they continually tested each other's thoughts and writings. When they were together, Franz said, they argued. They argued over the telephone. The arguments were only interrupted when Dietrich was abroad in Barcelona or the US, for they rarely exchanged letters. Franz said, 'We had twelve long years of unbroken friendship. We argued every day we were together. You could not be a friend of Dietrich if you did not argue with him.'

Franz was just beginning the studies that led to his doctorate as Dietrich was completing his (which he gained with high honours.) The oral examination was the final part and Franz used to say that if the candidate reached that point he was sure of gaining his degree.

When Franz took his 'First Theological Examination' in November 1930 Dietrich was abroad. Various lines were coming together at this time. Stimulated by a seminar with Professor Seeberg on the Lord's Supper he had been working on that theme for his own 'licentiate' thesis. He also had to prepare a catechism lesson on Luke 18.18–27 and trial sermon on Matthew 4.17–22.

His dissertation for his First Theological Examination was in 'dogmatics': an assessment of the Roman Catholic Church order, setting out its characteristic features and judging it by evangelical and biblical standards. It gave one sentence typical of Franz Hildebrandt: 'For the Lutheran Church it all hangs on this fact – to remain true to its principles and to establish the church not on organization but on the Word alone.' The examiners of this dissertation had an early taste of what was to be a foundation stone of his life. They were pleased with this piece of work.

However, his church history examination was a disaster. He was not happy with his theme, 'St Boniface, his work and its meaning for the Frankish church'. The examiner's comment was that it was the sort of essay any theological student could have written and showed no sign of special research. Initially it was marked 'unsatisfactory' but this was later changed to 'not fully satisfactory'.

The whole matter of the examination was delicate and difficult for Franz as he was also working on his licentiate thesis and this demanded much time. (It is not the first or the last time that a routine examination has been affected by special work to be done.) He pressed on.

When he submitted his licentiate thesis his professor, Reinhold Seeberg, at first referred him back saying there was 'too little text and too many footnotes'. He also said it was 'too simple and too literal'. Franz took this judgment hard as he felt it was a facile rejection of the whole work. It would need a year to put it right. Fortunately Dietrich came to the rescue, said it could be done and encouraged him to try. 'The result was that it took a year before I wrote again.' However with Dietrich's help and encouragement he passed and gained his licentiate. The title of the thesis is 'Est' and the theme is Luther's teachings about the Lord's Supper. He was awarded his degree 'cum laude'. On the strength of his doctorate he claimed he did not need further seminary training. He had hoped to go to Rome to serve as a curate but this did not come about and so he served in two other curacies and one area of special work.

It was at this time because of all the writing he had been doing that his aversion to writing in his own hand began. Later in his life he would apologize for typing letters and so being somewhat remote, but saying that he never liked to inflict his handwriting on a friend! He also retained a charming diffidence about his own work which may well have been the result of Seeberg's initial comments on his thesis.

At this time also he wrote to Bonhoeffer about his 'natural' tendency to 'pietism' which they had discussed before. He also wanted more and more study of Hegel, the 'problem of mediation' and the 'filioque' clause. This latter study was far from simply an abstract comment. Three years later in outlining the Bethel Confession, Bonhoeffer advanced the thesis to show: 'We cast aside the false teaching that the Holy Ghost might be recognised in the Creation and Ordering of the world *apart from Christ* ... Only because the Holy Ghost proceeds from the Father *and the Son* is 'Mission' the commission of the Church.'

It is highly probable that in this thinking Dietrich Bonhoeffer was influenced by the work and thinking of his friend Franz Hildebrandt just as in other ways he often drew on the fruits of Franz's remarkable memory. (Nancy, Franz's wife, once commented how frustrating it was: 'he remembered everything he read!'.) In his licentiate thesis 'Est', Franz had written: 'First of all the 'Filioque' makes possible an answer to the question how Immanence is defined definitively, namely where the Spirit of Christ is present in reality.'

On 26 February 1931 he defended his examination thesis in the Old Assembly Hall (Alten Aula) of Berlin University. Those who opposed him against whom he had to defend were his confirmation pastor, D. Albert Freitag, Professor Alexander Frederking and Professor Gottfried Niemoeller, who at that time was a follower of Barth and a member of the chapter-house of the Cathedral. The theses to be defended were characteristic of Hildebrandt's theological development and his clear theological position: later he kept returning to them in his thinking. His theses include:

- Lutheranism sees Church Authority only in the Gospel.
- Lutheranism has a 'Textus Receptus' the Luther Bible: as 'Canon' the New Testament up to III John; and as 'Introduction' the 'Prefaces of Luther'.
- Lutheranism recognizes the 'Old Testament' to be 'gathered up' in the New.
- Lutheranism teaches the unity of Word and Sacrament both for worship and normal legal assemblies.
- Lutheranism stands and falls with Luther's teaching on the Lord's Supper in its strict interpretation.

Here we see one who walks in the footsteps of Martin Luther in his scholastic interpretation of the Bible.

Already since May 1927 in the Old Prussian Church there had been a debate about the value of academically well qualified candidates doing a further period of seminary training. It was thought by some that such candidates had the ability to learn what was needed as they went along. Neither Dietrich Bonhoeffer nor Franz Hildebrandt was happy about the necessity of going to a seminary for further instruction in preaching or pastoral work in spite of the church requirement. They regarded it as something of a waste of time. In fact Bonhoeffer commented, in a letter to his brother-in-law Walter Dress, that he thought the authorities could have found a better way of developing those who had already completed strongly academic courses. (Already the protagonists in the Church battle were flexing their muscles!)

Franz, against the wishes of the church officials, agreed to work for six months with Friedrich Siegmund-Schultze's *Sozialer Arbeits Gemeinschaft.* (S.A.G.) in East Berlin. 'This', he wrote to Dietrich in New York, 'involved leading a youth group; education of the young unemployed; a study of the sects and free thinkers in Eastern Germany; lectures on St John's Gospel and a writing of Kierkegaard to theological students involved in S.A.G.; and helping Siegmund-Schultze in discussion groups'. Later Franz told how Dietrich and he had wondered why Siegmund-Schultze had not become a pastor in a parish in East Berlin but he remembered that when they had asked such a question all the reply they received was a shrug of the shoulders.

Both Dietrich and Franz owed a great debt to Siegmund-Schultze. He set internationalism above nationalism. He believed strongly in peoples and nations working together. He practised openness and edited *Der Eiche*, 'The Oak', a journal which was eventually suppressed by the Nazis in 1933. He was removed from the staff of Berlin University as 'unsuitable' and eventually was compelled to leave the country to live and work in Switzerland. From here he kept in touch with different Christian Church leaders, two of whom were Bishop George Bell in England and Mayor Carl Friedrich Goerdeler of Leipzig, Germany. (Later Goerdeler was a martyr for his faith, 2 February 1945). He gave sound advice and sometimes warned Dietrich of the dangers into which he was running. His attempts to work for peace and the overthrow of the Nazis met with little success with the Churchill government. His whole being is an illustration of Christian faith in action and Franz was ever glad to have worked with him.

Franz was never able to divorce his theology from pastoral work in the community. He wrote to Dietrich on 23 January 1931, that he now held that practical work (*Praxis*) was everything and pure scholarship worth little, but he did not intend to give up anything of his theology ('which was always ten times more concrete than existential wisdom'). His previous problems took second place in view of his new tasks and, apart from theology in action, he could see little to draw him back to the scholar's desk. Thereafter his theology was always related to, and relevant for, the folk in the working world.

In his own report on work submitted for his Second Theological Examination he expressed this point of view clearly. He saw that the church needed a change in approach between the individual members and the fellowship of the church. He was offering some radical thinking on pastoral care.

It was at this time and with these influences that the two friends developed the idea of a 'Team-Ministry' to work out their theology. In May 1933 two pastors' positions became vacant in the Lazarus-Kirche in East Berlin and such an approach to the work might have been possible. However, the changes in the church did not enable this to come about. Dietrich did not take up the invitation to go alone as he would not enter into a pastorate from which, for whatever reason, his friend was excluded.

Franz kept his contacts with S.A.G. into 1933 and continued to give lectures there. Some subjects were 'The present position of the church'; 'Responsibility and Freedom according to Martin Luther' and 'Albert Schweitzer'.

At the conclusion of his half-year of practical work with the S.A.G. the *Oberkirchenrat* (Senior church official) tried again to enlist Franz Hildebrandt into a 'Preachers' Seminary (*Prediger Seminar*). Franz however countered this with a report from his doctor and it worked out very well for him for he was allowed to go from April to September in 1931 to the little town of Dobrilugk (now called Doberlug-Kirchhain) to work with a pastor who had been one of his examiners at his First Examination. There was also another advantage with regard to his family. It was roughly half-way between Berlin and Dresden where his father was in a sanatorium.

His duties were not only in the town 'parish' but he was also to assist in the neighbouring village 'parishes' of Friedersdorf, Rupekersdorf and Gremho. Pastor Schade attested that he had an exceptional knowledge of the Bible and the Hymn Book and that he 'did far more work than a curate can be expected to do'. Franz himself expressed the view: 'I lived six happy months in his house with his family and learned to preach and teach and do pastoral visiting and other duties'. Indeed the pastor wished Franz to succeed him when the time came for his own retirement, but when that time came the Nazis were in control of things.

In October of that year there came a great contrast in work for him. He was appointed to serve in Berlin as curate to Leonhard Fendt who was a 'star preacher' at the church *zum Heilsbrunnen* (Church at the Holy Fountain). Fendt was a convert from Roman Catholicism. His own first sermon in this appointment was on the text of Eph. 4.25. The date was 11 October 1931 and it was the 400th anniversary of the death of Zwingli. He also preached here again on 15 November for the 100th anniversary of the death of Hegel. This was also the day of Dietrich Bonhoeffer's ordination. Fortunately the times of services did not clash.

It was here that he came to know Hans Herbert Kramm, later a companion in exile in England. Kramm's special interest was liturgical singing. Franz soon won the goodwill of the congregation by his pastoral caring and he stayed in this appointment for one and a half years. Fendt's assessment of Franz at the end of his period of service reads thus:

Licentiate Hildebrandt is gifted and mature beyond his years as a theologian, carer of souls, preacher, teacher of religion and in his personal character. His sermons are such that without any further ado he could be trusted with any important pulpit ... His clear cut theology is especially delightful. In addition he is possessed of indefatigable enthusiasm.

Franz's view of Leonard Fendt did not fall into the same terms. He records 'It was as well that I left just as the Nazis came to power because he turned out to be very much 'pro-Nazi'. 'His academic ambitions came to fulfilment under the Third Reich and he was made a professor. And we parted with not much love lost between us, certainly not on my part.' Franz saw the direction of Hitler's Nazi movement early in its course (although he said often, 'Not as soon as Dietrich'). He also had a sixth sense for recognizing those who might be influenced by it. Nevertheless he worked hard with all his senior colleagues and never gave them less than total loyalty and all his strength in service. In his entire life, fully dedicated to the work of God, he could never give less than his best.

Thus in his three curacy appointments, while still in his twenties, he had experienced a wide swathe of the church's pastoral life. But as Holger Roggelin points out, there were other things as well weighing on his mind as he approached ordination. What sort of career was there in his native 'land church' (*landeskirche*), disturbed as it was by the Nazis?

First to affect him was that the fact of international contacts, coupled with the social work in East Berlin, could bring the misfortune of expulsion from Germany, as neither of these found particular favour with the Nazi regime; then there was the question of those belonging to organized opposition. Also there were those who made their peace with the more or less Nazified church rulers and professors (his previous colleague allowed the Nazi Minister of Culture to call him to be a professor of theology in Berlin). For promotion it was neccessary to be unspotted by the radicalism of the Confessing Church or one must hibernate 'until the new time'.

Hildebrandt's feelings led to a confrontation with Fendt, who made it clear that his sympathies were with the new ruling party. This difference probably occurred on the evening after Bonhoeffer, in April 1933, gave his address to the *Jakobikreis*

(James Group) on 'The Church and the Jewish Question'. Fendt under protest allowed the group to continue to meet.

Hildebrandt was twenty-four years old when he had completed his church examinations. He had to apply for a special dispensation, for normally no one could be ordained until he was twenty-five years old. However, this rule was waived for him and he was ordained 'literally on the last Sunday when the decent old pre-Nazi church was in power'. He was ordained with three others. His journey from Naumburg to ordination was now completed.

CHAPTER 5

THE CHURCH UNDER THREAT

Officially Adolf Hitler came to power on 30 January 1933 but for some time before that his influence in Germany and on the German People and state had been considerable. For those who listened carefully his aims had been clear in his speeches and writings. Equally clearly did the actions of his followers show the way he would achieve these aims. His party the NSDAP (the National Socialist German Workers Party) had grown from the disaffected. Soon after this the Storm Troops had been formed (SA). They carried flags emblazoned with the swastika and marched through the streets in noisy demonstrations.

After the Munich uprising and march (the *putsch*) of November 1923 had failed, Hitler was imprisoned, where he worked on *Mein Kampf* until his release in December 1924. Friedrich Ebert, who had been elected provisionally as President of the Republic under the Weimar constitution, died in February 1925. As his successor Paul von Hindenburg, a Field Marshal and candidate of the right wing was elected. Though he disappointed the extreme right wing by acting constitutionally, he was an old man, a former soldier, and politically inexperienced. Hitler saw a situation ready to be exploited. Herein lay his genius. He re-established the NSDAP, which grew rapidly. In 1926 there were 17,000 members; in 1928, there were 80,000. His fanatical speeches stirred the people who did not hear the undertone of oppression as he spoke of lifting up the nation, giving it back its pride, and, more to the point, giving jobs to the unemployed.

There were those who thought they could use him for their own ends; that he would be in the control of the President, Paul von Hindenburg, and his wily minister and astute politician Franz von Papen. Some thought that General von Schleicher would control him and use him but they had misjudged this man. They had not taken seriously his words: 'For us Parliament is not an end in itself but merely a means to an end: we are not on principle a parliamentary party.' He went on to say that they were fettered by the constitution but one day they would set free the German people. This was in 1930. Those politicians and leaders who thought that they could control Hitler were tragically mistaken. Expressing his genius for manipulating people, he used them: von Papen, von Schleicher, von Hindenburg. Not even the brutal methods of persuasion used by his followers seemed to convince the majority that he was essentially dangerous.

There were some who in the early days read the signs and saw the danger in Hitler and the Nazis. Franz Hildebrandt recalled a conversation with his friend Dietrich Bonhoeffer in the days before the 1932 election. Dietrich surprised him by saying that he would vote for the 'Catholic' party – in those days a most unusual act for a Protestant pastor. When Franz asked his reason, he said, 'The Nazis have to be stopped and the Catholic party has the best opportunity.' In the event the Catholic party crumbled under Nazi pressure.

In July 1932 before the election Franz Hildebrandt himself preached in St Ann's Church, Dahlem on the text 'If you had only recognized the things that work for peace, but now they are hidden from your eyes'. (Luke 19.42) Dietrich was not alone in seeing the danger, but many wise Christian people did not recognize it.

Franz records how in the church elections in November 1932 the so-called 'German Christians' came to the fore as a party within the Protestant Church. The name was chosen carefully to trap the unsuspecting. This, at first, it did.* The idea was to wed the Christian church to the German national consciousness. In 1932 a conference of German Christians was held in Berlin which Hermann Goering attended. In its extreme expression the movement allowed the figure of a swastika on the Lord's Table (as for Dr Josef Goebbels' wedding, when the Nazi flag was also draped over it). Nevertheless to many it meant nothing more than the

---

*In January 1953 a pastor who had served as a missionary overseas in Brazil told how, at that distance, it seemed right and proper to join the 'German Christian' movement. Only when he returned home did he realize his error.

phrase 'the Church of England' means in the United Kingdom today. The lesson to be learned is that one should always read the small print in any document.

Franz recorded in his diary for his own interest and reference the simple statement to which he was asked in vain to assent : 'I declare my membership of the religious movement, the German Christians, whose programme I know and whose leadership I accept. In the case of a candidate I will carry out my duty in accordance with article 19.2 of the constitution for the church of the Old Prussian Union.'

He tells how his first reaction was to preach on the critical Sunday from Gal. 1.8. 'So even if we or an angel from heaven should proclaim to you a gospel contrary to what we preached to you, let that one be accursed!' Then he spoke with his senior pastors – he was not yet ordained – and one whose theological stance he found helpful said, 'When anyone is firing blanks, you can certainly leave him alone!' He, therefore, felt that the orthodox doctrine of the church would be a reliable guarantee, so he changed his text to II Cor. 13.5. 'Examine yourselves whether you are living in the faith: test yourselves'. It was a revision of thinking of which he confessed in later life to being ashamed. Hitler was not firing blanks.

Before the German Christians held their next conference in April 1933, their patron, Adolf Hitler, was in power. In fact Hitler came to power legally. He led the party which had most seats in the *Reichstag*, though a coalition of the others could have defeated him. He himself refused to back von Schleicher and so, at the suggestion of von Papen, President Hindenburg asked him to form a government. He soon called another general election (see voting paper, p. 39).

On 1 February 1933 Dietrich Bonhoeffer made a broadcast on German Radio. He tried to define the meaning of 'Leader' ('*Fuehrer*') but his broadcast was cut off the air before he had finished. He was already a marked man.

Demonstrations by Hitler's men (the NSDAP and their allies) continued – only now they had government approval. The Reichstag, their parliament building, was destroyed by fire just before the elections. This was blamed on the Communists though it was almost certainly organized by Goering, who lived in the Palace of the President of the Reichstag, which was just across the

Reichstagswahl 1933
Wahlkreis Potsdam II

1	**Nationalsozialistische Deutsche Arbeiter-Partei** (Hitler-Bewegung) Hitler — Dr. Frick — Göring — Dr. Goebbels	**1**	◯
2	**Sozialdemokratische Partei Deutschlands** Künstler — Dr. Löwenstein — Heinig — Frau Kunert	**2**	◯
3	**Kommunistische Partei Deutschlands** Thälmann — Ulbricht — Dahlem — Grosse	**3**	◯
4	**Deutsche Zentrumspartei** Dr. Brüning — Dr. Krone — Schmitt — Bernoth	**4**	◯
5	**Kampffront Schwarz-weiß-rot** Dr. Hugenberg — Steinhoff — Frau Lehmann — Timm	**5**	◯
7	**Deutsche Volkspartei** Dr. Croll — Frau Dr. Matz — Lüdecke — Gommel	**7**	◯
8	**Christlich-sozialer Volksdienst** (Evangelische Bewegung) Behrens — Weinitschke — Fräulein Wolff — Pietz	**8**	◯
9	**Deutsche Staatspartei** Dr. Schreiber — Colosser — Frau Dr. Lüders — Dr. Goepel	**9**	◯
10	**Deutsche Bauernpartei** Professor Dr. Fehr	**10**	◯
12	**Deutsch-Hannoversche Partei** Meyer — Prelle — Meier — Salfer	**12**	◯
15	**Sozialistische Kampfgemeinschaft** Erdmann — Schmidt — Happach — Renning	**15**	◯

street and linked by an underground passage. Such events, clearly used, helped Hitler's cause to a degree but in the election the Nazi party only obtained 49% of the votes and so, even then, did not have an overall majority. However, by blaming the Communists for the Reichstag fire and, subsequently, disqualifying them from office, Hitler gained the majority he needed. Then on 23 March 1933 by passing an enabling law he gained the power to make decrees without consulting the elected parliament.

In March 1933 Hitler said that his party held power throughout Germany. On 14 July after the offices of various other parties had been occupied and closed down by the Nazis, an official announcement was made that the National Socialist German Workers Party was the only political party in Germany and that anyone trying to form another political party would be subject to penal servitude of up to three years 'if the action is not subject to a greater penalty according to other regulations'. And this was signed by Hitler as Chancellor and by the Minister of the Interior and the Minister of Justice. Dachau and Sachsenhausen concentration camps were opened in 1933.

Von Papen believed, according to Alan Bullock, that when the Nazi party was harnessed to the state, it would be tamed. This proved to be wishful thinking. Nor could the prestige, position and status of Paul von Hindenburg hold Hitler in check. Hitler claimed that Hindenburg was the final authority – but millions soon realized that it was not so. Now that he had power, Hitler was ruthless in using it. He was the final authority.

Where was the Christian church in all this? In his large book on the German Church Struggle (*Kampf and Zeugnis der Bekennenden Kirche*: Bielefeld, 1948) Wilhelm Niemoeller, brother of Martin, points out that in many parts of Germany the strength of the organized church was faint and dwindling. Attendance had fallen. Nevertheless there were some fine leaders: Wilhelm Zoellner, Otto Dibelius and Theophil Wurm among them. The subsequent persecution revealed and produced others but in some ways the church was not too well equipped for battle on the ground floor. The pressures of the past – especially the 1918 collapse following World War I – had affected all morale. Wilhelm Niemoeller says that, nevertheless, although often uncoordinated and unorganized, there were some signs of spiritual quickening.

The Christian church did not comprehend what was happening, nor was she alone in this. Hitler had been very adroit in his thinking and planning. At the end of 1932 Wilhelm Niemoeller records, the Chief of Staff of the SA (the Storm Troopers) had a chaplain appointed to each of their commando groups. Franz Hildebrandt himself declares that there were few like Dietrich Bonhoeffer who had the gift of clear thinking, analysis and a view of the future: 'Dietrich saw the danger coming. Others like myself were probably too naïve.'

At first it seemed that the independence and freedom of the churches would remain untouched. Article 24 of the Nazi Party manifesto stated: 'The Party as such holds the position of a positive Christianity without binding itself to confessing any fixed creed.' People read this and, having read, were satisfied. However as Judge Jan Niemoeller (Martin's son) said in a lecture in 1995 'they overlooked the previous words "we further the freedom of all religious confessions of faith in the State *so long as they do not endanger the stability of the state nor work against the ethical or moral leadership of the German race"'*. This sentence contained, as Jan Niemoeller pointed out, all that was needed to justify the later anti-Semitism and the later persecution of Christians.

There was an also a more ominous sentence: 'She (i.e. the Party) is against the Judaic-materialist spirit within and outside us and is convinced that a lasting recuperation can only follow from within on the basis: beneficial for the community is beneficial for the individual.'

On 23 March 1933 in a sitting of the Reichstag Hitler said, 'The National Government sees in the two Christian Confessions (i.e. Roman Catholic and Protestant) the most vital factors for preserving our national character ... Their rights shall not be impinged upon. The state expects and hopes that the task of the national and moral reviewing which the Government has put in hand will receive in turn a like appreciation.' The entire speech merits study. It camouflaged his aims with specious promises which depended on the church complying with his orders. Some, however, had read and understood what Alfred Rosenberg, Hitler's philosopher for Nazism, had written – about 'faith in the blood line'.

Those who are critical of the churches and who blame them for inaction at this time forget that it is the Christian nature to be trusting, to accept until it is proved false, the word of anyone, especially when it is uttered publicly. In addition it is much easier for the side in power, prepared to attack, to make an assault on an unsuspecting opponent than for that opponent, unexpectedly attacked, to defend a position when unprepared. To coordinate any opposition it must be both discovered and organized. Under a totalitarian regime this becomes exceptionally difficult, for not only do the rulers have total power, but they hold the means of communication in their hands. Thus it is difficult, first to find out who opposes without that information reaching the ruling power and thus eliminating the opposition; and second, to gather that opposition together; for the more lines of communication there are, the greater the danger of being discovered. Coherent opposition is virtually impossible, and the Nazis were ruthless opponents. It is to the great credit of the churches that there was some, albeit somewhat fragmented, opposition.

In addition the idea of ecumenism – the different denominations working together – was in the 1930s in a very embryonic stage. The various Christian churches, large and small, were not accustomed to working together. They tended to exist separately and so were a somewhat scattered body. Nevertheless it was possible to read and know Hitler's main plan if one read carefully and understood *Mein Kampf* as well as his speeches and other writings. It must also be remembered that in 1930, 1931, 1932 and early 1933 he was making pronouncements to win votes. He spoke about rebuilding the nation and there were those who in the beginning thought he would give the German people a national identity, some pride to work to rebuild their country after the effects of the 1914–18 war and subsequent problems. At first Martin Niemoeller was of this number but he was soon disillusioned and afterwards was ready and willing to confess his mistake. His noble and brave witness with eight years confined in Hitler's concentration camps amply repaid his earlier error.

On 1 April, the first boycott of Jewish shops and businesses began. This lasted for four days. It was unpopular at home and abroad and was dropped 'for the time being', but the signs had been posted. From this point Jews began to be harassed and then excluded from parts of society: Jewish shops were looted and the police knew better than to interfere. Some brave souls like Dietrich Bonhoeffer's grandmother, aged 91, took action. She deliberately walked into one of the main Jewish stores in Berlin to make a purchase, daring the Gestapo to arrest her.The Bonhoeffer family saw clearly what these anti-Jewish acts portended. Was not Dietrich's close friend, Franz Hildebrandt, the son of a Jewish mother? Was not Dietrich's sister, Sabine, married to Gerhard Leibholtz who was also of Jewish blood? It is truly said that when you yourself suffer pain you understand the sickness more clearly.

While all these events were taking place Franz Hildebrandt was preparing for ordination. This took place on 18 June 1933, in St Nicholas' Church in Berlin; the church where his spiritual hero, Paul Gerhardt, the seventeenth-century pastor and hymn writer had been ordained. Gerhardt's hymns, along with those of John and Charles Wesley, were a constant source of spiritual strength to Franz until the day he died. It is also a fascinating coincidence that after his ordination Paul Gerhardt became minister of the church where he was ordained until he finally left it and went into voluntary exile in 1667 because he objected to national policy. 'In his hero's steps he trod ...'.

Thus the name of Franz Hildebrandt was entered into the series of books which contained that of Paul Gerhardt (albeit in a later volume). Franz always held this as a treasured memory and had a special affection for that church which, sadly, was destroyed in 1945 towards the end of the war. Dietrich attended Franz's ordination and so returned Franz's earlier act of friendship.

There was a problem over the Hildebrandt ordination. He was not yet 25 years old. He had taken his final exams but the ordination was delayed because he was not of 'the canonical age'. However he was given a 'tip off' by a Nazi who was an acquaintance to press on as 'something was in the air'. So he sought and was granted special permission to be ordained. He had in fact completed with fine endorsements the necessary tests both academic and practical.

The reason for the urgency became clear as events progressed. The week after his ordination the anti-Semitic laws came into operation. This meant that if his ordination had been delayed it could not have taken place because of his Jewish blood. It also meant that, as he later proudly claimed, he, and his three fellow ordinands, were the last Lutherans to be ordained *validly* in Germany until after the war for all other 'official' ordinations afterwards were marred by anti-Semitic regulations. The Confessing Church did ordain some ministers of their own in this period.

From 3–5 April the Assembly of the 'German Christians' met in Berlin. Amongst the many things said was the statement by Pastor Dr Wienecke that 'the swastika and the crucifix belong to one another'. Hitler also let it be known that in his view, in order to bring the Protestant churches together, one leader, a Reichbishop was needed. On 10 May the election of the Reichsbishop took place. The 'German Christian' nominee was Ludwig Mueller, a former military chaplain, a friend of Hitler who had been Hitler's adviser and representative on Church matters. He was leader of the 'German Christian' movement in East Prussia whose reputation was as 'an inflexible fighter for the National Socialist idea'. From the other possible candidates who might have stood in opposition, Pastor Dr Friedrich von Bodelschwingh, the younger, was named. He was the head of a remarkable caring work in Bethel bei Bielefeld which had been started by his pastor father some 60 years earlier. Pastor 'Fritz' as he was generally known had been little involved with political parties himself, but, because he believed that the church should not withdraw from the world but rather be involved in the whole of life, he felt he must accept the nomination. He was elected with a convincing large majority.

On 27 May 1933 he was installed as Reichsbishop. His counsellor/assistants were Pastor Gerhard Stratenworth and Pastor Martin Niemoeller, both of whom had in earlier days worked with him in the Inner Mission of Westphalia. As Reichsbishop he soon stressed humility, a will to seek the truth and a desire to be obedient to the Gospel of Jesus. Serving the people was his nature. On one occasion he said, 'I would rather be called the State servant than the State bishop'.

Although he was one of the best loved pastors in Germany he was not acceptable to the 'German Christians' and the Nazi party. They obstructed him in his work and made his life intolerable. He refused to lead the church into support of the Nazi party. He maintained the right of the church to be independent of all parties. The Nazis were not pleased. Almost certainly at the instigation of Hitler himself the 'German Christians' began to organize opposition to him. Some church leaders who were Nazi-

inclined were critical of him. Most Christian student groups at the universities appeared to favour Bodelschwingh but a stimulated vigorous and vocal minority made noisy objections. Dietrich Bonhoeffer was involved in trying to put over Bodelschwingh's views to students in Berlin. At some meetings the supporters of Bodelschwingh were so angry that they walked out in protest at a given signal. This was a tactical error and surrendered the meetings to those remaining. On 24 June a state official was appointed 'to put an end to the strife within the church'. Bishop Otto Dibelius protested at this appointment – and received support and applause. He maintained that within his diocese the church had given him the spiritual power. No secular power could take over that authority.

Bodelschwingh resigned on the same day of the State appointment. His work had been made impossible. Some including Martin Niemoeller tried to persuade him to stay but he said 'In the struggle if I take one backward step the battle is lost'. This gentle, saintly man saw what the notorious Judge Freisler said in 1944: 'Christianity and National Socialism have one thing in common and one thing only 'they both demand the whole person'. Some of the things he was expected to do he saw as 'backward steps'. In a moving word he explained his position:

> to all who love our German Evangelical Church ... I will willingly continue as Bishop and Deacon (servant) that is 'Overseer and Servant' of the German Church ... we want spiritual things to be handled in a spiritual way ... the confession (credo) and Proclamation of the church to remain free, independent from all power politics...this is a battle for the soul and the future of our people ...

It was said that the most prominent sacrifice the church made when it capitulated to Hitler was Pastor Dr Friedrich von Bodelschwingh, 'our beloved Pastor Fritz'. Dietrich Bonhoeffer, as a pastor to students in Berlin had spoken on behalf of Bodelschwingh ... Now he began to take an active part in the German church struggle. His close friend Franz Hildebrandt was with him in thought, word and deed.

Another election for Reichsbishop was arranged after Bodelschwingh's resignation and this time Ludwig Mueller was elected. All Hitler's powers and all the media were available to

him including personal endorsement and there was no doubt Mueller would win, but Dietrich Bonhoeffer and Franz Hildebrandt with all the burning energy of young campaigners threw themselves into the fray of electioneering. They wrote and published pamphlets. The Gestapo arrived and confiscated them. Eventually Bonhoeffer with Gerhard Jacobi managed to persuade the Gestapo to allow them to use posters with the title 'Gospel and Church'. Some of these they nailed to trees – particularly at the Autumn Synod. The big debate at the coming church assembly concerned the Aryan paragraphs. Would the church, now in the hands of German Christians, adopt them?

It would be fair to say that at first the majority of German people heard the words of the politician Hitler but did not listen to them and continued to live their lives without worrying too much about 'the small print'. But there were some in key positions in society who had heard and understood, and used his words to fill out their own prejudices.

Julius Streicher in early 1933 had said that the Nazis would take good care that, after them, people would live like proper Germans and not as folk who seemed like animals. On 1 March 1933 the medical journal from the provinces of Brandenburg, Greuzmark and Pomerania stated that the doctors felt it unthinkable 'that any Jew should have the possibility of spreading the poison of Jewish thinking as a doctor ...' They would work to see that Jews would be excluded from treating Germans because 'the Jew is the incarnation of lying and deceit'. Such ideas filtered down. As these ideas gathered expression the question was 'Which way will the church go?'.

In late 1931 Franz Hildebrandt first met Martin Niemoeller. From 1932 Franz Hildebrandt and Dietrich Bonhoeffer had been participants in a small circle of pastors meeting at the home of Pastor Gerhard Jacobi on the theme 'Church and Office'. This was the kernel of the opposition movement of 1933. It was to this group that Bonhoeffer read his paper 'The Church and the Jewish Question'. He made his position clear: 'The exclusion of Jewish Christians from the community of the church destroys the essence of the church.' An event which sharpened Hildebrandt's thinking was the resignation of Professor Edward Spraenger, a good friend of his family who on 25 April 1933 resigned his position as a protest against the measures the Nazis were introducing into the

universities and the 'disregard of religion, of the individual, of clear thinking and science'. More than 180 students and friends along with the Hildebrandt family signed a protest against this resignation being accepted. Franz Hildebrandt also added his name to a document sent from the Young Reformers group.

Franz in his turn had written a polemical pamphlet attacking the German Christians. Its format was very simple, just setting out the faith and the differences in a series of contrasting sentences:

- The German Christians say: The Voice of the People is the Voice of God. (a definition from Mueller 16 July 1933)
- The Bible says: He who is of the truth hears my voice. The people all cried together and said, 'Not this man, but Barabbas.' But Barabbas was a murderer (John 18.37, 40)
- The German Christians say: the appearing of Jesus Christ in the world is historical in its final form as a burning flame of a northern type (i.e. an Aryan) (Jaeger, 15 July 1933)
- The Bible says: This is the book of the birth of Jesus Christ who is indeed the Son of David, the Son of Abraham, i.e. of Jewish decent (Matt. 1.1).

In this way the document continued to expose the heresy of the German Christians.

The Aryan clause was being discussed and promulgated as policy in all parts of the State. It was being pressed on the church via the 'German Christians'. Concerning the clergy it read 'Anyone of non-Aryan descent or married to a person of non-Aryan descent may not be called as a minister or official in the general church administration'. A similar clause with reference to civil servants had been promulgated on 7 April. Would the church accept this?

On 30 July 1933 Dietrich had been invited to preach in the German speaking church in Sydenham London to which was linked a similar church in Aldgate (St Paul's German Reformed Church, Goulston St). He had been recommended to be the pastor. He insisted that he would not allow his name to be considered unless certain facts were known: that he was not a 'German Christian' and that he had a deep and strong link with the international ecumenical movement and England – although he stressed his loyalty to Germany. Chief Consistory Counsellor Heckel, to whom this was conveyed, replied that his work was to be pastoral and also that it would not be appropriate to bring to England and the German congregation in London the differences and divisions present in contemporary Germany.

Bonhoeffer wrote to Karl Barth at this time stating that he thought it would be good if he went into the wilderness for a time. He also invited his friend Franz Hildebrandt to come to England to join him in due course.

The two friends had worked together in Berlin. In 1931 they had written together and published a junior catechism to help young people (see Appendix 1, p. 213). It was an attempt to explain Lutheran teaching in the contemporary world, and was written initially for those in confirmation classes but not only for them. The questions and answers were in summary form. Wider explanations depended on those giving the teachings. The two friends were conducting confirmation classes and saw a need. The Catechism was reprinted in 1933 for discussions at meetings with ministers. Franz used to tell how the two of them joked about future textual critics looking to ascribe certain typical expressions to one or the other and, inevitably, guessing wrongly. It is indeed impossible to see the 'breaks'.

Bonhoeffer went to London to preach and to meet the congregations. At first he was uncertain about this move. Indeed it was only while he was at Bethel in August that he saw the London appointment as the next step to take. Also at this time his friend Franz Hildebrandt came to Bethel. He had been to Holland with a view to a possible appointment. Things had not worked out for him so Bonhoeffer told him that, in that case, he could come to London.

A group of theologians were meeting with von Bodelschwingh at his Bethel institutions. Bodelschwingh made sure that they all saw his caring work – which greatly impressed Bonhoeffer – and then they prepared a 'Confession of Faith'. After the initial draft was made copies were sent by Bodelschwingh to various scholars and church leaders for comment – to Bonhoeffer's disappointment. The result was, inevitably, a watered-down version. Eventually, after he was informed that Bonhoeffer would have nothing to do with publication, Niemoeller redrafted it himself. One objective was to state the Christian faith in such a way that nationalism would be compelled to take a back seat. In the end the 'Bethel Confession' served its purpose in that it prepared the way for the Barmen Confession which was a crucial moment in the life of the Confessing Church.

On 5 September 1933 the General Synod of the Old Prussian Church met in Berlin and passed a rule that only those who supported the National Socialist Movement and the German Evangelical Church and were of pure Aryan descent could be ministers. It was known as the 'Brown Synod' as so many wore brown shirts to signify their allegiance to the party. Gerhard Jacobi was refused permission to speak. Martin Niemoeller walked out in protest at the resolutions. One pastor claimed Adolf Hitler to be the final authority in the church in Germany. That was heresy enough.

Niemoeller and Bonhoeffer wrote to Karl Barth asking if he thought there would ever be more of a crunch time than this, Bonhoeffer asking if it were possible to remain in a church which was no longer Christian. With the Aryan resolution, he believed, the Old Prussian Church had separated itself from the Church of Jesus Christ. At this time the Pastors' Emergency League began whereby all who signed were pledged to support any who were cast out of their positions. In Sofia 15–20 September at the World Alliance Conference a resolution was passed deploring the state measures in Germany which were directed against the Jews and which stated 'that the Jewish race is considered a race of inferior status'. The resolution deplored the Aryan paragraph which puts 'serious disabilities upon ministers and church officers who by chance of birth are non-Aryan'. This resolution named particularly the Old Prussian Synod.

On 27 September the National Synod met at Wittenberg. Bonhoeffer and Hildebrandt were present with pamphlets appealing to the Synod about the freedom of the church to act, asking the Church to proclaim the Gospel and appealing against the Aryan paragraph. This pamphlet, they claimed, represented the views of 2,000 pastors and was signed by, amongst others, Bonhoeffer, Hildebrandt, Jacobi and Niemoeller. Bonhoeffer and

Hildebrandt had sent a telegram to Reichbishop Mueller asking him to make mention of the pamphlet but nothing was said – so they distributed it widely, nailing pamphlets on trees wherever they could. This action brought a reproving comment in the National Socialist report on the Synod 'Disturbances are occur ring in the city. It may seem unbelievable but it is true. Our oppo- nents are making themselves noticed. Leaflets without printing house approval are doing the rounds. But with unerring certainty and sureness our leaders will take measures ...' Bonhoeffer and Hildebrandt had helped to stir up matters. As the two of them sat in the Wittenberg church and heard one of the leaders of the German Christians, Hœssenfelder, say to Bishop Mueller over Luther's tomb 'Greetings! Reichsbishop!' Hildebrandt whispered to his friend that he now believed in the doctrine of the revolution of Luther's bones for assuredly they must have turned in his grave at those words.

Niemoeller, Jacobi, Bonhoeffer and Hildebrandt were the only ones who had been involved in every event since May in various meetings, preparing statements and drafting resolutions. They were described by one supporter as 'the essential seed corn' of the movement. Now after Wittenberg they felt, as Hildbrandt remarked, they had seen the end of the German Evangelical Church. Franz knew that, after the Church had accepted the Aryan clause, his days of service would be numbered so when Dietrich made the suggestion that he also should travel to London and they work together in caring for the congregations in Sydenham and Aldgate, he began to make plans for that move. At this time he had also been sounded out about a post in the Pastors' Emergency Union. He waited a while. During this same period he was less than pleased with the attitude of Karl Barth whom he thought was not enthusiastic about what he called the 'Dibelius-church' and seemed to a degree to be sitting on the fence – waiting.

On 1 October with Dietrich and some other young Christians he went to a church where they saw the Swastika flag flying from the church flagpole. During worship there was no mention of oppo- sition to the Nazi regime. At this period Franz found little support for his suggestion that Christians should move out and create a church completely independent of the state. He saw problems for a 'state-linked' church, ties financial and otherwise which could make thought and action difficult.

The Pastor of the German Church
of Sydenham and St. Paul's in London.
Lic. Dietrich Bonhoeffer.
23, Manor Mount, S.E.23. London.

London, 3.XI. 32.

This is to certify that I have invited my friend,
Pastor Lic. Franz Hildebrandt, to come to London
and to stay with me as long as he wants. He will
during the time he is here take up studies of
the English language and of English Churchlife.
I garantee for him in any respect.

Lic. Dietrich Bonhoeffer, Pastor

I beg to repeat this
invitation for the month of
August and September. Being
myself on holiday in Denmark
where my friend is coming from
I am unable to confirm this Invitation
with my church seal.
August 23rd . 34.

Letter from Bonhoeffer for Hildebrandt to present at immigration.

On 24 October he wrote a letter to Martin Niemoeller who had sent a telegram to Hitler on the occasion of his walking out of the League of Nations. The idea of Niemoeller's telegram was to support Hitler's plea for equality of status between countries – which had been rejected. Franz made the point that this same Hitler denied equality of status *within the church in his own country*. Franz ended his letter to Niemoeller by saying that he had no wish to harm the cause of the Pastors' Emergency Union by repeating yet again what had been his constant refrain. Henceforth his part was to keep silent.

Dietrich Bonhoeffer journeyed to Forest Hill, Sydenham to take up his London appointment on 16 October 1933. On 10 November 1933 Franz Hildebrandt arrived in England to join him. He reached Victoria Station in London where Dietrich was to meet him, but Dietrich was nowhere to be seen. So he tried to telephone the house where Dietrich lived. Later he loved to tell how with his minimal knowledge of English he tried to obtain the services of the operator to find the number but while he was struggling in the telephone kiosk there was a tap on the kiosk window. Turning round he saw Dietrich, who had arrived a little late. Franz had a problem in that for him French had been the second language taught at school. Now learning English was revealed as a number one priority. In this Dietrich took charge. A good English speaker, he had his own ideas of teaching it.

By arriving on 10 November Franz was in time to hear Dietrich preach next day on 11 November, Remembrance Sunday. Later in his life he said he could vividly remember the sermon on the text 'but they are at peace' from Wisdom 3.3. He told how Dietrich related the story of a patient given up by the doctors, losing consciousness, hanging between life and death who was looking, as it were, across the border and who exclaimed 'My God! This is beautiful!'

On 12 November Dietrich was officially elected as the minister of the German congregation. Thus there came about in Forest Hill London one of the main sources of power of what later became the German Confessing Church. Others were gathering strength and becoming witnesses in the churches of their homeland. In London were two young keen pastors who in spite of saying they would take a break from the struggle because they felt the church was not always bold enough, risking enough in pursuit of her calling, were thinking about the challenge every day. One would love to have a full record of their conversations and activities during the three months they were together.

This was the time when Dietrich's *Cost of Discipleship* took shape. Franz always maintained it was the finest of his writings, albeit he made some critical comments about it to his friend. It was only later he saw the touch of genius in the English title 'The **Cost** of Discipleship'. The title, thus, said so much about both book and author. He remembered their conversations together when they discussed themes which later appeared in the book.

Dietrich tried to teach Franz English. Franz used to laugh whenever he talked of Dietrich's methods of instruction: how he gave to Franz his first English Bible; how he sent Franz to do the shopping, for shopping will always teach the 'essentials'. Reading the Bible is a good way of learning a language as some can testify but it is important that the edition of the Bible which is read is carefully chosen – otherwise one can end by speaking in the language of the 'Luther Bible' or the 'King James Version'! Dietrich also believed that it was easier to learn a foreign language when half asleep. He had various ways of instruction when Franz was sitting in a chair and dozing. Later Franz became as much a master of English as he was of German.

By letter and telephone they remained in touch with Martin Niemoeller. This relationship with Niemoeller developed as they passed on ideas. Indeed at times they told him what they thought he, as leader of the church opposition to Hitler, should do. One is rather amused and somewhat amazed that these two young pastors, residing and working in London, both in their mid-twenties, both fine scholars, should take it upon themselves to instruct and sometimes to correct and criticize the words and deeds of a senior pastor. It says much for the character and perception of Martin Niemoeller that he listened to them and used their thinking. So a great abiding friendship was formed by him with them both.*

So, slowly in thought and action in Germany and in London the

---

*That this friendship meant much to Niemoeller was obvious when one talked with him. The Franz Hildebrandt of whom he spoke to me was the same person I had grown to know and love. I accept his portrait of Dietrich Bonhoeffer as equally accurate. (ASC)

theology of opposition to the Nazis was being worked out, and slowly the 'confession' of the Confessional Church was growing. It may have seemed to some that Dietrich and Franz were silent, but underneath there was a growing rumble of thunder. The surface water may have seemed calm, but beneath were strong currents never ceasing to pull them along.

CHAPTER 6

THE STRUGGLE INTENSIFIES

What some 'German Christians' feared would happen if Dietrich Bonhoeffer became a pastor to the two German congregations in London did in fact take place. Dietrich Bonhoeffer had first met George Bell, Anglican bishop of Chichester, in 1933, and his friendship deepened. He was pleased to be able to share his concern about the unfolding events in Germany. The bishop had a growing reputation in ecumenical circles in the days before the World Council of Churches became an official organization in 1948. Bell also became a strong advocate for all who were refugees from the Nazi regime. Having been well-briefed by Bonhoeffer and others, he understood what was required in their situation.

Dietrich introduced Franz to the bishop and the whole friendship so developed that Bell, who had no children of his own, would refer to them as 'my two boys' – and the two boys passed on to him what they knew about the situation in Germany. Bishop Bell's interest was such that later, when the flow of refugees increased, he pondered deeply if he should resign the see of Chichester and be appointed 'Bishop of the Refugees'. In fact he remained and continued his noble and honoured work while Bishop of Chichester.

As Hitler's powers grew in 1933 the opposition to the Nazis in Germany was, of necessity, scattered and erratic but amongst Christians there were those who stood for the faith and for Christian values as a few brief pictures will show. It is important to note that the situation of the Roman Catholic Church in Germany was different from that of the Protestant churches. The centralized structure of the Roman Catholic Church reaches beyond national boundaries. In the 1930s, before the alliance of Protestant Churches in the World Council of Churches, it was international in a way unrivalled by any other confession. Its centre is the Vatican, and even though the Vatican is an independent state, it is located in the city of Rome which is the capital city of Italy. This territorial link is underlined by the fact that the Pope, head of the world wide Roman Catholic church, is also localized as the Bishop of Rome. Thus there can be consciously or subconsciously an influence on the international church by the nation where its headquarters are located. In the 1920s and 1930s the fascist Duce or dictator of Italy, ruling from Rome, was Benito Mussolini. After Hitler's accession to power in Germany, the two became allies. Rome and Berlin were linked.

Although the evidence suggests that Hitler was never happy with the Christian faith and teaching, he realized that, if possible, he needed to have the churches on his side or at least that they should remain politically quiescent. The 'German Christian' movement allied to his own specious ideology had worked to a degree with the Protestants. The appointment of a Commissar for Church Affairs had been a major factor in bringing about the resignation of Pastor Fritz von Bodelschwingh, the popular independent Reichsbishop, on 24 June. Ludwig Mueller, the new bishop, had solid party support. Hitler therefore turned to the Roman Catholics.

On 20 July 1933 Cardinal Pacelli, who later became Pope Pius XII, signed a Concordat on behalf of the Vatican, which was intended to establish good relationships between the Roman Catholic Church and the Nazis. While he did not agree with the tenets of its faith, Hitler admired the Catholic church structure, organization and control of the tenets of the faith, down to the last detail of what loyal Catholics must believe. The Concordat was also part of Hitler's plan for gaining recognition in the wider world. On 14 September, 1933, Hitler, acting as Chancellor, held a meeting of the Government to explain the advantages of the Concordat: a) the Vatican had negotiated with a country ruled by what it had claimed was an unchristian government; b) in establishing good relations with the National Socialist state, the Vatican, to his surprise, had committed the bishops to working with the Nazis and had given unequivocal recognition to their government; c) on signing the Concordat the Roman Church would withdraw its support from other parties and organizations, e.g. trade unions.

On his accession to power on 30 January Hitler, having wanted an agreement like the Concordat, had not thought it could be achieved so quickly. Now, within a year, the Roman Catholic church had effectively withdrawn from German party politics (there had been a 'Catholic' party) and Hitler had removed one possible great and influential opposing force.

However, not all Roman Catholics found it easy to accept the terms of the Concordat even though it did give Hitler decisive power against Catholic opponents. Bishop Clemens August Graf von Galen, the Roman Catholic bishop of Muenster, was one who could not be kept silent. He was in fact the first Roman Catholic bishop appointed after Hitler's accession to power. He gave spiritual help and counsel to many, including Martin Niemoeller. In 1941 he stood alongside Pastor Fritz von Bodelschwingh on the issue of euthanasia when the SS wanted to destroy the handicapped and disabled residing in the Bethel hospitals of which Bodelschwingh was the head (Leiter).

Some other Roman Catholic leaders such as Bernhard Lichtenberg, the Dean of St Hedwig's Cathedral in Berlin, who led prayers for the Jews, and ordinary priests like Alfons Wachsmann and Alfred Delp were amongst those who gave their lives in testimony to Jesus and the Gospel. In St Hedwig's Cathedral there is a chapel with a wall on which the names are inscribed of those Roman Catholic priests who resisted and died. In Muenster there is a statue dedicated to von Galen. However, all in all Roman Catholic resistance was weak and scattered. The Concordat prevented officially organized and effective opposition.

There were Protestants too who faced Nazi idolatry with unselfish courage. Paul Schneider, a pastor of two churches in Dickenscheid and Womrath, would not allow the Nazis to use his church with their 'pagan' liturgy. They arrested him three times. The last time was after the Harvest Festival service in October 1937. This led him to prison and concentration camp. Professor Heinrich Vogel commented, 'He was imprisoned with bars of paper' for he had only to sign a piece of paper saying he renounced his action and he would have been freed. When asked, in Buchenwald, to do this he replied, 'I know why I am here' and his wife, equally devout, supported his action. She understood the nature of his faith. He died in Buchenwald concentration camp on 18 July 1939, almost certainly as a result of an injection of poison. His opposition had begun at the beginning of the Nazi rule and he was one of those whose family the Pastors' Emergency League was pledged to support.

Like Schneider other pastors fought lonely battles, especially in the early days. Ludwig Steil of Westphalia on Whitsuntide 1933 gained 100 signatures to a document which contained the words 'the Lord of the Church himself calls. He whom we confess as the Son of the living God, the God of Abraham, Isaac and Jacob, the Word become flesh. He summons us to confess Him today'. Steil eventually paid for his opposition with his life. He died in Dachau concentration camp in January 1945 after a time of incarceration. In thinking of these brave Christians, many of whom he had known personally, Franz would sometimes quote the verse from the letter to the Hebrews 'of whom the world was not worthy'.

Later, during the war, Jochen Klepper, scholar, poet, hymn writer and journalist, went to his death on 10 December 1942. He had married a Jewish widow who, with her daughter, had become Christian. In his work as a journalist, with his ear to the ground, he heard things about the concentration camps. He also learned that his wife and step-daughter were to be arrested and deported and he knew what that meant – death in a gas chamber in one camp or another. If he disowned them he might save his own life. But he loved them and they loved him in a deep reciprocal love. What to do?... In Hitler's Berlin in 1942? So, knowing the inevitable, they chose voluntary death together. As the last verse of one of his hymns, an evening hymn which serves also for the evening of life, Klepper wrote:

> You close my eyes with touch so light
> I sleep at peace till dawning:
> For He who leads me into Night
> Will lead me through to Morning

And, trusting in Jesus, they walked together through the night to morning.

On 30 January 1935 in Hagen, Westphalia, a play by Edmond Kiss was being performed. It was both racist and pagan. It attacked Christianity. This was the second anniversary of Hitler's coming to power; Dr Josef Goebbels the Minister of Propaganda commended it, so people were afraid not to attend. During the performance a man stood up and protested. He was soon arrested by the Gestapo, beaten, and dragged half-conscious from the theatre. That man was Kurt Gerstein, a Christian who had worked with boys in a Bible group, who had joined the Nazi party in hope of good things and then had been critical of the Nazis, finally having his membership downgraded to provisional membership. He became a supporter of Martin Niemoeller. His wedding service was conducted by Otto Dibelius. Then he became re-established in the Nazi party – and had little to do with the church. His pastor was surprised.

This was part of Gerstein's solitary plan. On 22 February 1941 he had attended the interment of a relative's ashes. They had been returned from the hospital to which she had been transferred a little time before with the information that she had died of a cerebral thrombosis. He became very angry saying that she had been murdered. She had been suffering from mental illness and Gerstein said that part of Hitler's plan was to eliminate all such persons. This sharpened his determination to unveil the evil. From that time he worked actively in the Gestapo and the SS. Later he gave a dossier to a member of the Swedish legation in Berlin detailing what he had discovered in order that they could pass it on to the Allies. Nothing was done and a message came back effectively saying that they wanted facts and not horror stories. At the end of the war Gerstein was arrested as a war criminal. So a man who had helped prisoners to live, who was tortured spiritually and mentally by what he had to do to obtain facts, died, probably by his own hand. An investigation found that in the Allies' files under his name was the entry 'Dossier mislaid'.

Judge Jan Niemoeller said that his father knew what Gerstein was about as did some others whom he consulted about the spiritual and moral issues of his carrying poison gas to the concentration camps. Pastor Martin Niemoeller, Jan's father, spoke up for him but immediately after the war anyone wearing the 'Death's Head Cap', the mark of the SS, was fighting a losing battle for freedom. 'A very special kind of saint,' Niemoeller said of him.

Gerstein said that it was difficult for any German who was an enemy of the Nazis to find a way to discredit the government. Outside Germany few would believe the horrors they had perpetrated, until the gates of Belsen, Dachau, Buchenwald and Auschwitz were opened by Allied soldiers. Germans have been accused of taking no action concerning such camps. In answer one ordinary German said, 'The Allies couldn't believe it until they saw it. Is it surprising that we found it difficult to believe? All we knew was that people who asked questions disappeared.'

The Nazis were strong and powerful, well-organized and ruthless in opposition. In addition Goebbels was a master of propaganda who used the lie as his weapon. We must not make sweeping condemnations of the church but be thankful that there were people for whom Jesus Christ and He alone was Lord. There were those who proclaimed this message in spite of the Gestapo. Many of these found their way to concentration camps and to death.

Niemoeller now became the focal point of that Church opposition. Later Hitler said of him: 'A man like Pastor Niemoeller cannot be allowed to remain at liberty', so awkward to the Nazis was his opposition. The initial aim of the Pastors' Emergency League was to help those pastors and their families who had been deprived of their living either because of their non-Aryan blood or because of their opposition to the Nazis. On 13 November, a few days after Franz Hildebrandt had arrived in London, the German Christians held a large rally in Berlin. The senior Nazi of the Berlin area, Dr Krause, addressed them. He said that non-Aryans must be removed from the church which must have everything 'non-German', i.e., non-Aryan removed from the worship and the confessions. 'The church must be freed from the Old Testament ... with its stories of cattle dealers and pimps ...' He was following the teaching of Alfred Rosenberg, the philosopher of the Nazis. There was little comment in the meeting but later even some German Christians were shocked. Two days earlier Niemoeller, Dr von Rabenau and Professor Scharf from Sachsenhausen had been suspended from their positions. On 16 November the Aryan clause in this present setting was withdrawn. Mueller even postponed his consecration which had been set for 3 December in Berlin. When the Dahlem congregation were told Niemoeller was suspended they refused to accept the decision nor would they accept any other pastor – so he stayed.

On 30 November Bonhoeffer and Hildebrandt in London learned of a gathering of some of the church leaders meeting with Bishop Mueller in the north of the country. From London they urged Niemoeller not to hand over 'control of the ship' to those who would guide her astray. They came to realize that Niemoeller's sense of national pride was still real: but whereas the 'German Christians' said 'I am a German and I am also a Christian' Niemoeller was saying 'I am a Christian. I am also a German'. The two friends continued to bombard Niemoeller, especially when they heard that Jacobi had resigned from the Council. They were upset. Jacobi and Niemoeller had found it difficult to agree on an assessment of the situation. Meanwhile the two friends had persuaded the German pastors serving in London to join the Pastors' Emergency League. After receiving their message of disquiet about Jacobi, Niemoeller replied to London assuring them of his joint action with Jacobi, commenting that things were very difficult, asking them not to create problems. Nevertheless they continued to press him with telephone calls, letters and telegrams making various comments particularly about the Aryan clause.

This information, relayed by Niemoeller to other anti-Nazi colleagues, drew attention to Bonhoeffer and Hildebrandt. Ideas were constantly being sent over and Franz Hildebrandt often spoke about the unity of their views, usually saying that Dietrich was always ahead of him in thought. There is no doubt that Dietrich had a personal charisma and having been about and in action for two or three years before Hildebrandt, he was more established as a theologian, but , with his incisive and analytical mind and with his remarkable memory, Hildebrandt was his equal in many ways.

The telephone account for the two friends became very large indeed. They were keeping in touch with Germany on several fronts including the Bonhoeffer family, who gave them encouragement. They also kept in touch with Gerhard Jacobi, and, of course, Martin Niemoeller. So large was the account that according to Franz, 'the post office decided they couldn't cope with these figures and cancelled the bill'. The telephone calls were important as they helped to clarify the news which came from Germany. Normal press avenues were restricted because of Dr Goebbels and his propaganda machine. This hoodwinked many nations and their leaders even up to and after the outbreak of war in September 1939. Reliable news of the church opposition came from their telephone contacts. Much of this was passed to Bishop Bell to keep him informed.

Their plans to keep out of the battle in Germany had not been successful, partly because they kept in touch with relatives and friends, partly because their sharp active minds were devoted to battling against any evil philosophy. Dietrich was already exhibiting signs of that restlessness which was to bring him back from the USA to Germany in 1939. His landlady Miss Sharp, who proved to be a good friend to them both, came to know and understand them very well. In 1935 she commented, about Dietrich: 'I shall always remember him pacing up and down in our lounge, trying to decide whether to remain here or to give up his church here and return to the persecuted church in Germany. He longed to visit Gandhi and India and felt a premonition that unless he seized that moment he would never go. I knew how he, being who he was, must decide ...'.

After the meeting in Berlin on 13 November and Dr Krause's speech, which surprised neither of them, Franz Hildebrandt commented that 'the German Christians let their mask fall and in an unconcealed way landed on the New Paganism'.

Dietrich and Franz were disturbed that Niemoeller and Jacobi still seemed to be at odds with one another. They tended to side with Jacobi. Hildebrandt wrote to Niemoeller expressing his perplexity as this division gave 'German Christians' a cause for rejoicing (15 December). They also differed from Karl Barth who was critical of the idea of forming a new free church. They believed the danger lay not in creating a new structure and hierarchy but in the task of trying to save the Christian church. Niemoeller gave assurances that there was nothing personally wrong between him and Jacobi and they were not going to settle for half measures. It was an honest disagreement where it existed.

At Christmas time Dietrich sent out Franz to buy the Christmas tree to help his learning English and for a present gave him an English Bible. They had a surprise visitor on Christmas Day, Wolf-Dieter Zimmermann, who brought a surprise present, a Bonhoeffer family speciality, homemade Strassburg liver pâté. The friends had a lively theological discussion. Julius Rieger remembered how Franz enjoyed it all and the argument ended in great friendliness. Zimmermann later wrote joyfully about this Christmas Day.

They took heart that the trend in Germany seemed to show that the German Christians had been in retreat. They hoped to hear further news in this direction. Similar sentiments were expressed in a meeting of the Pastor's Emergency League under Jacobi's leadership in Berlin on 24 December .

On 4 January 1934 a 'muzzling' decree was issued under the influence of Bishop Mueller, effectively forbidding the church to speak about or become involved in politics. Niemoeller and company responded. On Sunday 7 January some 3,500 members of the Pastors' Emergency League read a statement to their congregations accusing Mueller of bringing strife into the church. At this time the Church Youth Organization was handed over officially to the Hitler Youth Movement.

Now events began to change direction radically for Franz Hildebrandt. Martin Niemoeller had written at Christmastime mentioning that the treasurer of the Pastors' Emergency league was retiring. (As far as Franz could remember later, he was a layman, a retired Admiral who was a friend of Martin Niemoeller.) In January Franz received a letter from Niemoeller asking him to return to Germany to take up the Treasurer's post.

He telephoned Niemoeller at once and asked three questions:

> Did the job require a pastor?
> Did it require him (F.H.) in particular?
> Did it require him at once?

The answer to all three questions was 'Yes!' and so he took the next available boat home and arrived in Berlin just three days before the historic – and only – meeting between Hitler and Niemoeller. Church leaders met with Hitler on 25 January. In the group Niemoeller was 'at the back'. As Hitler came to shake hands with him prior to leaving the meeting Niemoeller spoke words which effectively were a direct challenge to the Fuehrer: 'Herr Reichskanzler, you said just now "I will take care of the German people". But we too as Christians have a duty and neither you nor any power in the world is in the position to take it away from us'. Earlier conversations in the meeting had revealed that Goering had had Niemoeller's telephone 'tapped' as he quoted what had been said in a private telephone conversation. Later Niemoeller used to say that he realized that this might be his only opportunity to speak his challenge to Hitler. He felt he must make his stand clearly and unambiguously.

On 26 January, the day after the confrontation, Niemoeller was again suspended. On the previous evening his house had been raided and files of the Pastors' Emergency League removed. On Sunday 4 February , which also happened to be the birthday of both Dietrich Bonhoeffer and Bishop Bell, the congregation arrived at St Ann's Church, Berlin-Dahlem, now without the senior Pastor, expecting to hear a pro-Hitler preacher. A young pastor was in the pulpit, a younger 'Niemoeller' by name Franz Hildebrandt. After about a month Niemoeller was back and then, in the words of Franz, 'we preached side by side'.

The *Morning Post* in London carried a report of how on 4 February a full church heard the sermon by Franz Hildebrandt on the text of Psalm 16:2 'You are my God: I have no good apart from you', which challenged the government, put spiritual before temporal authority and showed that these are people 'by no means satisfied' with the German Christian Church. A few days later a bomb exploded in Niemoeller's home. Police appeared without having been called – which suggested to Franz, who was looking after the house, some collusion. He protested about the bomb but nothing was done by the police.

Two days afterwards Franz was called to Gestapo Headquarters. They were upset by the *Morning Post* report and wanted him to withdraw what had been said. He maintained that it was a 'pure Biblical sermon'. It dealt with the proclamation of the Word of God and nothing else. The theme was the elementary statement of Christian faith that God is the Lord. Both he and Niemoeller, he said, were upset that the Pastors' Emergency League had been regarded as a political movement to discredit the relationship between church and state in the Third Reich. He was aware that there were those who wanted to attack the Pastors' Emergency League as enemies of the state and he was trying to offset these malicious designs without surrendering his own beliefs. It was an occasion when he was trying to be diplomatic. If pressed he would probably have referred to the words of Jesus about being 'as wise as serpents', with a smile on his face.

The Pastors' Emergency League for which Franz was now treasurer had been created a short while before the two friends had left for England. It was a voluntary union of those who opposed the new Nazified church regime. Those who had signed the membership cards were bound together in fellowship to be 'actively' faithful to their ordination vows (Franz stressed the word 'actively'. He wanted no sleeping partners). They had singled out the Aryan clause as one of the issues to be taken up with the new commitment. To them it violated the confession of the church. Those who joined also undertook to make contributions for the upkeep of those pastors and their families who because of their stand were dismissed or suspended. Niemoeller wanted a good, careful treasurer who was totally committed to the cause and he knew well the qualities of the young pastor in London.

Franz would sometimes talk about how from time to time he would meet one or another of the dispossessed pastors who would say 'I am Pastor so-and-so from such a place' and he would say 'Yes, I know: and your monthly salary is so much'. The man would look surprised until Franz told him he was responsible for sending it. There was, naturally, much need for secrecy in the whole matter. Franz's superb memory helped to keep written records to an essential minimum. Pastors were not always compelled by the Nazis to move out of the parsonage when they were suspended. The Nazis wanted to avoid too much chaos. Sometimes they would stay. Some would attempt to defy the suspension order by not drawing any regular salary and simply continue with their pastoral duties, officially unpaid. In this kind of situation the scheme helped immeasurably. The state would sometimes close its eyes to the scheme, for in this way there was no claim on the state 'church tax.' The reaction varied. One could never be sure. Sometimes it would mean imprisonment or exile. At one time Paul Schneider was placed in another church for six months. Some Nazis were fairly tolerant towards the churches. Others like Martin Bormann regarded the churches with 'a venomous hostility'.

Franz recalled later that for a time the situation became a kind of endurance competition. The Gestapo would arrest a pastor. Then the Confessing Church (as it became known) would send a replacement. This replacement would be arrested, so another was sent. In the end the Gestapo would weary of it and give up and the latest Confessing Church nominee would be allowed to stay.

This was becoming very like the organization Bonhoeffer and Hildebrandt favoured – 'a free church' – which meant a church free of any link with the state, a church financed independently with its own structures and Government.

The normal way of financing the church in Germany was through a church tax collected by the state along with other taxes. The individual opted for Roman Catholic or Protestant main churches. If the individual opted 'in', he or she had a claim on the church for baptisms, weddings and funerals. The pastors were paid through the state, hence the state's area of control and right to speak. Baptists, Methodists, Pentecostalists and others were not in this system. Hildebrandt and Bonhoeffer were not the only ones who saw this system as a stranglehold on the national church.

Events now began to move quickly. The early months of 1934 may well be the low point in the story of the church opposition to Hitler. On 2 February the Reichsbishop suspended some fifty pastors. Pastors who disagreed with the Nazis were also transferred from their parishes to others and 'German Christian' pastors assigned. Some senior pastors were removed by retiring them early. Propaganda was put out that the battle was simply about pastors, their status and prestige. Niemoeller and company continued to proclaim Jesus. Many were imprisoned, albeit for a short time in most cases.* And in 1934 for the first time the gates of concentration camps opened to take in pastors.

A call went out early in the year 'to our parishes' and 'to our members in the parishes'. The response was unexpected and incredible. Many parishes did not want to give up their pastors. Some 5,000 people travelled to Ulm. There on 22 April 1934 Bishop Theophil Wurm, who was under threat from the German Christians, preached in the Minster on the text 1 Pet. 2.11–17. He was a church leader who had been attacked by Reichsbishop Muller and had been vilified by the Nazis. He said 'We serve God if we take office in the running and ordering of the state. We serve our people if we are other than the world.' After the sermon Bishop Meiser of Bavaria read to the congregation, all of whom

*In 1953 (twenty years later) I stayed and worked with a pastor named Kurt Storck who had been imprisoned by the Nazis for three months. He claimed to have been only one of many: 'They tried to frighten us' he told me. 'We relied on the Lord Jesus Christ, knowing our faith was vital. The weak ones were the ones who relied on their emotions and good feelings'. (ASC)

remained, a 'Message from the Confessional Front of Germany'.

Franz Hildebrandt, who was there in his new position as treasurer of the Pastors' Emergency League, maintained that the opening sentence was the most important thing in the declaration. Others have agreed that this was the sentence which infuriated Hitler (coming as it did so soon after Niemoeller's challenge when face to face with him). The offensive words, as Franz Hildebrandt records them, were:

> We, the representatives of the churches of Wuerttemberg and Bavaria, of the Free Synods of the Rhineland, Westphalia and Brandenburg, as well as of many confessing congregations and Christians all over Germany declare, as the lawful Evangelical Church of Germany before this assembly *and before the whole of Christendom* ...

The last words contained the challenge, because to speak out like that to the world at large while being a group in defiance of Hitler and the ruling power of Germany was tantamount to treason. The statement then continued to contradict things said by the government about living at peace – 'Their deeds contradict their words'. Niemoeller and Hildebrandt were amongst the signatories to this statement.

Ulm had been chosen as the venue because if trouble came it was possible to cross the river Danube and so move from Wuerttemberg into Bavaria and into another jurisdiction (Germany still having various 'regions' of government). Jan Niemoeller still remembers how thrilled the young boys in the church in Berlin were when Franz, now his father's curate, returned, having travelled from Ulm to Berlin by aeroplane! In 1974 Franz was invited to preach at a special service '40 years later'. He said that this had been a tremendous step forward to a church without frontiers of language, race or nation, leaping over all barriers on the way to a united Christendom on earth.* After this somewhat spontaneous act of resistance at Ulm the leaders of the church organized a meeting at Barmen-Wuppertal. It became the first nationwide organized Free Synod of the Confessing

---

*Those who later in British Methodism of the 1960s thought his view and perspective on church unity to be narrow were completely wrong. He had a broad vision.

Church and concluded by presenting a statement or confession of faith for the people.

Earlier in the year, in February, Pastor Fritz von Bodelschwingh had called upon the church to take time away from the tumult to pray for a clear sight of the way to go and to walk in it together. The only way, he suggested, is to follow obediently the path of opening wide the gates, lifting high the doors so that the King of Glory can come in. Five weeks after this word one of Bishop Mueller's men said in an open meeting: 'The state has opened a sanatorium for its opponents, the concentration camp'. The state, having used the teaching 'Render unto Caesar' against the protesting Christians, was now openly using violence. Opposition would be snuffed out, if possible.

Franz Hildebrandt was Martin Niemoeller's official representative on various committees. After a meeting in Berlin of the Pastors' Emergency League, he put forward 'the arguments in favor of an Independent Free Church'. He pressed this because he had a vision of a church without frontiers and cited Gal. 3.28 in support. But they (Bonhoeffer and Hildebrandt) were still very young men and their point was heard but not taken up. On 3 May Bodelschwingh had said in a sermon on Mat. 11.29: 'We can carry the yoke of Jesus together, Lutherans and Reformed. We do not "unite". A farmer who has two animals yoked to his cart doesn't care if they are the same colour, if they are willing to bow and work under the same yoke. We can only begin a new chapter in German church history if we learn from Jesus.'

The first Synod of the German Confessing Church met in Barmen on 29 May 1934. They needed a clear statement of what they believed and at the conclusion of the Synod they had done precisely that. It is probably one of the most important statements made by any group of Christians living in a country where the state government is hostile. Franz Hildebrandt always stressed its crucial importance. He was one of the youngest present. The Synod drew its strength from the Bible, the Word of God. Perhaps it was from this time that reliance on the Bible as the Word of God took such strong hold on Franz Hildebrandt's thought – though he had always been a 'Bible-based' Christian and later easily became a John Wesley Methodist, 'a man of one book'.

Hans Asmussen and Karl Barth did the major work in preparation of the Declaration which states unequivocally: 'The impregnable foundation of the German Evangelical Church is the *Gospel of Jesus Christ as it is revealed in Holy Scripture ... He is the one Word of God* which we are to hear, which we are to trust and obey in life and in death'. The italicized words are inscribed on the Barmen memorial which stands today in the pedestrian precinct in Barmen-Wuppertal near the church where the Synod met. The Declaration also has paragraphs beginning 'we repudiate the false teaching ...' and outlines the Nazi heresies. The Declaration was signed by a selected number of the 139 representatives though all supported it. Dietrich Bonhoeffer was not present and consequently did not sign it, though he was continually in touch with the whole event.

In 1984, 50 years after Barmen, Eberhard Bethge, Bonhoeffer's biographer, gave a lecture in Seattle, USA. It was published in a symposium of papers one of which was given by Franz Hildebrandt. Bethge says that there was no way in which Christ and Hitler could be combined. The Barmen declaration made this clear. Karl Barth revised the document and produced the final version 'fortified by strong coffee and one or two Brazilian cigars'. In an open correspondence with Professor Kittel of Tuebingen, a Nazi sympathizer, he made this issue clear. Christ was and is the centre of all things.

Franz Hildebrandt was still uneasy. He didn't think it had gone far enough. He still desired an independent church without any links with the state. 'The so-called "People's Church" has no promise in the Bible, no fulfilment in history and no meaning in the present day'. He believed that only a free and independent church could exist and concentrate not on political activity but simply on saving souls. So, yet another of John Wesley's influences is seen to be on his heart.

Franz was a man always ready to 'go out' in faith. His friend Dietrich was another. Later, for example, in the Anglican-Methodist conversations (see ch. 16) in the 1960s Franz advocated the same. In the 1930s his friend Martin Niemoeller thought differently from him: 'When a burglar breaks into your house, you turn him out. You do not go away and let him take over the house'. This was the great dilemma and to the end of his life Franz Hildebrandt believed that at Barmen, by not taking this act of faith and going out with a clean break, the Confessing Church missed a great opportunity of really decisive action.

CHAPTER 7

AFTER BARMEN

Barmen had given the Confessing Church its official beginning and its creed. Franz Hildebrandt was ever pleased that he had been present and had shared in the deliberations, though for him and for Dietrich, who was not present, it did not go far enough towards the total independence of the church. Nevertheless it was a momentous occasion in the life of the Christian community. Franz continued as treasurer of the Pastors' Emergency League but other events were beginning to take place which were to change the pattern of his life. Here his diaries both excite and disappoint. They note only a time, name or a place. Of course had the Gestapo seized them, they would have seen simply the kind of data anyone would keep, betraying nothing. Yet, one wonders: how were those items filled out? what did those names mean? what issues were discussed?

On 4 June 1934, he and Jacobi telephoned Dietrich Bonhoeffer. On behalf of the Emergency League they were seeking a seminary principal to train pastors, curates and students and they wondered if Dietrich would take it on. It was yet another feeler on the road to independence. Fifty years later Franz assessed the situation saying: 'We needed a Thomas Chalmers* who would lead Dissenters into a separate Free Church. "The time is not ripe" was the answer, one of the most powerful weapons of the enemy.' This was a favourite criticism of his when the decisive action he thought necessary was not taken by those who led the church – and at times he was right.

*Thomas Chalmers 1780–1847, a Scottish divine who, in 1843, led a secession from the Church of Scotland to form the Free Church of Scotland. The issue was over the authority to appoint ministers.

Now however, there was in fact a separate Confessing Church in Germany and for Bonhoeffer in London this became a matter of great importance. He kept Bishop Bell informed. Hildebrandt in Berlin was also following the development of ecumenical relationships. Preparations were in hand for an ecumenical conference at Fano. Both Bishop Bell and Dietrich Bonhoeffer were involved. This was a troubled year in German political life with the death of President Paul von Hindenburg in August. He had been regarded as a controlling balance to Hitler, who, in the eyes of some, was 'playing out' his hand and would soon be finished. Hitler however decreed himself 'Fuehrer and Reichschancellor' and became unassailable. It was another 'misreading' of Hitler, who was far more astute than his opponents realized.

Barmen had upset the 'German Christians'. The big question for those organizing the Fano conference was 'which church in Germany should be invited?' Bonhoeffer, who was involved together with the other church leaders, insisted that the Confessing Church was the true Christian church and not simply 'another' church. He refused to go unless he was invited as a member and representative of that church. He travelled to Berlin in June to meet Martin Niemoeller and President Koch, who had presided at Barmen. As it turned out neither Koch nor Bodelschwingh attended. Franz Hildebrandt pressed Dietrich to go to Fano and travelled to Esbjerg to talk with him. Together they proceeded to Fano. Franz explained that no others were coming and Dietrich felt very isolated as Franz, not being an invited delegate, left, but before he left they had had a deep discussion including an examination of Ps. 85 on which Dietrich later gave a fine talk in the conference. Dietrich gave his celebrated address on 'Peace' as his main word to the assembly.

Franz Hildebrandt travelled to London to take his friend's place in the Sydenham church during the time of the Fano Conference and preached on Acts 28.30–31:

And he [Paul] lived there two whole years at his own expense, and welcomed all who came to him, preaching the Kingdom of God and teaching about the Lord Jesus Christ quite openly and unhindered. (RSV).

Before he returned to Germany he had again spoken to Dietrich and on his return he carried in his luggage Dietrich Bonhoeffer's agreement to lead the seminary for the Confessing Church of Berlin-Brandenburg which proved an event of major significance in the opposition to Hitler.

During the period after Barmen, Franz had invitations to minister in various churches. He was sounded about going to Montreux – no less a person then Bishop Otto Dibelius had proposed him. Then the pastor, father of a young curate he knew, asked him to consider being his successor. He replied that at present he saw his duties in the work of the Confessing Church. (Later in the year this invitation was pressed with the comment that the Superintendent had said that nothing would stand in the way – presumably referring either to his Jewish blood or more likely to his work in the Confessing Church – or both.) Meanwhile he continued his work in the Berlin parish in a pastoral and preaching role as needed, acting as curate-assistant to Martin Niemoeller. As treasurer he received the contributions from the brethren who were members and from this fund helped those in need. The League also fought a number of cases for pastors who had been ejected from their parishes. They fought the cases on the grounds that the pastors had been dismissed for reasons contrary to the law of the church. The Nazis then created a *Spruchkammer* to which such cases had to go. This was a court separate from the normal courts of law.

Reichsbishop Ludwig Mueller was consecrated in Berlin Cathedral on 23 September. Hildebrandt sent to Bonhoeffer in London a postcard on which he had written only the recommended text for the day in the Lutheran calendar: Luke 14.11a: 'All who exalt themselves will be humbled'. It is doubtful if the text was used in the Berlin service! Bishop Theophil Wurm had been suspended before the Reichbishop's consecration. Shortly afterwards he was put under house arrest. A week later so was Bishop Meiser. These events, along with the arrests of other pastors, created protests. It was decided, therefore, to call another Synod of the Confessing Church at the end of October. Barmen had worked out the *credo*. Dahlem, where this Synod was to be held, would work out the constitution and organization.

On 11 October Franz visited Dietrich, who was not well. He brought Dietrich and Bishop Bell up to date with the situation in

Germany. On 15 October when Franz met the bishop he was over-whelmed by the friendly welcome. He urged the bishop to come to the Dahlem Synod but Bell was reluctant since he felt that an official representative should be obviously neutral. He suggested that the Swiss Church President Alphons Koechlin should attend. When Franz arrived at Duesseldorf on the way back home he was told that the date of the Synod had been brought forward. Nevertheless Koechlin was able to attend.

The Confessing Church was in need of thorough and careful organization. In the summer Bonhoeffer had said in conversation, 'I am more afraid of many of our own supporters than I am of the "German Christians."' Many suggestions were 'in the air' and many doubts accompanied them. The comments critical of Bishop Mueller were penetrating the Hitler coterie. Hitler had summoned the Minister of Justice to discuss the resolutions of August of the National Synod about the centralization of the church. They were all hopeful of change but their hopes were not fully realized.

August Jaeger, the troublesome Nazi Church commissar, resigned on 26 October. The two bishops under house arrest were freed. Indeed they were received by Hitler. They returned to their dioceses triumphantly. But Hitler was playing a shrewd game. His apparent yielding caused cracks to appear in the fragile unity of the Confessing Church. Reichsbishop Mueller had not been completely set aside. The Bishop of Chichester, accompanied by the Archbishop of Canterbury, went to the German Embassy in London to be apprised of the situation; but Dietrich Bonhoeffer, with his private sources of information including his brother-in-law Hans von Dohnanyi in the German civil service, was able to keep Bishop Bell accurately informed of the true situation.

At the Dahlem Synod Pastor Fritz Mueller (not to be confused with the Reichbishop), one of the three pastors in the Berlin-Dahlem parish, was given the task of building up the Confessing Church. Niemoeller was obviously very busy. Mueller did what parish work he could and, to help, Franz Hildebrandt became a member of the pastoral team. Mueller was paid by the congregation, and Hildebrandt by the Pastors Emergency League, now a part of the organization of the Confessing Church. Hitler's gentler words and invitations to some church leaders led them to wonder if some kind of compromise with the government was possible, but the pressure for Reichsbishop Mueller's resignation was not effective. He remained in office and at the end of November forbade all pastors and church officials taking orders from the 'Provisional Church Government'. Dietrich Bonhoeffer had produced a resolution from German pastors in England speaking of their support for the Confessing Church but later this was shown not to be unanimous. Nevertheless it was worrying for the 'German Christians'. More and more Martin Niemoeller came to the fore as leader and, as his brother wrote: there were other friends who knew 'Alexander Platz' and 'Prinz-Albrecht-Strasse', people not unknown to the headquarters of the state police. Amongst the names he mentions are Franz Hildebrandt and Helmut Gollwitzer. After Dahlem many were marked men and women.

At Dahlem the discussion about training ministers in the 'Confessional way of thought' had been seriously undertaken. They had to be prepared for ordination, receive ordination and be installed in their appointments. When the next Synod was held in Siegen on 28 March 1935, the matter of training was taken up responsibly. 'The Church has the duty to proclaim the Word of God clearly, purely and unabbreviated.' A statement was made that both Lutheran and Reformed churches should be serviced in this way and a group was set up to arrange and implement the resolution. Training was to commence on 1 November 1935 and amongst those nominated to teach were Pastor Asmussen, Pastor Vogel and Licentiate Hildebrandt. But this was in the future.

After the Dahlem Synod Franz Hildebrandt said that he must be committed to the Dahlem parish and undertake his own set of duties. He was bound to this congregation and their pastoral team. Since the new Confessing Church was paying him he had nothing to do with the 'official' state church and he was happy with that arrangement. He continued to be Niemoeller's representative. He turned down the opportunity to be Bonhoeffer's successor in London, happy that on his friend's return to Germany they could work together again. They both viewed the new position of the church with mixed feelings. Franz wrote that they must hold close to the New Testament in order to be crystal clear about winning the battle within the church. Dietrich expressed his fear of a second battle for the church when all would know clearly the meaning of 'confession' and 'discipleship'. Franz had a busy time lecturing in houses, parishes and fellowship groups on various subjects. In one lecture on Luther, given in April 1935 to a group of thirty students in Berlin, he maintained that only a church which clearly denounced false teaching and the Antichrist could be truly 'Lutheran'. He reiterated his view that a 'folk church' in the Nazi sense had no grounding in the Bible or history.

Hans Kerrl was Hitler's newly appointed Minister for Church Affairs. By proposing the creation of certain committees, he was sowing dissension with the aim of taking control of the Confessing Church. Marahrens, along with some others, listened. They were deceived. Niemoeller was disturbed and began plans for another leadership group of the Confessing Church to take the place of those talking with the Government. All of this gave added impetus to the work of providing a Confessing Church training scheme. They had to take over the First Examination, which was normally cared for in the universities (Biblical Languages, Theology, Church History and kindred subjects) and the Second Examination (for which incidentally neither Dietrich nor Franz had studied in seminary) which normally meant studying in a special seminary. Franz was to teach Reformation and Post-Reformation Studies.

There were no premises where they could easily meet and few facilities for their work. According to Franz, they met 'in all sorts of places: in flats, in the back rooms of cinemas and pubs'. The groups were small but the teachers were excellent. Martin Albertz, a pioneer of Form Criticism and later professor in Berlin, taught the New Testament. Heinrich Vogel who, after the war became a professor in Berlin, taught dogmatics. Hans Asmussen became Chairman of the Confessional Church in 1943. He was the founder of the Academy. All were solemnly ordained to this office in addition to their regular ordination.

Examinations were conducted orally and the times for each examination varied from one student to another. The authorities spied on them but couldn't prevent the work. Franz told the story of how Niemoeller, not himself a member of the examining board – indeed he used to smile at his lack of theology – once made an announcement from the pulpit that the place and time of the examination had to be changed three times because of pursuit by the authorities but he was happy to say it had been successfully completed. This announcement was to tease the ever present

Gestapo agent in the congregation. This work of education, along with his pastoral work, continued until 1937. Many came under the influence of those witnesses of the Barmen declaration, recognizing the Word of God as supreme. Slowly, in Westphalia, Rhineland and Berlin, examination centres were established. Figures given by Wilhelm Niemoeller are: for the First Examination in 1934, 28 students; in 1935, 333 students; in 1936 (until spring) 155 students. For the Second Examination in 1934 there were 10 candidates; in 1935, 155 candidates; and in 1936 (until spring), 120 candidates.

In East Prussia the Prediger Seminar was directed by Professor Hans Iwand, and the better known seminar in Finkenwalde by Dietrich Bonhoeffer. Dr Gloege led the one in Naumburg. Iwand and Gloege moved to other duties after a time. Gloege was made a bishop in the Confessing Church. The Naumburg parish, however, which had 600 members of the Confessing Church amongst its number, took the work of the seminar to their hearts and kept it going through all the difficulties. Dr Gloege used his private house as a meeting place and lecture room.

During these difficult days Franz Hildebrandt used the prescribed lectionary texts in his preaching. They had been of service to the church long before Hitler. He used to say how amazed he was that they were always so relevant to the contemporary scene. After one sermon on the text in Mark (6:18) where John the Baptist challenges Herod, he was advised to 'go underground' for a few days. Not long before this, 500 pastors had been arrested! He had some favourite texts of course, and in Autumn 1935 he preached a series of sermons on Paul's letter to the Philippians. His homiletical gifts, his love for unusual texts and his pastoral care made him not only a well-known but a well-loved preacher. Some forty years later people still remembered the time when he was the preacher in the Dahlem pulpit.

Not only was he involved with training ministries; he also ran classes for the lay members of his congregation – a series on the parables of Jesus for example – and another on the poet and hymn writer, Matthias Claudius. He also took an active pastoral role along with another pastor in a maternity home. Dietrich wrote to Franz saying he was worried that his fears for the Confessing Church would come true. He was not happy that the Confessing Church was looking to the state for help in carrying out its mission. 'Confessing Church' pastors still in charge of churches and allowed to remain were being financed by the 'church tax' collected by the state. Thus the state, the Nazis, still had a finger in the Confessing Church pie.

Both men were pleased when Martin Niemoeller invited them along with fifty others to a discussion in the Dahlem parish hall. They were worried that the conviction necessary to maintain the unity they had known in Barmen and Dahlem was lacking. They found that there was nothing clear on the freedom of the church, the Jewish question, the Nazi party lie about 'positive-Christianity' and their opposition. The statement on 'positive-Christianity' was the one in which the Nazis stated the supremacy of the state over church affairs, in cleverly worded language. The Synods at Barmen and Dahlem had made it clear that they were called to Jesus Christ alone as Lord, so they must put aside every thought of compromise with that which was clearly 'non-Christian'.

Just two months after Niemoeller's meeting the Confessional Church held a Synod in Berlin-Steglitz at the end of September 1935. The Nuremberg laws, justifying persecution of the Jews, had been passed by the Nazis not long before (Hitler announced them at the Nuremberg Rally on 15 September). These laws and the reaction of the Confessing Church were the main subject for discussion. On the only occasion that a minister of the state appeared at a Confessional Synod Dr Stahn represented state minister Kerrl. Franz, fearing that some sort of compromise would be made, first told Niemoeller that he would resign his post in the Pastors' Emergency League and be compelled to leave the Confessing Church if the new laws were not rejected. Secondly he passed the word to his friend Dietrich who brought students from Finkenwalde to be a pressure group. They did not have seats in the Synod so they went to the gallery and heckled various speakers. Heinrich Vogel complained that the assembly held back comment so much that they were in danger of saying the minimum possible and then added 'perhaps not even the minimum'. The Nuremberg decrees made by Hitler had further tightened, restricted and attacked the Jews and all non-Aryans. The Synod was trying to hold a link with the state so that they could receive their normal finances and some were prepared to concede the right of the state to legislate about the Jews. A palliative statement was issued. This revealed yet again to Franz

Hildebrandt and Dietrich Bonhoeffer the need for a totally independent church. They believed that the Confessing Church had
missed an opportunity of speaking up for those whose voice had
been taken away.

The resolutions were somewhat toned down. Vogel,
Niemoeller, Hildebrandt and others were unhappy. Niemoeller
said that he doubted if they would ever understand the position
of the Jews until they themselves suffered persecution. For the
Confessing Church it was a 'missed opportunity', a 'Pyrrhic
victory'. Hildebrandt said consistently that the Jewish question
was the real test of the ethics of the Confessing Church and 'the
swastika is the flag of anti-Semitism'.

Franz returned to his pastoral duties. His texts were more challenging. His preaching had more belligerence. He enjoyed his
work with young people and children and underlined the
Apostles' Creed as doctrine. And he continued his teaching of
church history to the pastoral candidates. He was becoming more
aware that his own 'racial defects' would eventually catch up
with him. He knew that the danger in Germany would soon touch
his own life. He talked with some of his closest friends. Their
advice was that he should prepare to leave Germany. On 26 June
his father's authorization to teach was withdrawn by the state.
Though his father was not at that time teaching, the move was
significant. His father was married to a Jewess and was the father
of a 'rebel'.

On 1 July 1937 Martin Niemoeller was arrested. He had been
apprehended several times but this time he was re-arrested as he
left the court having been declared innocent. Hitler did not wish
him to be at large any longer. 'He is my personal prisoner', said
the Fuehrer.

Everyone who called at the Niemoeller residence on the day of
his arrest was detained there. This meant that they were all under
suspicion. Jan Niemoeller, his son, still recalls how as a boy of ten
years he found it mystifying that this happened and all callers were
detained. 'The house became full,' he says, 'as people called. Not
even casual callers were allowed to leave to go about their
business.' Franz was amongst those in the house at the time of
Martin Niemoeller's arrest. He immediately stepped into his
friend's place as pastor. His views were known, as was his
mother's Semitic lineage. The Gestapo always had representatives

in the congregation (Martin Niemoeller would sometimes refer directly to them and say 'please pass a hymn book to our policeman friend').

After Niemoeller's arrest one friend who had just completed a term of imprisonment told Franz, 'You had better go now while you still are able'. The friend told how when he himself was arrested he was carrying a sum of money. His wife asked the police for it as it was their own money and was told that she could have it if she surrendered his passport. This she did. However, unlike Franz, he had no Jewish blood. The lifting of passports made Franz take the suggestion seriously. There was an ecumenical conference planned for Oxford. Franz hoped to go but the Confessing Church was not able to send representatives because passports were withheld and the State Church was given instructions not to send anyone. Franz was prepared to try to go as a 'silent observer' but when the Conference took place he was himself in prison.

On 18 July 1937 during worship, an extra collection was taken at Dahlem for the Confessing Church. It was a departure from the normal procedure because, until this day, such collections had been 'retiring collections'.

Franz Hildebrandt had sensed that something was 'in the air' and he had ordered that the extra collection be taken as a clear part of the act of worship and that it be placed on the Lord's Table to be dedicated for the Lord's work. So it clearly belonged to God. Usually the purpose of the collection was announced at the end of the service. This was done. Franz later could not remember precisely what it was for (probably to train and maintain the ministry of the Confessing Church) 'but certainly' he said, 'it was an illegal one'. The Nazis had been allowing such collections to be taken, knowing their purpose, because, by turning a blind eye, they kept the so-called hidden work under some supervision.

On this day the Gestapo came forward at the end of the service and took the collection from the Lord's Table. The symbolism of the act was not lost on the congregation. It also signified a 'step up' in the persecution of the church. They now intended to cut off the training and maintenance work. They claimed that in any case the money belonged to the state since the state supported the church through the 'church tax', an argument which had some validity as both Dietrich and Franz had recognized in earlier discussions. Franz was not altogether surprised when at the same time the Gestapo arrested him. He protested that they were preventing him from conducting the children's worship, claiming that by this act they were infringing the approved minister's rights and duties. It made no difference. He was marched off to the waiting police car while the congregation protested shouting, 'We want our pastor!' To every onlooker's amusement the police car would not start and the frustrated Gestapo officers marched him along the street with the congregation alongside protesting as they went.

This method of arrest in public view was a departure from normal Gestapo procedure (they preferred a quiet arrest, preferably at night). Combined with the appropriation of the collection it suggested that the Gestapo desired to make a public statement about their attitude to the Confessing Church. However, on this occasion things went wrong. Not only did the police car refuse to start, but whether because the Gestapo were angered, confused by the congregation's shouting or simply because they were officers who were strangers to the area, they marched him away in the wrong direction, away from the police station. Franz, knowing this, kept quiet. The Gestapo appeared foolish to the onlookers and later they added to the charges against him one of 'recalcitrant behaviour'. They complained that he had allowed them to lose their way.

He was eventually taken to the Gestapo Headquarters in Alexander Platz and later on to the prison at Ploetzensee – which had an execution chamber, and from which many never returned. The next day the Gestapo took him to his flat where they made a search. They found another 'illegal' collection which they confiscated. Then, and Franz would smile as he told the story, the officer in charge had a bad spasm of toothache and the search was called off. So a third 'illegal' collection was not discovered. This money was eventually delivered to its intended destination.

In after years Franz would sometimes relate that in one sense it was a great relief when eventually you were arrested. You had seen the Gestapo, known of their actions, seen their prison vans about and wondered when they would 'pounce'. His wife Nancy told of an occasion when they were in the USA and they went for a walk. As they turned the corner to approach their residence they saw a van parked outside their house. It reminded Franz of a

Gestapo van. The memory was so vivid that he stood still and for a time couldn't move.

He was reasonably well-treated during the month he was in prison. Fortunately he was in the hands of the ordinary magistrates and police. The chaplain to the prison was a relative of a Baltic Lutheran bishop, (one of the clergy attending the Oxford Conference) over whom Hitler had no control. From this bishop news filtered through, together with a message of Christian solidarity with the persecuted church. No specific reference to the German situation was made in the final report of the Conference, assuredly a tactful move to avoid adding to the difficulties of the Christians there.

While in prison Franz had a toothache. It was unpleasant but led to a good contact. He was sitting in the prison dentist's waiting room and there were some Communists present. He asked, 'What is the news?' and received the reply 'Which do you mean? The official news? or the real news?' He discovered that they had a well-organized network for receiving underground and foreign news. (It is a fact that a Communist cell in Buchenwald concentration camp built a radio receiver from bits and pieces which was on display in the museum in 1983). Prison throws up unexpected friendships.

While in prison he also began to work on some ideas which had sprung out of his own experiences. Eventually it became the thesis 'The Gospel and Humanitarianism', which he presented to Cambridge University and for which he was awarded the degree of Doctor of Philosophy. He used to say 'the work was begun in a German prison and completed in a British internment camp'. It began with a letter, sent to Hitler in 1936, from Niemoeller and other leaders of the Confessing Church. Franz Hildebrandt had been involved in its drafting. The letter made the point that the existence of secret police and concentration camps gave the church great cause for concern: 'the gospel is not simply neutral on the humanitarian issue and humanitarianism is not a mere and equally heretic compliment of nationalism ... "God hath showed me that I should not call any man common or unclean (Acts 10:28)"'. He could not do any effective research while in prison but he could use his phenomenal memory and make his plans for the work.

At this point there was an unusual confluence of events. The

Nazis needed international currency. They had a rule that people of Jewish background could 'buy off' part of their sentence at a price, providing the time of the early release was paid for in good currency and that the prisoner then left the country. This policy lasted until the outbreak of the war in September 1939.

Two days before his arrest Franz, now convinced of the wisdom of leaving Germany, had visited Dietrich in Finkenwalde. He had said 'farewell' to his friend (they next met in England in 1939) and explained his plans.

However he had been 'unexpectedly busy' and had not collected his passport from his parents' home as he had intended, so he had planned to pick it up after the morning service on Sunday 18 July. His arrest during that service had made this impossible. When after his arrest the Gestapo took him back to his flat for the purpose of a search, they naturally did not find his passport. They saw some cases packed but strangely were not inquisitive. Perhaps they thought he was anticipating arrest or preparing to go on a journey within the country. Perhaps they were distracted by finding the 'illegal' collection – or was it possible that the spasm of toothache of the officer in charge threw them off? The cases were left untouched. His parents were already in possession of a permit for the three of them to take a vacation together in Switzerland. This vacation was planned to begin after morning service on 18 July. In the mind of Franz this was now to be the springboard for his journey into exile. The permit remained valid though this plan was now impossible. His parents waited quietly on events.

Hans von Dohnanyi, brother-in-law of Dietrich (and later to be executed on the same day as Dietrich in 1945), worked in a government office. He discovered how the payment worked and how much was required. He also helped in clearing the way through the regulations. The money was collected and paid by his friends and so Franz served twenty-six days imprisonment instead of the prescribed twenty-eight, thus anticipating his release by two days.

But Franz was no ordinary 'Jew'. He had been a key player in the trouble which the Confessional Church was causing the Nazis. He was a 'watched' man. Therefore, on the advice of his friends, he went to the Bonhoeffer home rather than to his own flat. His luggage had been collected and on the twenty-seventh day the Hildebrandts left for Switzerland on their permitted vacation. 'I did not tell them I would not return', he used to say. His landlady, in the meantime, had displayed a Nazi flag with swastika from the balcony of her flat. She may have been a Nazi sympathizer or she may have been attempting to camouflage Franz's activity.

On the twenty-eighth day some thought the Gestapo were ready to re-arrest him. This 're-arrest tactic' had been used before. Earlier that year the Gestapo had re-arrested Martin Niemoeller on his release after trial. However all things, planned and accidental, had worked together for his good. He was not there. At the end of the vacation, his parents returned to Germany without him. Franz, meanwhile, spent a little time in Zurich with his friend, Siegmund-Schultze, also in exile from the Nazis. He wrote to Karl Barth saying that he had exchanged the Ploetzensee prison for a place which was more pleasant (i.e. Switzerland) but that his end destination was London. Barth replied that, in the final analysis, all things hung on the Aryan anti-Semitic paragraphs. In this both he and Franz were in agreement. From Switzerland he flew to London to the home of Julius Rieger, pastor of St George's German congregation, one whom he had grown to know well since his days in the manse with Dietrich in Sydenham in 1933.

CHAPTER 8

REFUGE IN ENGLAND

Franz Hildebrandt the refugee was not arriving in an England which was unknown to him. His visits to Sydenham to and for Dietrich had given him some knowledge of London. Bishop George Bell was a friend of some years standing. There was also Pastor Julius Rieger. Rieger had arrived as pastor of the Lutheran Church of St George's in East London in 1929. Initially, like many German pastors serving abroad, he had looked with interest on the Nazi movement rising in his homeland and like others overseas had regarded the 'German Christian' movement as nothing more than a movement of Christians in Germany – just as Nazi propaganda intended. Naturally any pastor serving overseas belonged to his homeland and cared for the things of home.

However, when Dietrich Bonhoeffer and Franz Hildebrandt met him in 1933 and explained to Rieger the philosophy which lay behind the movement with its anti-Semitism and the repression of non-Nazi opinion, his views changed. On a recent visit to Berlin early in 1937 Franz and he had spoken about the direction in which events seemed to be moving. Julius Rieger assured Franz that if ever he had to flee for safety, there would be a haven in the Rieger home in London. Therefore to Julius Rieger, Franz travelled.

Refugees who arrived in England were dependent on others for help until they could find some kind of employment which brought remuneration. Various charitable organisations helped. Franz later commented that the Quakers in particular made contributions and Bishop George Bell set up a 'Church of England committee for "non-Aryan" Christians'. Bell himself became a 'sponsor' responsible for thirty or forty families who had fled to England because of the 'non-Aryan' paragraph. Some of the refugees had already identified relatives and friends to whom they could go. Very few were financially independent.

Julius Rieger appointed Franz as the assistant pastor at St George's. This was how in 1934 Rieger had helped a previous refugee, Pastor Wolfgang Buesing, who had fled Germany because he married a non-Aryan bride. Before very long the church accepted Franz officially as Rieger's representative. This could be only a temporary position because of Franz's status in Germany. He was not *persona grata* with Lutheran officialdom in Berlin, indeed in January 1938 a message to this effect came through to Rieger and the Lutheran Church in London. (The situation had been highlighted when Church President Koch visited London in October 1937 on the occasion of the 175th anniversary of the founding of St George's.) Nevertheless during this time Franz became the pastor especially to German speaking Jewish Christians and on Wednesdays he held discussion sessions for refugees within the society at St George's. As a consequence St George's received the nickname 'The Jews' Church'.

The problem which lay behind this was that while there were *Jewish* organizations caring for *Jewish* refugees, Jewish *Christians* fell through the caring system. Franz tried to encourage the Confessing Church in Germany to recognize this and to send help, but the Confessing Church in Germany had its own problems. Some congregations were tolerated by the Nazis, for their pastors had not yet come into immediate conflict with the Nazi authorities. The system of church financing applying in Germany meant that they received funds from the Nazi state. This in turn raised the ethical question whether it was – in the Christian sense – right to use any of that Nazi-originated money for supporting persons who were refugees because they had been driven out by that same Nazi state order. Franz believed that the Confessing church in Germany should take this question in hand and see if some help could be given. He wrote, of the situation at St George's: 'The whole misery of emigration came together in the people who took refuge there: Jews and Christians; church members and "non-church members"; normal folks and "cranks"; all who were left in the lurch found their way there.'

All the while the pressure was building up on Julius Rieger for taking in Franz. The German representative of the NSDAP in London, a man by the name of Karlowa, denounced Rieger in the summer of 1938 as a 'fanatic' and 'heading for martyrdom'. The reason for this report to his Berlin HQ was an appearance on 8 May 1938 by Rieger and Hildebrandt in the Methodist Westminster Central Hall in London, the church right opposite Westminster Abbey and across the road from the Houses of Parliament. The *Methodist Recorder*, the weekly journal of British Methodism, reported a major meeting at the Central Hall and then continued in reporting the meeting in its issue of 12 May 1938:

> On Sunday, Dr Julius Rieger (Berlin) and the Revd Franz Hildebrandt (a colleague of Dr Niemoeller) spoke to a deeply inter-ested audience, and afterwards many Westminster students and other friends signed an affectionate message which Mr. Hart is sending to Dr Niemoeller's wife.

Rieger received advice from Germany that 'Herr Lic. Hildebrandt' was a cause of problems. 'We would suggest that Herr Lic. Hildebrandt should not be entrusted in the next few weeks with the preaching and advocacy in your parish. The tension which has already arisen in certain circles, has not been resolved.' Rieger at one point was accused by Heckel of not behaving correctly and he replied that Heckel was 'not a bishop but a Nazi-agent'! Bishop Heckel had for years been trying to put the best picture of the 'German Christians' before the 'outside' churches, but in the end even he realized the Nazi party was determined to destroy the churches.

There is no doubt that the Germans worshipping in London had their sympathies torn apart by Hildebrandt's presence and recent experience. They were becoming more and more suspi-cious of the Nazis in their homeland and the Nazi representatives were annoyed. Pastor Gustav Schoenberger from the Lutheran church in the Hamburg region was serving in Dalston, London. He was linked with the Seaman's Mission. He became a member of the NSDAP just after the First World War and saw in the movement an ideology which was 'above parties and which brought a moral and religious base' to life. He had also at first felt the influence of Bonhoeffer when he was at Sydenham, but now in 1938 with Bonhoeffer back in Germany he was spreading the support for the Nazi party. Franz felt that he damaged the public view of the pastor's calling and duties.

Since 1937, according to Canon Max Warren who was vicar of

Holy Trinity Church in Cambridge, that city was increasingly becoming a reception centre for refugees from Nazi Germany. Up until this time there had not been a German Lutheran congregation in Cambridge although for years there had been Lutheran groupings and congregations in different cities of the UK. These congregations came about as a result of trading relationships which had begun as far back as the Reformation and developed over the last three hundred years. Hitler's persecution of dissenters, particularly those of Jewish ancestry, had increased the number of refugees tremendously. Cambridge with its well-known university became a focal point for those of high academic standing such as atomic physicist Lisa Meitner and her nephew, Professor of Physics, Otto Frisch. Those who were Christians sought fellowship in the various churches in the city. Early in 1939 Franz was living in Ridley Hall, Cambridge, an evangelical theological college for training Anglican candidates for the ministry. He was there by the kind invitation of the Revd Dr Paul Gibson, the Principal. He soon became a part of this circle of exiles and he saw his duty clearly. He began to gather his distressed countrymen and women around the Word of God, offering them the comfort and safety of a Christian fellowship in their own language and tradition.

On Sunday 23 April 1939 the first service of the German congregation in Cambridge was held in the chapel of Ridley Hall by kind permission of the principal. The text of the sermon was Ps. 23. Thirteen days earlier on Easter Monday, Franz had preached in German in the parish church of nearby Hitchin. Shortly afterwards with the unanimous support of the Parochial Church Council, Max Warren welcomed the German congregation to Holy Trinity Church to hold a regular late Sunday evening service according to the Lutheran rite. Soon a monthly joint service was held with the congregation of the parish church with a ten minute address in German as part of the service. By the outbreak of war in September 1939, there were 100 members. It was known as 'The German Evangelical Congregation' – though Franz said the word 'Lutheran' applied equally well.

He remembered his duties consisted of baptisms, marriages, and funerals. There was no established constitution. He had a group of very loyal church elders who held office for some years and kept the whole congregation stable. Amongst these were the

Roubiczeks (the husband followed his wife in office), Professor Kestner, Mrs Baercroft (who was at the same time a member of Holy Trinity). At her death Dr Olive Wyon took her place. Harold Fleet, the organist of Holy Trinity, helped them tremendously. They made a short-lived experiment with children's worship but their strength lay in the fellowship meeting every fourteen days in the home of the Roubiczeks. The themes included: the Sermon on the Mount; Luther's Greater Catechism; the prophet Daniel; the hymns of Paul Gerhardt (a Hildebrandt favourite) and the Psalms.

Franz stayed at Ridley Hall apart from the vacations when there was no provision for anyone to remain in the college. At Easter he was the guest of the great Congregationalist minister and scholar, the Revd Professor C. H. Dodd and his wife. He had to find somewhere in the summer and so he went from Ridley Hall to the Oratory of the Good Shepherd. Franz loved Ridley Hall because Paul Gibson took it for granted that he would receive the sacrament of Holy Communion and was only grieved that the Church of England would not allow Franz – a Lutheran ordained pastor – to be a celebrant.

The Oratory of the Good Shepherd was an Anglo-Catholic seminary and here Franz learned what the 'umbrella of the Church of England' meant. He was told clearly that he could not participate in the sacrament of Holy Communion, nor did he wish to do so, since it was an Anglican celebration of the Mass. He did, however, join in the non-sacramental worship, reading the Psalms and using the *Book of Common Prayer*. Here in Cambridge in the Anglican seminaries began his 'love affair' with 'the Prayer Book of Cranmer'.

Wilfred Knox, a noted New Testament scholar, used to lead the worship. Franz had great difficulty in following the worship when Knox was conducting it. He blamed his own poor mastery of the English language for this until he discovered that Knox read the service so fast that no one could either understand him or keep up with him. Indeed Franz reckoned that his own contribution to worship at the Oratory was to make this fact known to Wilfred Knox who, out of courtesy to the German refugee, slowed down his reading considerably. The British could then also understand and follow. In Cambridge he also met and made friends with Bernard Manning, the Senior Tutor of Jesus College who was a Congregationalist layman. He attended some of Manning's lectures at Cheshunt College. He found him very witty, sometimes bitingly sarcastic but truly humble when talking with his friends. He also began to share Manning's deep love for Wesleys' hymns – another love affair which lasted to the end of his days.

In 1938, shortly after his escape from Germany he had met his parents in Lucerne, Switzerland. They had been pleased to hear of the possibility that he might give occasional lectures in the University in Cambridge. His parents felt this could be an environment which was suitable for him. Early that year an article had appeared in the *Hibbert Journal* with the title 'A Confessional Pastor: the Church Struggle in Germany'. The article was anonymously credited but many believed Hildebrandt to be the author. In the summer a small book appeared, published in Switzerland in German but later translated into English and other European languages. It bore the title *Pastor Niemoeller and his Creed* and told the story of the leader of the Confessing Church, his struggles with the Nazis, his 'fixed' trials and his imprisonment. It was published anonymously but after a while it became understood that Franz Hildebrandt was the author and that he had written it while staying with Julius Rieger.

The book was banned in Germany and was soon on the proscribed list of Heinrich Himmler, head of the Gestapo. However, an extract was circulated in Germany with a printing of 60,000 copies under the title *Dieser war auch mit dem Jesus von Nazareth* (This man was also with Jesus of Nazareth). The book's strength was its 'popular' style which contained many illustrations of the struggle. His picture of Martin Niemoeller is a vital, living one. The author obviously knew his subject well. Some of the words of Niemoeller, selected with great care, are trumpet calls to the Confessing Church. A paragraph written in January 1938 illustrates Niemoeller's conviction:

> Somehow during these last six months the ship of the Church has set sail again. Her ensigns are damaged, her masts are broken, her whole appearance is far from beautiful; but the Lord Christ is still at the helm and the ship is afloat. Who would have dared to hope for this when Ludwig Mueller believed 'he had captured a fine prize'? ... I believe my arrest is a part of the sacred humour of God. First comes the mocking laughter, 'Now we've got him!' – then the

arrest – and the result? Fuller churches and praying congregations … The might of God watches over me … To grow bitter would be base ingratitude.

Niemoeller himself is described in this way:

The Bible is a part of him … the pastor in all his doings and undoings must be the servant of God's word.

The brief introduction says all that is needed:

On July 1st 1938 Martin Niemoeller completed one year in prison. The following pages are intended as a reminder of this fact. They contain no biography and are not a chronicle of Church History. They just show by a few examples what he stands for. And again: 'He set his whole heart upon the Lord; he raised up the true service of God once more, for the land was full of idolatry' (Ecclus. 49.3) This is his witness, that may not be forgotten, among us.

                                                            The Author

Its publication in Britain gained much publicity and opened many eyes and its message was underlined by Bishop George Bell, who wrote the foreword and widely commended the little book. The story bit hard into the Nazi hierarchy. Three thousand people wrote with good wishes on Niemoeller's birthday – this produced a popularity poll which even the hostile Nazis had to heed. The public attention in many countries resulting from this book probably helped to keep Niemoeller alive when many Christians suffered death in similar concentration camps.

The 'German Christian' church was greatly challenged especially by the story of the prison chaplain who visited Niemoeller and asked 'Brother, why are you in prison?' and received the reply 'Brother, why are you not in prison?' Perhaps the writing of this book was the most valuable work Franz did during these years. The English translation was published early in 1939. Ordinary people bought the book and talked about Martin Niemoeller.*

*I remember, as a small boy in a mining village in Staffordshire, being told by my father – who had been a soldier fighting for Britain in the First World War – about this great Christian in Germany and, as a boy of twelve, was encouraged to pray for him. Years later I had the thrill of taking Martin Niemoeller who was staying with us, to visit my father and mother who were overjoyed to meet the one for whose witness they had prayed. (ASC)

Professor Hildebrandt, Franz's father, had been examined after Franz's escape, 'tried' by the Nazis, and thereafter moved to Dresden, then a beautiful city with art galleries and museums (much of its beauty was destroyed by bombing at the end of the war) but the climate was too damp for him. So his parents returned to Berlin, to a flat near where Franz grew up. Now however, due to increasing claustrophobia, the professor could no longer go out to concerts and operas. Bruno Walter, the great conductor, heard of this and would invite him to rehearsals. Otherwise the radio had to suffice. He could manage the cinema, however, for in the darkness his claustrophobia was not so bad – and he thoroughly enjoyed Disney cartoons.

In January 1939, at the age of 64, Franz's father died suddenly of an embolism. Franz heard of this by telephone – he was still at the home of Julius Rieger – and immediately he began to make arrangements for his mother to join him in England. Had his father's health been better he would almost certainly have had them both over before, but now he could not allow his mother, a Jewess, to remain in Germany. He hurriedly applied for the requisite papers though it meant leaving behind furniture, glass, china and much else which his parents had collected during their marriage.

When she first arrived, Franz, now living in Cambridge, found a place for his mother in a small hotel. Then they heard that their furniture and some of their goods were being sent over from Germany. They never fully understood the mechanics of the act but they believed that some of their friends paid for this surreptitiously. Since they had not been able to bring any of their money out of Germany they reasoned that maybe some of their friends had gained access to the account and so managed to finance the transfer, perhaps by bribing the Gestapo to turn a blind eye.

Franz found a house to rent in Cambridge where he installed his mother with many of her own possessions around her. He was happy to be together with her. To his great joy his piano also arrived. Later he wrote that they were most fortunate for so many of the refugees were separated from members of their families. In numerous cases they never met again. 'One only needs to remember Auschwitz and Theresienstadt', he said. The house was small and cost one pound per week. At the time Franz was being given an allowance of 250 pounds per annum from the British Council of Churches. His mother, who had been kindly offered a home by her brother and his wife in Loughborough, chose to be with Franz. Only one box of her treasures had gone astray. They were not able to obtain their silver, which was hidden in Germany by their friends to avoid the Nazis taking possession.

Franz found that more and more people were interested in hearing about the German Church Struggle with the Nazis. Nevertheless there were those who believed that such sympathies were out of place. The Rt Revd A. C. Headlam, Bishop of Gloucester, was out of sympathy with the Confessing Church and believed that Martin Niemoeller was justly imprisoned, that the theology of the 'German Christian movement' was 'much more in harmony with the teaching of the Church of England than was that of the Confessional Church, which has been influenced by Calvinism and the teaching of Karl Barth'. This he wrote in a letter to the *Manchester Guardian* (2 September 1938) which was translated into German and published by the Nazis. He also wrote to *The Times* in a similar vein, a letter which Professor Owen Chadwick, a church historian beloved by many of his students, described as 'the most lamentable letter ever written by an Anglican bishop to a newspaper'.

Franz also had a debate (by letters) with Karl Barth about the right course of action: peace or war. He believed Chamberlain, the British Prime Minister, was right in working for peace, but it must be a peace conditional 'on the confession of the Name of Jesus to bring about peace between the two countries'. Barth was against 'peace at any price' but that was not exactly the point which Franz was making. Later in 1940 he outlined his views on loyalty and pacifism to a friend:

> I am convinced that Hitlerism has to be fought against as the system of the Antichrist and this is what we in the Confessional Church in Germany have actually been doing long before the outbreak of the present war.
>
> As a Christian and as a minister of the church I consider my means to fight Hitler different from those employed by the world. I cannot reconcile modern warfare with Christianity though I respect my fellow Christians who are conscientiously able to do so. I would not object to an ordinary police force doing away with the Nazi party, but I fail to see how the killing of thousands of lives on both sides will harm the guilty; on the contrary I have reasons to

fear that once again Hitler will manage to unite even his opponents in Germany for the cause of the defence of the country and that war will offer to him a convenient opportunity to solve the church problem too by the calling up of pastors. I need not say how I feel about any colleagues of mine now fighting in Hitler's army.

When my pupils in the confirmation classes at Berlin asked me about a practical advice, I used to recommend the Samaritan service of the Red Cross now as the least evil in what must be an indissoluble dilemma, and I would take the same attitude myself when I had to face the decision. Pacifism, therefore, is to me a practical, not a doctrinal question; it is the question of what means the Christian citizen should have in the service of his country ...

I have not referred to my personal pacifist convictions unless I have been asked about that. My object is to preach the Gospel and to assure my fellow Christians of the prayers and solidarity of our suffering church with them; it is for the cause of Christ I want to work.

As always Franz Hildebrandt took his stand on the Gospel, on Christ alone. He felt Karl Barth was to a degree temporizing, using the methods of this world to fight the battles of God's eternity, even if as a last resort. His own attitude was 'NEVER dilute or compromise the Gospel of Jesus Christ'. In his book *This is the Message* he wrote 'If you and I want to remind the church at this time that Christ means peace, then we must make it clear to the world that peace means Christ'.

The times were disturbed. Hitler's move for *lebensraum* (living space) led to events in 1939 that were to have serious effect on the status of the German refugees in England. Disregarding previous treaties, on 1 September, German troops launched a *blitzkrieg* invasion of Poland. France and the United Kingdom, honouring their agreement to defend the Poles, declared war on Germany on 3 September. Poland fell in a few weeks. Then followed six months of relative quiet known as the 'phoney war'. In the spring of 1940 Denmark was overrun, followed by the invasion of Norway. In May Holland and Belgium were attacked. Paris fell to the Germans in June, signalling the collapse of France. Britain stood alone against the Nazi menace. Winston Churchill succeeded Chamberlain as Prime Minister. The energy, eloquence and resolve with which he undertook the defence of Britain inevitably led to measures that would limit the activities of

German nationals who were living in Great Britain, regardless of their attitude toward the Nazis.

Fear of air raids meant that a few days before the outbreak of war, the government gave an order that there must be a 'black-out', i.e. all lights must be covered during hours of darkness, all windows had to have thick, opaque curtains (black dye was in great demand) and lights on cars must be shielded within specific limits. When it involved churches, there were so many windows to cover that most churches moved their 'evening' services to the afternoon, and continued so for some months.

The German service normally held at 8.30 p.m. was now under a question mark. Canon Max Warren met Franz Hildebrandt and suggested that the German and English services be combined. 'Think it over,' said Franz to his friend, 'It will not be very popular now.' Warren replied 'there is nothing to think over' and the following notice appeared in the next issue of the *Cambridge Daily News*:

> Germans specially invited
> Holy Trinity Church
> Sunday September 3rd
> 3.15 p.m. Evening Service

'As the German Service announced for 8.15 p.m. CANNOT TAKE PLACE all German speaking people are invited to the above service during which there will be prayers and an address in German. Pastor Hildebrandt will give the address.'

The service used was an abbreviated form of that in the *Book of Common Prayer*. The hymns, prayers and sermon were first in English and then in German and it so happened that the Gospel for that particular Sunday was the parable of the Good Samaritan.

Max Warren described this as 'one of the most moving services I have ever attended' and similar services took place regularly throughout the war, the high point being a visit of the Archbishop of Canterbury, William Temple, not long after his appointment to the archdiocese honouring a promise made sometime earlier. (This was in June 1942. A photograph of the event was published in the *Cambridge Daily News* and copies were sent to Germany!) Warren also wrote that the mutual encouragement and under-standing that this and other services like it around the country were a pledge that the anti-German hysteria of 1914 'which so disgraced the nation' would not occur this time.

Warren himself helped by writing to adherents of Holy Trinity and to the citizens of Cambridge in a circular:

> The first thing we have to remember is that in the great majority of cases they are the unwilling victims of the Nazi regime. In the second place we have to see them as men and women in need of help and encouragement. To the Christian the answer to the question 'who is my neighbour?' is clear: my neighbour is anyone, anywhere, in any kind of need which I can meet. That fact determines that we as Christians shall see these refugees not as a problem but as men and women and children in need.

In the meantime a Refugee Club was opened at 55 Hills Road, Cambridge, sponsored in the main by the Quaker lady Hilda Sturge. As it was not easy for all activities to continue at Holy Trinity, Professor Charles Raven, Master of Christ's College, made the chapel of his college available for the refugees and a notice was put out – for the benefit of the refugees in Cambridge – that a Bible Study for them would be held every second Tuesday in Christ's College, next to Lloyds Bank. Christmas 1939 approached and an invitation was given by Holy Trinity congregation to join in a Christmas Eve celebration at 4.30 p.m. after the service in the church at 3.15 p.m. This was to be held in the Henry Martyn Hall.

Events with the congregations moved fairly smoothly until the men, including Franz, were taken to the Isle of Man for internment. Thereafter for a time sermons were only preached in German when Professor C. H. Dodd, the Norris Hulse Professor of Divinity, was able to preach. On one occasion when he was preaching a lady left the church and shortly afterwards a letter appeared in the Cambridge press protesting that a German was preaching in 'that language' in these critical days. Max Warren wrote to the paper replying and pointing out that the sermon preached in 'the horrible German language' was preached by none other than Professor Dodd, one of the greatest scholars in Britain, who happened to be fluent in German.

On Whit Sunday 1940 Franz Hildebrandt, along with many German men in Cambridge was interned. Franz later commented that, whereas in general the climate was different from the hostility shown in the First World War, the invasion of Holland and Belgium and the change of Government from Chamberlain to Churchill sharpened issues. There was a fear of spies and of a 'fifth column' – and so 'enemy aliens' were interned.*

*The 'fifth column' was the name given to those who were planted in a country some years before and worked at first secretly and then openly for the enemy. Some were in fact 'planted' as refugees.

CHAPTER 9

INTERNMENT 1940

Forseeing the possibility of internment, Bishop George Bell had already written to Sir Alexander Maxwell and had visited the head of the Aliens Department to plead the cause of the genuinely honest refugees from the Nazi terror. Nevertheless on that Whit Sunday in 1940 the order for the internment of aliens took effect. Among them were Franz Hildebrandt, Julius Rieger, Werner Simonson and many refugee friends. The influence of the 'fifth column' had aided the Nazis in overrunning Norway, Holland and Belgium and there was evidence of a hidden enemy at work in Britain. Bishop Bell wrote to Franz an encouraging letter, intended for circulation amongst the refugees, in which he said, 'I regard you all as colleagues and allies in our cause.' He had known Franz and some of the others very well and trusted them, but of course he was not the Government.

The police officers who came to arrest Franz in Cambridge were also sympathetic towards him. They knew him well. Indeed they allowed him to leave the police station to preach at Evensong at Holy Trinity Church that afternoon under pledge to return later. Some present commented that it was a very powerful sermon and Franz seemed unaffected by the fact of his arrest. His friend Dr Werner Simonson, a lawyer who was a fellow refugee, was at the time a student at Ridley Hall, hoping to become a priest in the Church of England. He had heard the call to ordained Christian ministry during his time as a refugee in England. His account of the arrest and internment is very moving and confirms that of Franz Hildebrandt. Later Franz confessed that he wished he had kept a detailed diary because in those days, he said, he was apparently a 'very important person'.

All were gathered at the Town Hall, Cambridge. Lists were checked and they were allowed to return home to collect things they wished to take with them. Werner Simonson had had his case packed ready for some time, for the move to internment was not unexpected nor was it resented by many of them. They were taken first to Bury St Edmunds, then to Liverpool where the internees from the country were gathered and thence to Douglas on the Isle of Man. Bishop Bell wrote to Franz (via the Aliens Internment Camp, c/o Police Office, Cambridge) trying to help the internees to understand why a government, hitherto kind and welcoming to them, was acting in this way. He mentioned 'the difficulties and anxieties of the situation which made the internment of so many, who are truly ememies of the Nazi regime, the price to be paid for the help of this country, their host at the present moment'.

Hotels and houses in Douglas were requisitioned. Simonson and Hildebrandt shared a room until Franz was recognized as Camp Leader. Each building elected a representative and these met and chose Franz as 'number one'. Hence his reference to being a 'very important person'. Deep down he was very proud of this appointment but Nancy often said that he was reluctant to talk about it. He was always a very humble man and never could accept easily that others held him in high regard. When Bishop Bell heard of it he wrote 'I am delighted to learn that you are head of the whole camp and how absolutely you are trusted.' He spoke to Franz of the need for his ministry of pastoral care and consolation. This Franz, the pastor, practised. The bishop and his representatives kept the government departments 'fully conscious of the difficulties and hardships' in the camp. Many of the internees accepted their situation knowing that it was far better than the deceit and treachery they had experienced at the hands of the Gestapo, but there were some for whom it was all too much. They had lost everything under Nazi rule and this experience was seen as yet another loss and deprivation, and their despair led them to commit suicide. Franz's energies were stretched helping loved ones in such cases.

To stimulate the minds of the people in the camp, professors and teachers organized classes in their own subjects. Franz's friend Willi Gross had been elected deputy leader. He was an Austrian scientist and he helped in the organization of classes. Julius Rieger and Hans Herbert Kramm were two of a group of pastors who organized services of worship, Bible study groups discussions and prayers. Some Jews came along and were warmly welcomed. Some indeed became Christians and were baptized. Rieger had been interned, then released, then interned again. He was a class 'A' prisoner and he and his wife had a child born during internment.

Every kind of emergency came to them: from illness, birth and death to shoe repairs. They were so busy that they had to make a request to be allowed at least one free 'off duty' hour in the day. Franz loved to tell of the amusing occasion when he and one or two of the other leaders went to see one of the camp guards for a second broom to keep the camp clean. He did not know what prompted the guard to act as he did. It may have been a lack of understanding of the speaker or just obtuseness but they received a lecture on the use and misuse of army equipment. If this misuse was accompanied by disobedience of military rules it could result in severe punishment. 'The extreme penalty is death', he said. Franz and his friends shook with laughter. The threat of death seemed somewhat exaggerated for the request of a new broom, or even its misuse!

Sometimes a rigid officialdom did not help – and often pastoral care was of paramount importance, for at times the Government's right hand did not seem to know what the left hand was doing. There were sons who were sent to Canada while fathers were interned on the Isle of Man. Nephews and uncles in like manner were also unnecessarily separated. Once, sadly, while trying to rectify this, a transport ship carrying some separated internees was torpedoed in the Atlantic and sunk. Intensive pastoral care was needed then.

All the while Bishop Bell was helping as he could. He visited a prison in Liverpool where nearly 200 internees were detained: Czechs, Norwegians, Russians, Belgians and others. He wanted them all to know they had not been forgotten. He was actively pressing for a review of the internment cases. He wrote to Franz saying that he had enlisted the help of both archbishops (Cosmo Gordon Lang of Canterbury and William Temple of York) to write in support to the Home Secretary. In addition Bell wrote to the USA and Canada to see if they could help – not specifying what help he expected. He also kept a caring eye on Franz's mother who, having broken her leg, was not interned. He made sure that the interned wives and children were not separated, though they were usually kept separate from the men.

Canon Max Warren of Cambridge into whose care Franz had committed his Cambridge congregation, wrote encouragingly to him. He had enlisted support for his case from friends at the University including Professor Canon Charles Raven; but he pointed out that, although they were working hard for his release and that of others, if the bombing of Britain by the Germans intensified, the climate of opinion might become hostile. Dr Paul Gibson also wrote to both Franz and to Werner Simonson from Ridley Hall. Bishop Bell then discovered and obtained some forms which were needed. He enlisted Franz's help in completing them for the internees. Dr Ehrenberg, an older refugee, had been released earlier because of sickness. The bishop said Franz's help 'in the position of trust' was crucial but 'the machine grinds slowly.' There were many categories under which internees could apply for release. Bishop Bell tried unsuccessfully to have pastors treated as a group. Franz was asked to use his discretion but to make very clear those who had been members of the Confessing Church. Franz himself, having been treasurer of the Pastors' Emergency League for a time, was in a good position to know these details. The bishop also made use of the book *Pastor Niemoeller and his Creed* to help Franz. Its wide circulation in many countries had given it great influence.

There were some strange and humourous incidents in the camp. One man, an Anglican vicar, had been born in Germany. He had, in fact, been a British Army chaplain in World War One but had no idea that he had never received British nationality. So he was interned as a German in Britain until it was sorted out. Another was the son of the German Crown Prince who had been a student at Cambridge when the war broke out. He took a full part in all activities and duties in the camp, sharing the most menial tasks with a good and willing heart.

Towards the end of 1940 Franz was released from his internment and returned to Cambridge. He was ever thankful for the letters, love and care of his friends, particularly Paul Gibson, Max Warren and George Bell, who himself had visited the Isle of Man and with some anger had cleared the way for letters to reach the internees (He had discovered that for some weeks only one postcard, from himself, had been delivered).

Franz always held that Bell should have become Archbishop of Canterbury on the death of William Temple. To him there was no doubt that Bell's stand for the Confessing Church in Germany, his working with and for the German resistence, his aid to refugees and caring for them and his bold speeches in the House of Lords on the conduct of the war counted against him. Churchill and Eden had rejected overtures which Bell brought to them from Bonhoeffer and his friends. It might have meant an earlier end to the war. It might also have meant giving up the idea of 'unconditional surrender'. In Britain the final recommendation for Archbishop of Canterbury had to travel to Buckingham Palace, to the sovereign and via the Prime Minister, in this case Winston Churchill whom Bell had opposed. To Werner Simonson Bishop Bell's caring and compassion gave the impression that he wanted to apologize for the Government's treatment of German refugees 'as if he suffered with us'. In retrospect Franz would say, 'He did – for he was passed over for Canterbury'.

CHAPTER 10

CAMBRIDGE, MARRIAGE AND METHODISM

Towards the end of 1940 Franz Hildebrandt returned from the Isle of Man to the German congregation in Cambridge. With the return of their minister and other men in the congregation, regular services in English and German gained renewed energy. They were now, so to speak, 'in the clear' and soon became 'officially' established.

In November 1940 Bishop Bell met a group of German pastors and charged them with the task of interpreting the witness of the Confessing Church in Germany to the churches in Britain. From this unofficial start grew the German–British 'Christian Fellowship in Wartime'. A leaflet was circulated asking British congregations to invite the pastors to tell about the battle the church was fighting in Germany and to show solidarity with the Christians there. It was also hoped that in this way links would be forged for the day when peace came. On 30 June 1941 a service was held in the church of St Martin-in-the-Fields, London, to remember the fourth anniversary of the imprisonment of Martin Niemoeller. There was much debate about it. Would it help or hinder the Christians in Germany and their witness? The final decision was that silence would help Hitler more than speaking out.

During this time there was a burgeoning of groups working with a similar purpose. Franz was invited to be a representative on a Church of England committee supported by the Ecumenical Council through which some pastors were maintained. His friend Werner Simonson was a representative of the Church of England with whom he had thrown his lot. He had been a judge in Germany, had come as a refugee to Britain as a layman and later became an episcopally ordained clergyman. Franz and his friend H. H. Kramm were pleased because this was the normal way of ordination in the Church of England. Kramm, who claimed to be more at home with 'high church Anglicans' was very upset at the idea of *ordained* Lutheran pastors being *re-ordained* as Anglican clergymen. This denied the validity of their own ordination – yet by the end of 1942 ten refugee pastors had been so 're-ordained'.

During 1941 there were two events in his ministry in Cambridge which Franz remembered with particular pleasure. A circular letter was sent out inviting the children of refugee families in the refugee communities of East Anglia to a special Children's service in Christ's College chapel. This was followed by a guided tour around Cambridge and then tea and games. The refugee community in Cambridge had been given permission by Professor Canon Charles Raven to use the college chapel when needed until the end of the war. The other event was that on Whit Sunday he was invited to preach at a Parade Service at the Royal Air Force station near Huntingdon. Appropriately he preached on the third article of the Creed. He remembered that he concluded his sermon: 'Now you will say "we go out to defend this faith". You are mistaken: this faith is going to defend you.' And this was a pacifist, a refugee from Germany speaking!

There were other small groupings which were unofficial but which had much influence on the background thinking of the refugee situation. After internment as the German refugee congregations began to work, closer links were aided by the 'Group of Four' who met informally from time to time. They were Buesing, Hildebrandt, Kramm and Rieger. From these meetings came gatherings of congregations first in London in 1942 and then in Cambridge in 1943.

Another group was known as the 'Cloister Group' which was started by Archbishop William Temple, then Archbishop of York, and Canon Charles Raven, an informal group which gained its name from the first meeting place at the home of Thompson Elliott, who was a canon of Westminster Abbey and lived at 4, Little Cloisters. The idea was to prevent division in the church on the issue of pacifism. George Bell was a member as were Henry Carter, a fine representative of Methodism's social conscience, and W. T. Elmslie, the General Secretary of the Presbyterian Church in England. Franz Hildebrandt was invited to join. He sometimes said that the only thing he was prepared to fight for was the right to be a pacifist.

In Germany pacifism was not tolerated. Pastors were conscripted into the army just as ordinary citizens. Indeed the common belief was that those who were known to be out of sympathy with the government and their sons were sent to the most dangerous places such as the Eastern Front. Sometimes soldiers who were pastors would 'break ranks' and stories were told of the sacrament being given to men before battles or across national barriers to prisoners of war. The situation was vastly different from that of Britain.

Topics other than pacifism were discussed. On one occasion, Franz remembered William Temple telling Henry Carter that after the address he had just heard Carter give, he now had the finishing touch for a lecture he himself was due to give. It was through this group Franz had met William Temple and invited him to preach at the united service in Cambridge. Temple had agreed but when in 1942 he became Archbishop of Canterbury, Franz wrote to him saying he would fully understand if, in the changed circumstances, the archbishop could not fulfill the appointment. Temple replied that of course he would still come. William Temple was consecrated Archbishop of Canterbury on 23 April 1942. Franz was invited but Hitler's forces were just across the channel and Canterbury was a restricted area. He, a German, was not given permission to attend, albeit his name was announced on BBC radio as one who would be present. Later, towards the end of the war, when Temple died suddenly, Franz was given permission to attend his funeral but by then the Allied forces were driving across France to Germany and the situation was easier.

Just eight weeks after his consecration William Temple preached at the German-English service in Christ's College Cambridge on 28 June 1942. He later wrote that for him it was 'one of the most effective testimonies that have been given to the reality of our fellowship in Christ during these days of war'. After the service was concluded refreshments were provided but the tea was too hot to drink. Franz and his mother, being Germans, had to observe the curfew and be home by 10 p.m. The archbishop noted their predicament, grinned at them and said, 'Don't you always saucer it?' and he promptly poured his tea into his saucer and drank it.

In the pre-war year of 1939 there had been discussions about the BBC broadcasting a Christian service in German to the continent. Franz Hildebrandt had been involved as was Julius Rieger. At that time the opinion of Hans Lilje, an influential pastor in Germany, was sought since all religious broadcasting in Germany came to an end in April 1939. The issue, clearly stated, was: 'Is it a religious Christian broadcast or is it an addendum to political propaganda?' It was now raised anew. Franz and Julius had done an occasional broadcast and they were consulted again. News broadcasts in German had been going out since Munich 1938. The BBC, now moved to Bedford, took as models the German-English services in Cambridge and broadcast a fifteen minute service in German every Wednesday morning. Some queries were raised that Franz, an open pacifist, should be used although this was countered by the fact that it would mean the broadcasting would be religious and not political. Franz records that all the preachers were anonymous (though maybe some listeners in Germany recognized the voices). He also tells that 'after the war we learned that these broadcasts were heard over there in the "catacombs" often at great risk to the listeners'.

As the different refugee groupings met, various ideas were proposed. Julius Rieger supported the idea of a training institute. A number of names of men and women interested were known. Franz Hildebrandt was the name suggested to teach 'Dogmatics and Ethics' but he declined. Vacation schools were organized by the International Fellowship of Reconciliation – under the inspiration of Canon Raven. Raven and Hildebrandt ran a course on 'The Situation of the Church on the Continent' and they in turn conducted morning devotions. From these developed the 'Christian International Service' (the CIS) with Raven as chairman and Hildebrandt as secretary. While at one of these schools in autumn of 1942 Raven had the idea for his book *Good News of God*, and he warned Hildebrandt that it would annoy him greatly. When the book was later published it did just that – with unfortunate consequences for their friendship.

Dr Olive Wyon was giving a lecture at the Quaker Meeting House in London under the auspices of the CIS and a young woman attended who as a student had known her in Cambridge. Nancy Wright was a student of Bedford College, London, which was evacuated to Cambridge at the beginning of the war. Olive Wyon had been persuaded by Raven to become chaplain to the womens' colleges in Cambridge, Girton and Newnham. She was a Presbyterian and so was Nancy. They became friends.

Nancy, who was now doing practical studies in social work in London, went to see her friend and after the meeting waited to speak to her. As Dr Wyon happened to be speaking to another, Nancy stood nearby and waited. Also waiting was Franz Hildebrandt. Nancy remembered that he had spoken at the invitation of Olive Wyon at a Student Christian Movement meeting. She was then just 'one of the crowd'. Now they spoke to one another while they waited. The date was 24 September 1942. Six months later on 1 April 1943 they were engaged to be married (Remembering that it was April Fool's Day Nancy often says 'and before midday'!)* Then her plans had to be altered. Her passage to Hong Kong where she planned to go as a missionary worker was cancelled.

Nancy's family welcomed Franz warmly. Her father's family in Bristol were evangelical Anglicans who prayed regularly for Martin Niemoeller. Franz had worked with Niemoeller and himself had suffered for the faith. That he was joining the family was a happy, joyful event. That he was a German, therefore technically an alien, mattered little. Her mother took to Franz immediately and her family accepted him without demur. It was only much later that she heard from her sister who was serving in China that she had received one or two letters from her parents which raised some doubts – doubts never voiced to Nancy, who saw the whole event as a most happy one.

Franz's mother also received Nancy warmly, but Nancy was aware that for a senior lady seventy years old who was deaf, it was another element of confusion. She had seen her son flee as a refugee to England, lost her husband, and she herself had left the country of her birth, endeavouring to learn a new language in spite of deafness. Her son with whom she had been reunited had been taken away by police into internment. Then he returned and now had decided to marry a British girl. Fortunately a number of

---

*In Britain the best fools are those caught before midday.

her own relatives had come to England and she had a brother and sister-in-law who lived in Britain who showed her great kindness. Their Jewish tradition of caring for the family made a great impression on Nancy.

In April 1943 there was a meeting with Bishop Bell in London of pastors of the Confessing Church now living in England. Franz took Nancy with him and she met a number of his friends: Julius Rieger, now the centre of the opposition in Britain to the 'German Christian Church,' Wolfgang Buesing, now in Wembley, engaged to a girl with Jewish blood whom he intended to marry while in England, and Hans Herbert Kramm who cared for the congregations in Hampstead and Oxford. Kramm was a scholar of some note who died not long after the war ended. He was a clear thinker and not afraid of debate. It was because of Kramm that some bishops had exchanged letters about the validity of Lutheran confirmation and the rightness of their taking the sacrament in the Church of England. Bishop Bell was the most open to 'treating them as guests'. Later, at the end of the war, Kramm believed that the German Lutheran Church should be maintained in Britain for the benefit of succeeding generations. At the time Franz Hildebrandt did not agree, believing their future was with British churches. Later he admitted that his friend did have a point.

Werner Simonson had escaped from Germany alone. He hoped his wife and son would follow but the war began before they could get away. His son was conscripted into the German army but managed to escape into the hands of the Allies. He was then reunited with his father to the great joy of both. His wife joined them after the war. Nancy was welcomed by them all. She treasured their friendship as did Franz. It was during this period that Franz paid a return visit to the Isle of Man as a pastoral visitor to the internees. He felt strange revisiting the place where he had been held prisoner, but he talked with the people and came back with a case full of problems which he set about solving as soon as he returned.

A wartime marriage with rationing of food and clothing presented numerous problems. Many things associated with weddings in peacetime were simply impossible to obtain. Friends rallied round gathering the necessities for a home. Friends also promised to take care of the wedding reception. Mrs Baercroft, a bilingual member of Franz's congregation, helped to organize the wedding presents. One day she discovered a tea trolley and was seen trundling it from one side of Cambridge to the other.

25 September 1943 was the date fixed for the wedding. The Revd W. T. Elmslie was to conduct the service assisted by Julius Rieger. It was to take place in Finchley, in the Presbyterian Church to which Nancy belonged. However, one evening as Franz was returning from a speaking engagement he felt a pain in his leg. At first he thought it was rheumatism but, fortunately, went to see the doctor. On hearing that Franz had broken his leg when he was sixteen, the doctor sent him for an X-ray. This ascertained that the metal plate which was then inserted had begun to move. 'No hurry', said the surgeon. 'Lots of hurry', said Franz. On being told that the wedding was to take place shortly, the surgeon said, 'It can be done; but you'll be walking in plaster at your wedding.' This meant a change of venue to Christ's College, Cambridge. New invitations were sent out. Somehow *King's* College was mistakenly printed on the invitation. The error was spotted by Canon Raven who knew where the ceremony was to be. A third lot was sent out.

His good friend Max Warren was best man. With his wife Mary, Max invited them to hold the reception in his house. Both Elmslie and Rieger could manage the change of venue in a day. Sadly, Bishop Bell and his wife could not, but Franz's Cambridge congregation were overjoyed. Amongst the hymns in the service were two by Paul Gerhardt sung in German. Julius Rieger arrived late, and rather than interrupt the ceremony, sat at the back of the chapel. He did cap the whole event, however, by saying, 'It is better for him to enter into matrimony with only one leg than to be cast into eternal fire with two.'

The proposed honeymoon included walking in the Cotswolds. In the event it meant travelling in the guard's van in a wheelchair with Nancy sitting on the mailbags. On arrival the new wife pushed her husband around in a wheelchair. They worshipped at the local parish church and met the vicar who invited them to tea and to see the vicarage *Ampelopsis*. Neither of them knew what it was. They discovered it was a lovely creeping plant. Nancy maintains Franz would have preferred it to have been a new breed of cat!

The marriage created a problem. Nancy had married an alien

and therefore lost her British citizenship. Her husband was techically an 'enemy'. However after six weeks she was granted re-naturalization. The 'aliens officer' in Cambridge was friendly. He told her not to worry about the curfew herself, so long as Franz was at home by 10 p.m.! She also had to adjust to Lutheran worship. Apart from the black gown and preaching bands worn by the pastor, it was very different from the Presbyterian form. Franz jokingly described her feelings 'as though she were shaking hands with the edge of the Scarlet Woman.'

Nancy again had problems when Franz later became a Methodist minister. The adjustment was not easy. Her Presbyterianism was deeply rooted – but she came to love Charles Wesley's hymns as did Franz. His attempt to teach German to Nancy, a non-linguist by her own confession, foundered. Not only did Franz tease her by teaching her words used in the nursery but all their German friends spoke such good English. Nancy tried to find work in Cambridge. She was a qualified social worker but she was young and inexperienced. In Cambridge jobs were at a premium since there were so many evacuees and refugees looking for work. So they continued to receive £250 a year from the Ecumenical Council.

During 1943 Max Warren was moved from Holy Trinity to be in charge of the Church Missionary Society. He continued to live in Cambridge for another three years since London was being bombed, and their relationship with him continued. The change did bring a new friend, for his successor, the Revd Howard Cruse, who later became Provost of Sheffield and Suffragan Bishop of Knaresborough, warmly embraced the German–English relationships.

During the winter of 1942–43 news came from Germany via Geneva of Hitler's war on the Jews. Some in Britain like Archbishop Temple and Bishop Bell tried to make a protest heard and explored what could be done to help. On 28 and 29 December a group of German pastors met in London. They had heard the news and decided to join the action. They wrote a telling letter to *The Times* headed 'Nazi War on Jews'. It was signed by Buesing (London), Deutschausen (Birmingham), Ehrenberg (Manchester), Hildebrandt (Cambridge), Kramm (Oxford) and Schweitzer (Oxford). It appeared in *The Times* on 2 January 1943. Some of these sentences reveal their thinking:

> We ministers of the German Lutheran Church in England feel in duty bound to call our congregations to solemn prayer and intercession for the Jewish people in their unparalleled sufferings. It was the anti-Jewish legislation which brought the Lutheran Church in Germany to its first witness against idolatry and barbarism and caused it to become a 'Confessing Church'. Some of us wish that the protest then made would have been stronger ... it is not for us who live in safety to criticize those who under fire have done their utmost not to bow to Baal ...

The letter ended with a text used by Dietrich Bonhoeffer: 'Open thy mouth for the dumb.' (Prov. 31.8)

These German pastors, aware that their protest could have been stronger and realizing they were speaking for many in Germany who had difficulty in speaking out, were upset when their friend William Temple, himself preaching at a service in London to remember Martin Niemoeller's birthday, and broadcast by the BBC, said that 'as far as we know there has been no protest against such crimes as the attempt to exterminate the Poles or the horror of the massacre of the Jews', and suggested that any protest was somewhat in self-defence.

Kramm prepared a memorandum which was sent to Temple whose words had also reached Geneva. He commented that a sermon which was intended as a sign of friendship and unity had stirred the political waters. On receiving Kramm's evidence Temple apologized and confessed that 'these extracts represent a greater volume of protest than I realized had been uttered.' It was to make clear the position on such questions that Julius Rieger prepared a tract published in 1944, 'The Silent Church: the Problem of the German Confessional Witness'. Here he spoke of 'apparent silence' when the church seemed quiet but was working and speaking quietly; 'functional silence', when the church did not speak officially, saying nothing which would prevent the work being done; and 'guilty silence' when the church compromised the Gospel through cowardice. 'In compromising the Gospel the church lacks charity ... the silence of the church is guilty silence.'

Many German pastors felt that the situation in Germany was not understood clearly by people in Britain. In 1996 a German Methodist pastor, from Chemnitz, who had lived under Nazi and Communist domination began an answer to a British questioner:

'Your question shows that you have never lived under a totalitarian dictatorship'.

In 1938 a group of refugee pastors made the suggestion that the help and friendship of Bishop George Bell should be acknowledged by publishing a book of essays, a *Festschrift*, in his honour. It took some time to develop and organize. The task fell to Franz Hildebrandt. The Cambridge University Press agreed to publish it if 250 subscribers could be found. This had to be done in secret for Bishop Bell was not to know of it. Eventually it was published in 1943 with contributions from a most learned group of pastors and scholars. These included the 'retired' Dr Ehrenberg along with Dr Kramm, Dr Rieger, Dr C. G. Schweitzer and, of course, Dr Hildebrandt. There were contributions, on the Bible on the Church of England and, naturally, on Luther. It would be interesting to know what Bishop Bell thought of some of the contributions, viewing them from his episcopal seat.

Dr Kramm's essay on Luther's ideas about church structure is still challenging: 'on principle all ministers are bishops'; 'he would have kept ordination by bishops only for the sake of peace'; 'His theology shows that the apostolic succession in the Roman sense had no great value ... all ministers could ordain others.'

Franz Hildebrandt presented various interpretations of Luther and tore apart that of the Nazi philosopher Rosenberg that Luther's Reformation was in its essence the fruit of the German spirit. 'Luther is a prophet *to* rather than *of* Germany, giving constant warning to a nation which is disobedient to God's voice ... the Word of God, as Luther says, is like a shower of rain which comes here today and goes there tomorrow and no nation should think she could have it forever.' Canon Jasper in his biography of Bishop Bell quotes the 'moving tribute' written by Franz Hildebrandt: 'Today there are thousands of refugees who would wish to thank you for what you have done for them ... Let us pastors speak in their name.'

The book is a veritable treasure and deserved and still deserves wide reading. The title *And Other Pastors of Thy Flock*, was taken from a prayer used regularly by the Revd Dr Paul Gibson. Franz searched for it in the *Book of Common Prayer* without success. Only when discussing it with Max Warren did he learn that it had been inserted by Paul Gibson into the prayers for bishops and clergy and was only used at Ridley Hall. Nevertheless it was a happily inspired title.

One delightful memory of 1943 was the day when Franz was present at the University Church in Oxford for the confirmation of his 'adopted' niece, Marianne Leibholtz, daughter of Dietrich Bonhoeffer's twin sister Sabine and her husband Gerhard.

During 1943 another book was published which brought to an end Canon Raven's friendship with Franz Hildebrandt. Raven, a naturalist, scientist and a theologian published *Good News of God* in which he stated his philosophy and theology. He saw his science and his faith bound together in an 'evolutionary process'. This alone would have disturbed Franz but Raven also attacked continental theologians. Franz was goaded into replying in a book of his own, *This is the Message.* He felt he must answer 'only from the Continent no reply is likely to be received at present and it is in this direction that many of Dr Raven's statements are aimed'. The subtitle of his book is *A Continental Reply to Charles Raven.*

He begins with an apology, admits all the kindness he had received from Raven but says 'against all my habits and inclinations I simply had to sit down to write this reply'. He refers to Raven's earlier warning that he would not like the book being written and he answers Raven's argument effectively by stating 'Faith alone, grace alone, Christ alone – based on the revealed Word of God in scripture.' Franz could never be less than courteous in argument. On almost every page he begs Raven's pardon for daring to answer, but, firmly and politely, strongly answers Raven point by point. It is significant that when he was being considered for a professorship at Drew University, this book was cited in his favor. So the man who argued regularly with Bonhoeffer in an ever-deepening friendship, who dared challenge Niemoeller on policy while drawing nearer to him in affection, who always enjoyed a good debate – in the continental way, was sad to find that this statement of faith had destroyed his friendship with Raven.

Not only had Raven regarded his own book as a distillation of his own faith – and the attack had been a personal hurt – but while the Hildebrandt book was in preparation the gracious and kind Mrs Raven died. Her presence would certainly have helped the relationship and would probably have soothed the troubled waters. Franz had allowed his wife and Olive Wyon, who was a good friend of Canon Raven, to read his manuscript and adopted the suggestions they made. Franz Hildebrandt had not realized that a theological argument like this could destroy a friendship. Olive Wyon spoke to Raven and tried to heal the breach as did others. Franz himself wrote to Raven full of sorrow thanking him for help in the past (Raven had opened doors for him.) and saying that he realized these doors would close. Nevertheless he could not take back his defence of the German Protestant theological position. Franz always admitted that he was spoiled by his arguments with Dietrich Bonhoeffer. For them, friendship and strong argument went together. So he remained bewildered.

At first Franz had thought that after the war he might return to Germany but after a few years he wrote to Bishop Bell that a return to Germany seemed more and more unlikely. Not long after his marriage he was asked to represent the British and Foreign Bible Society. Gordon Bennett, a much loved minister in Cambridge, had represented subsequently the BFBS in 'Cambridgeshire, Huntingdonshire and the Public Schools of England and Wales'. However he had died unexpectedly and the vacant post was offered to Franz. Nancy was asked to help with the Woman's Work. Now he needed a car to cover the area. For the schools and colleges he tried to use public transport; Nancy remembers how at times public transport in the war years and just after could be unreliable and she had some emergency calls to collect Franz at some strange hours. Nevertheless the Cambridge congregation still held services regularly on alternative Sundays at 8 p.m. and he was their pastor. Folk still wanted to hear about what had happened in Germany but he expounded the Bible in the pulpit and gave talks as an extra. One subject was 'The Bible in the Churches in Germany'. He believed that it was not possible to transfer situations. 'You cannot transplant their faith but you can transplant the Word which has created their faith, the message which has produced it.'

After the failure of the plot to assassinate Hitler on 20 July 1944 and, knowing how Hitler and his gang would react, he worried about his friends. Bishop Bell had pressed Anthony Eden again and again to see if there was any way Hitler's opponents in Germany could be helped – without success. Obviously there were great practical difficulties but Eden saw no reason to help and referred to Bell as 'that pestilent priest'. Niemoeller survived.

Bonhoeffer didn't. Whether anything could have been done to help, no one knows. It is just possible that, had Eden and Churchill been more open, the war might have been shortened and many lives saved. William Temple died unexpectedly in October 1944. Bell, popularly expected to be his successor, was not nominated.

On 9 May 1945, the day after the end of the war in Europe (VE Day) a united service for German and English congregations was held in Holy Trinity Church with Howard Cruse and Franz Hildebrandt leading the worship, the congregations united as they were on the day war was declared. The theme was rejoicing in 'the delivery from tyranny and oppression' and dedication to 'the unbroken fellowship in the Church of Jesus Christ', under the heading of 'Thanksgiving for Victory and Prayer for Peace among all nations'.

In the days and weeks after the war ended the German pastors tried to gather information about their friends in Germany and on 30 May 1945 from Geneva came news of the death of Dietrich Bonhoeffer. Julius Rieger travelled to Oxford to be with Sabine Leibholz and her husband and family. Franz passed on that news as well as any other he gathered, to friends and relatives. He also wrote to Herbert Johle in the USA: 'Dietrich Bonhoeffer is dead. It is too awful to put this down in cold blood. What his loss at this moment means for the cause of Christ and peace I need not tell you. With us here all is well. We live in comfort and safety, but it is all so unreal'. Eventually the news came through that Martin Niemoeller was safe.

On 27 July in Holy Trinity Church, Kingsway, London, a special memorial service was held in German and English for Dietrich Bonhoeffer. Bishop Bell and Franz Hildebrandt gave the addresses. Franz took as his text II Chron. 20.12: 'O our God, will you not execute judgement upon them? For we are powerless against this great multitude that is coming against us. We do not know what to do but our eyes are on you', a text he had once offered to Dietrich in the 1930s and which had produced a powerful sermon. He spoke simply about Dietrich's discipleship, imprisonment and martyrdom.* After the service Sabine said, 'No one else could have given such a lovely address', and her

*Appendix 2.

husband Gerhard said that Dietrich's death made Franz's friend-ship more precious than ever.* The service was broadcast by the BBC to Germany as well as in Britain and in this way many people in Germany learned of Dietrich's death. Indeed the BBC broad-casts gave Germans most of their accurate information. Many were thankful for the bonds established in the united witness. For some time Cambridge and the surrounding area had been receiv-ing German prisoners of war. Franz with other pastors took on the responsibility of caring for them. The matron at Addenbrooke's Hospital where some were billeted cared little for the 'no fraternization' order and allowed worship and practical teaching in their own language. Franz notes that it was in the American prisoner of war camps where the 'red tape' was most difficult to bypass.

After the end of the war some of the refugees began to move from Cambridge. Slowly the congregation declined in numbers. Franz thought deeply about the future of the church and his own situation. The older Germans were returning home. On 17 February 1946 he preached in English at a service in St George's Lutheran Church in London. They were remembering the 400th anniversary of the death of Martin Luther. The BBC broadcast the service. Later in the year the Lutheran congregation moved to worship in the smaller college chapel of Wesley House, the Methodist Ministerial Training College in Cambridge – and its last regular service in German was held on 28 July. The German Lutherans continued to worship there in small numbers for some years.

Franz, with a British wife (half English, half Scottish) and a son, David, born in 1944, did not see a return to Germany as the way for him. He also had in his mind the discussions with Dietrich in Sydenham about witness in the struggle and he remembered what Dietrich had said when he returned to Germany in 1939. It was not his fault that he had been in exile and therefore not in the greatest heat of the battle during the war years. He had to believe that he was part of God's plan. Believing it was not the right course to return to Germany, he could see two possibilities. He could either work as pastor to a German congregation in Britain,

*Four members of the Bonhoeffer family were executed by the Nazis: Dietrich, his brother Klaus and his brothers-in-law Ruediger Schleicher and Hans von Dohnanyi.

and this he was rejecting, or he could join a British Free Church which would recognize his ordination as valid. The Church of England would insist on a second, episcopal, ordination and his views on the implications of that step had been expressed often enough. The Methodist Church seemed the obvious place to go. To him it was 'a translation from one language to another'. This is clearly shown in a reading of his great book *From Luther to Wesley*. He saw the battle for the faith 'perfect, full and present salvation through Christ' as only being won 'by the united forces of Luther and Wesley'.

Later, in September 1956, he wrote Eberhardt Bethge that in Methodism one could still be a follower of Luther and sing the appropriate hymns for one's sermons. The English Luther was to be found in Charles Wesley. How often he said words like these! He also needed a ' regular' congregation where he could preach and teach systematically. The BFBS work made him a touring preacher and he was not at ease in this. He needed to preach from the Bible and not talk about it. The BFBS had asked him if he would be prepared to take some Bibles to Germany but he pointed out the incongruity of taking Bibles to a country which so recently those same nationals had devastated with their bombing. And so, after much thought and prayer, he offered himself to the Methodist Church to become one of Mr Wesley's preachers.

CHAPTER 11

FRIENDSHIP WITH DIETRICH BONHOEFFER

It was a remarkable friendship: unusual, deep, inspiring for both of them. When talking about it Franz would say with a smile, 'It began with an argument. We argued every day of our time together. You could not be Dietrich's friend if you did not argue with him. After Dietrich's death arguments were never the same again'. In words like these Franz would talk of his friendship with Dietrich Bonhoeffer.

While waiting in the University of Berlin for Professor Seeberg's seminar to begin, Franz Hildebrandt became involved in an argument with his fellow student Dietrich who was also waiting. They both knew the great professor, Adolf von Harnack, and had read his book on Marcion. Franz putting Harnack's point of view found that his opponent, who also greatly revered Harnack, had a critical view of him as well. He soon discovered that Dietrich loved the Old Testament, Harnack and arguing. Neither was to know how great a friendship was to begin or what would lie ahead for them both. Franz Hildebrandt was soon introduced to the Bonhoeffer home and became a welcome member of the family. It was already a large family. He was an only child. He called it 'a second home by adoption'. His entree was to a talented family where every member thought clearly, pushed aside prejudice, recognized evil and, though not always in a completely orthodox way, accepted the challenge and power of the Christian gospel.

The friendship was unusual because Dietrich Bonhoeffer and Franz Hildebrandt were in some ways very different while in other ways they were much alike. They joked about the fact that when they were in Berlin together as colleagues their telephone numbers had the same digits but in reverse order. It seemed to them to be a parable of their own friendship. In the basics they were completely united but the approach of either to any subject was likely to be different from the approach of the other.

The occasion of their first meeting is just another illustration of this. Both had been greatly influenced by Harnack. Franz always remembered how as a teenager he had met Harnack. He had been completely won over. Dietrich, also greatly influenced by him, gave a eulogy after Harnack's death and both were caught by some of Harnack's epigrams. Later, when talking of Dietrich, Franz would often refer to words which Harnack used when his friend Holl died: 'Part of my life is buried with him in the grave.' He also kept a note of a telegram which Harnack not long before his death in 1930 had sent to Dietrich: 'The content of eschatology is but this: that we come to understand that we are God's children.' (Was this in the back of Bonhoeffer's mind when he wrote 'we are all children of the resurrection'?)

Franz stood nearer to Harnack in theological thought. Dietrich was more in the line of Barth. Their initial argument was over the place of the Old Testament in Christian worship, for Bonhoeffer loved the Old Testament. Surprisingly, Ps. 119 was one of his favourites. Later when in prison he found the Old Testament and the Psalms a source of strength. In their discussions Franz Hildebrandt learned much about the power of the Old Testament and at times suggested texts to his friend for sermons. He also came to love the Psalms. There is no doubt that each helped the other in spirituality. Franz's approach to the Psalms was always from a critical background. Later when he had become a lover of the Wesleys he would tell how their mutual friend Julius Rieger once complimented Dietrich on his exposition of Ps. 27 as he preached in St George's Church, London. He would then comment that it contained a verse which John Wesley once said was 'highly improper for the use of a Christian congregation'.

Franz Hildebrandt and Dietrich Bonhoeffer both had birthdays in February; Franz was three years younger than Dietrich. Three years is not much between friends, especially friends such as these, but Franz also used to say that Dietrich was years ahead in the perception of men and events. Though he himself was not a chess player, he thought Dietrich must fit his image of a clever chess player, always thinking several moves ahead of his opponent. Bonhoeffer's vision was part of his genius. The fact that in the 1930s he, a Protestant, was prepared to vote for the 'Catholic Centre' Party in the national elections because he saw it to be the only party with the possibility of stopping Hitler and the Nazis, shows his foresight and openness.

The whole Bonhoeffer family saw the Nazi danger. Later Franz would smile as he told how grandmother Bonhoeffer- a doughty anti-Nazi in her 90s – used to say when a member of the family answered the telephone with 'Heil Hitler' before speaking – a customary greeting introduced by the Nazis – 'Drop that! lest you grow accustomed to using it'! This appears to have continued as a running joke in the family. Marianne Leibholtz remembers that when she was about eleven years old her Uncle Klaus and 'Uncle' Franz greeted one another laughingly in the Bonhoeffer house with 'Heil Hitler!', only to be told by her grandmother, 'Children Children! Enough of that!' and then all burst into laughter.

When Franz was introduced to the Bonhoeffer home he was welcomed and came to love it. He called it 'An Oasis of Freedom'. And what was true of the parents was true of the other members of the family. Friendly chats, musical sessions – both Franz and Dietrich were excellent pianists – times to relax. Indeed in the years 1934–37 he would be found on most Sunday afternoons in one or other of the Bonhoeffer homes.

The Bonhoeffers were a truly German family, pure enough in the blood line to satisfy any Nazi, but there was nothing of the 'Aryan' about them. From the beginning they had no time for the false Nazi thinking. As it happened Dietrich's twin sister Sabine married Gerhard Leibholtz who was of Jewish blood and Dietrich introduced his friend Franz Hildebrandt, a man with a Jewish mother. Neither Gerhard nor Franz ever felt out of place. Franz would sometimes say that the key word for the family in general and for Dietrich and his father in particular was 'consideration for others'. He would cite in support the fact that Dietrich's father, a professor of psychiatry, would be very angry if anyone laughed at anything silly which a mentally disturbed patient might do or say. Dr Bonhoeffer was so courteous that if he entered the bedroom while his wife was reading or telling a story to one of the little ones he would not interrupt to say 'Goodnight'. Such was his code of behaviour.

Shortly after they met, Dietrich Bonhoeffer went to serve in a curacy in Barcelona (1928) and they next made contact on Good Friday, 1929. Drawn by their love of music, they met by chance at a performance of Bach's *St Matthew Passion* in Berlin. In later years, when asked, Franz found it difficult to remember particular incidents of this time. He could remember going to hear Dietrich preach in July 1930. The text of the sermon was Luke 17.7–10. (It happened to be the text which Bishop George Bell used when he preached in Denmark in 1958 shortly before his death.) He also remembered Dietrich being present in turn when he himself conducted children's worship in the Bonhoeffers' home church in Gruenewald.

One of his specially treasured memories was of the way Dietrich helped him over the matter of his 'Licentiate'. Franz had worked hard at Luther's teaching on the Lord's Supper. And he always remembered how when it was rejected with the comment 'Too little text: too many footnotes' and he was quite prepared to give up, Dietrich stood by him, talked with him , encouraged him and suggested that the faults could easily be remedied. Such encouragement was vital to his flagging spirit. He set to work with Dietrich's advice and help, rewrote it and presented it again, this time successfully. Later it was published under the title of *Est* in the series: *Studies in Systematic Theology*.

He aims to show that the word 'Est' is the Luther principle which assumes all Lutheran theology. He saw the position of Karl Barth and his followers as one of questioning with 'uncertainty regarding the sacrament' whereas true Lutheran theology underlines the 'givenness', the certainty or assurance of God. In using the word *realpraesent* with regard to the sacrament perhaps it is possible to hear already words from his book *From Luther to Wesley*. He was not uncritical of the Lutheran church, nor of Melanchthon. He stressed the importance of faith in the 'word became flesh' and suggested that each 'Why?' disappears before the 'Est'. He concludes by underlining a reliance on the Scriptures – always a strong point with him. He is uncompromising and positive in what he sees as the truth – always a characteristic. 'With Franz', said Martin Niemoeller on one occasion, 'it is either black or white. There is no grey.'

Franz in childhood.

Franz and his mother.

St Anne Kirche, Darlem, where Franz shared his ministry
with Martin Niemoeller.

A meeting of the Refugee Congregations.

Douglas Camp, Isle of Man, 1940, where Franz was elected as
'Camp Leader'.

Franz and his mother,
September 1942.

The wedding of Franz and Nancy,
25 September 1943.

Franz with the Archbishop of Canterbury,
William Temple, Cambridge, 1942.

Franz and Nancy with David and Ruth on-board the *Italia*,
September 1953, their 'voyage into the unknown'.

Swanwick, England, 1954.

Franz and Martin Niemoller in the USA, 1962.

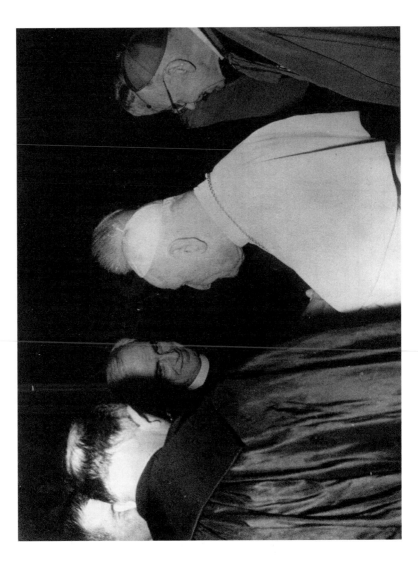

Franz with Pope John XXIII at The Second Vatican Council, 1962.

His thesis foreshadows his later work, written in England in the 1940s, on Melanchthon and also his taking up of the teaching of the Wesleys and the hymns of Charles on the Real Presence – which he came to love so much. When it is remembered that Dietrich Bonhoeffer worked with him on this thesis and that they discussed often the ideas of Luther and others, perhaps we should not be too surprised if some notes, later found in *Letters and Papers from Prison*, seem to contain echoes of *Est*. For though they argued much, deep down they were united in their faith in Christ and in their understanding of that faith.

Reviewers praised Franz for his sharpness of thought and his clarity of expression but they had reservations about his linking of Luther with Hegel and Zwingli with Barth. Hans Iwand, Lutheran scholar and also a strong opponent of Hitler, who himself headed an 'underground seminar' of the Confessing Church, praised his statement of the Lutheran position but thought his sharpening of the Lutheran–Reformed relationship was not helpful and the mingling of polemic with history was dangerous. (Was this a foretaste of the tough logic shown later in the Anglican–Methodist Conversations debate?)

After rewriting this thesis Franz wanted never to write anything else by hand. Indeed it was in part his dislike of writing by hand which developed his own special idiosyncratic way of preparing sermons. He would select a text after careful thought. Then he would go for a long walk, pondering it and thinking, drawing on his remarkable and voluminous memory. He would write down only what was absolutely essential. Sermons which needed recording on paper were usually written down from memory after they had been preached. Dietrich used to quote to him some words of Harnack that 'he hoped his pen would be more clever than his head'. Franz in reply readily admitted that in his case it was not so. Of course when they were working together in Berlin and London the preparation of each sermon by either could become an area for debate. But that was a special setting with two friends working to bring out the best in each other, for the good of the Gospel.

That this was indeed truly a two-way movement is seen by the fact, recorded by Roggelin, that Franz collected and wrote two notebooks of useful quotations for his friend, one from the Bible and the other from Luther, so using his marvellous memory to help Dietrich. His own modesty would prevent him from telling this. Franz was pleased when Dietrich returned to Germany from Barcelona. He confessed that several German pastors seemed to hear 'the call of the south' to places with a warmer climate. He was not entirely happy with the way Dietrich sometimes extolled the power of the sun and felt his words needed care. It is interesting that in one letter in *Letters and Papers from Prison* (30 June 1944) Dietrich makes some observations about being in the sun and the warm countries and one can see why Franz was cautious. It also shows that Dietrich had eyes open wide to see God wherever God showed Himself. The beauty of nature tended to pass by Franz.

Dietrich's attitude to bullfighting also disturbed Franz, for he actually said a few words in defence of it and did not condemn it out of hand – an attitude which Franz could never hold.

There were times when Dietrich found that the Roman Catholic church had its attractions. Some of these ideas are expressed in *Letters and Papers from Prison* 'Outline for a Book. Chapter 2'. The best of Catholicism has always been helpful to many non-Catholics. We remember too that Bishop von Galen, the Roman Catholic bishop of Muenster, gave strong support to Pastor Dr Friedrich von Bodelschwingh when he needed help to keep open his hospitals for the mentally sick at Bethel bei Bielefeld. Martin Niemoeller also received valued support from Roman Catholics during his imprisonment.

Franz said he never discussed the Roman Catholic church seriously with Dietrich. His own position – as usual – was clear. He could understand people growing up in the Roman Catholic church in which they had been baptized and nurtured, but he could not understand anyone moving from Protestantism to Roman Catholicism. In his later years he used to say that he could not understand how men like Hans Kueng could remain Roman Catholics.

Dietrich used to tease Franz as their friendship developed. He would complain that Franz would not read 'popular' books on society or history (which was largely true to the end of his life). On one occasion he doubted if Franz would know the date of Bismarck's birth. Franz immediately gave a date, day, month and year. Dietrich was so surprised he had to look it up and found that Franz was exactly right. Sometimes when they were both involved in an argument Franz would produce his trump card, his clinching point. At this moment Dietrich would look up and say, 'What was that? I'm sorry I didn't hear a word!' Then, as Franz said, 'even the best rejoinder falls a little flat when it is repeated a second time'. So they would usually dissolve into laughter.

Franz would tell how Dietrich used to tease him. With his idea that you learned a language if you were half asleep, he would speak English to Franz when his eyes closed for a few moments on a tube train in the underground in London or when he was relaxing at home. Dietrich would also say if they were in a restaurant or going to the cinema, 'It doesn't really matter who pays does it?' and follow it with 'You pay then!' And sometimes when they were in a cinema watching an exciting film, at the crucial moment he might turn to Franz and ask 'Shall we go home now?' But sometimes his humorous remarks contained an edge such as 'I take no responsibility for Hitler: I never voted for him!'

Laughter was a part of their relationship and they would tell one another stories of humorous events. Franz remembered Dietrich coming one day with the story of a young 'German Christian' pastor who knew more about the Nazis and their ideas than he did about traditional Christian thought and practice. A christening came along and he read the rubric in the prayer book as it stood, ending the prayer 'through Jesus Christ our Lord, I baptize thee N or M'.

Dietrich was obvious material for a university teacher in theology. Franz also had gifts as a teacher for his curacies proved this. Both of them held firmly to the belief that a good university teacher in theology must also be a pastor of a congregation. In the pre-Hitler period this line of thought was far from obvious. Professors began their careers as junior lecturers not as pastors and, as they were able, moved up the ladder of promotion to become professors. Theology however is different from other subjects in that students of chemistry, physics, languages and the like continue to work in their chosen field. Students of theology have to take what they have learned into churches and congregations and also have pastoral care of the people. The resulting situation was that congregations and churches tended to look with suspicion on academics. 'That anyone could be at the same time a university teacher and a pastor was an exceptional idea.' Otto Dibelius who caused Dietrich to be the student pastor at a technical college in Berlin said to him 'You are a man of Praxis', i.e. practical work.

The Third Reich changed the picture completely. With few exceptions the universities gave in to Nazi pressure. Dietrich because of his opposition lost the appointment to which he had been directed in 1936. Then the illegal seminaries such as Finkenwalde came into being with the solemn calling of the lecturers who were also doing pastoral work.

Later, when a Professor of Theology at Drew University in New Jersey, Franz Hildebrandt remained true to this idea. He took pastoral charge of a small church near the university campus. He never changed his view that any teacher who shares in the training of ministers must himself or herself be 'active' in pastoral work. Such forging of ideas was an essential part of the friendship of Hildebrandt and Bonhoeffer. Anything and everything was open for examination and argument, so that when any idea finally emerged it had been tested and refined: and by this examination they knew the answers to most of the criticisims likely to be levelled at them.

Wolf-Dieter Zimmermann edited a lovely little book *I knew Dietrich Bonhoeffer* which is an anthology of writings from Bonhoeffer's friends. Zimmerman has two articles of his own. One is a priceless chapter about his visit to the Forest Hill parsonage at Christmas 1933. He talks of the mice. (Franz used to tell how he was woken up once when a mouse ran over his face.) He speaks of Dietrich and Franz living 'in a state of permanent dispute'. It was at once 'serious and humorous, aggressive and witty' and this continued the whole day, every day; but they were 'united by a very deep friendship'.

They argued over everything, each coming back at the other. It seemed it must end in estrangement. It often ended with them playing the piano together (Dietrich had had his own piano brought to London). Dietrich was more a Barthian than Franz; Franz put the Scriptures as his ground of being and might by some have been regarded as a fundamentalist; though he never disregarded sound modern scholarship. They were in fact deeply united on the Bible. Franz later remembered how they discussed the Sermon on the Mount and related subjects which discussions became the basis of *The Cost of Discipleship*. They regarded some of the ideas then as somewhat dangerous to proclaim. In later years Franz admitted that he now recognized its great value as never before, and always said it was Dietrich's finest work.

If their arguments helped their ideas to become clearer, their faith in Christ as Lord was the rock on which they stood firm. This was the rock on which they desired the Confessing Church also to stand firm. They thought and discussed and together wanted the Confessing Church to think clearly. They dared to tell Martin Niemoeller what to say and do. He recognized that he had two fine minds working with him and for him and he held them dearly in his affections.

In Berlin they had worked together for a short time. Indeed they had produced together a catechism* to help younger people. They had joked over the textual criticism which might ensue over who wrote what, little realizing that it would be part of the literary deposit of both of them. Dietrich had refused to take one position in the church because his friend, Franz, could not share it with him owing to the Aryan law, even though the two of them were prepared, there in that parish, to live on just one stipend. They had constructive ideas as to how a church and a pastorate might be developed and it is a tragedy they were never able to try to achieve their aims. When Dietrich was invited to Sydenham, 'You must come with me' he said, and after a short time Franz did just that. However, time in Sydenham was brief. Franz, knowing his own standing in Germany as a non-Aryan, was quite prepared to stay and work in England had the opportunity come along. The single stipend in Sydenham could not maintain them both for long, but Franz was soon recalled to Germany to hold the key position of treasurer in the Pastors' Emergency League. Niemoeller had chosen well.

From this point in January 1934 they were never to work so closely again, though they kept very close bonds of friendship. They still planned together in matters to do with opposition to the Nazis. When Dietrich went to conferences, he talked with Franz. This was especially true with regard to Fano. They met, and after their meeting Dietrich went to Fano and Franz went to Sydenham to hold the fort until Dietrich returned. Niemoeller regarded them both as his 'lieutenants'.

Dietrich was suggested to be the Director of the Seminary at

*See Appendix 1.

Finkenwalde and Franz headed the group who tried to persuade him to take up the task. Franz visited London to do this. Dietrich very much wanted to visit India and Gandhi but when Franz returned to Germany he carried with him Dietrich's assent. Doubtless the pressure of the moment was an important factor in making the decision. Sometimes the two friends said they would publish a little book of 'Biblical sayings which were of use to Satan'. The first would be 'the time is not yet ripe' (Hag. 1.2) It was a saying never used as an excuse by either Franz or Dietrich.

The closeness of their friendship and the 'belonging' which Franz felt with regard to the Bonhoeffer household was such that when he was in England one German pastor said 'They say in Berlin that Bonhoeffer is engaged to your sister.' Franz, an only child, relished the story.

He did keep in his heart a comment made by Dietrich when he heard of the document which some Confessing Church pastors sent to Hitler (1936), a document which Franz helped to draft. This document prompted the work which later became his Cambridge Ph.D. thesis. In a letter (they did write letters from time to time) Dietrich said that this event had built up his hopes. He wondered what the future would hold as a result but he assured them of his prayers. In February 1937 Franz went to preach in Greifswald. He believed Dietrich was behind the invitation. He also was invited to examine Confessing Church students in Breslau – the farthest points East that he visited. In this period they met when and where they could.

When Franz had decided that he must go into exile, he had fixed on a Sunday in July 1937 and in the previous week travelled to visit Dietrich and to apprise him of his plans. (How we would love to have an account of that conversation!). After his release from prison in August, for his own safety's sake he went to stay at the Bonhoeffer home rather than to court possible danger and re-arrest in his own flat. The 'Oasis' became a 'place of refuge'.

After his exile to England, they exchanged a very occasional letter, one with coded names and another in which Dietrich referred to the night of 10 November 1938 when 'the worst pogrom that had yet taken place in the Third Reich', the Night of Broken Glass, took place. Jewish shops were attacked and destroyed. Dietrich wrote that Franz's decision in the previous year was 'the right one'. The Jews and folk of Jewish blood were now directly targeted.

They met in England on two occasions. In March 1939, Dietrich, in England, journeyed to Cambridge to visit Franz and in July Franz travelled to London to the home of Julius Rieger to meet his friend who was travelling from the USA to Germany. Later in 1942 Dietrich met Bishop George Bell in Sweden and amongst other messages the Bishop brought a personal greeting from Dietrich to Franz.

In 1967 Franz received from the author a copy of the German edition of Eberhard Bethge's biography: *Dietrich Bonhoeffer*. By now the two friends of Dietrich had themselves become good friends. Franz wrote in his letter of thanks to Eberhard that he had read the book straight through at a sitting. He described it as 'masterly'. 'It will belong to the great historical and theological biographies ... you alone are competent to give the correct portrait of Dietrich'. He also thanked his friend for putting himself, Franz, in the correct place in the life of Dietrich. 'I have never since had such a friend nor such a partner in discussion'. He referred to Dietrich's word 'better isolated than untrue' and spoke of the yearning both of them had had for a 'quiet appointment'.

But there are two points which create a puzzle when thinking of this friendship. In Eberhard Bethge's great biography of Dietrich Bonhoeffer he tells that Dietrich in the early years of the 1930s had a powerful spiritual experience. Bonhoeffer refers to this in guarded terms in one of his letters to Eberhard Bethge. Bethge quotes from three letters where, to different people, Bonhoeffer makes the point that his calling is now crystal clear and he is completely in the hands of God. He knows that now he is on the right track and the Bible 'this strange word of God' is working on him. (cf. *Dietrich Bonhoeffer* by Eberhard Bethge, Collins Fount, pp. 154–6). Franz Hildebrandt at this time was Bonhoeffer's closest friend and said he knew nothing of this until he read the biography. He had noted no additional spiritual power or intensity. He records the texts of two powerful sermons in that period: 'Because your goodness is better than life, my lips will praise you' (Ps. 63.3) preached in October 1931 and another in May 1932: 'We do not know what we should do, but our eyes are on you' (2 Chron. 20.12) – a favourite verse of them both. The latter text lived with Franz as a summary of Dietrich's life and faith. Indeed he used it when preaching at the memorial service for Dietrich in July 1945.

So Franz was puzzled. Yet there are lines of thought which might help an understanding.

Franz came into theology and the Christian faith because of a gripping experience he had in Naumburg as a teenager. One hour changed the direction of his life. It was a major spiritual moment.

Dietrich came to be a theologian along another way. His family were surprised when he opted to study theology. They were not anti-church, indeed they were linked with the church in Gruenewald but they thought he might well follow another line of study. However theology fascinated Dietrich and his interests and studies developed. Then, awaiting the oral examination for his doctorate, he met Franz, a student with a vital faith, an equally sharp mind and abundant enthusiasm. They argued. The friendship grew and enthusiasm increased. Later Dietrich sensed he had moved – during this time – from being a theologian out of interest to being a Christian theologian out of conviction. It is not unknown for people studying the Christian faith or the Bible to find their way into the faith as the subject grips them. John Wesley, we are told, was exhorted by Peter Boehler to 'preach faith until you have it and then you will preach faith'. In his later years Franz would sometimes smile and say 'Dietrich was a true Wesleyan'.

But if one adds the joint study of the scriptures, the joint work in Berlin, the co-authoring of the Catechism, the growing opposition to the Nazis, the sharing in the creation of the Confessing Church, the struggles it involved, the 'call' to London, the growth of ecumenical relationships set in the background of a deep committed friendship, it is not too surprising if Franz, caught up in the same enthusiastic pursuit, missed out on the noting of a change in his friend or if Dietrich caught up in the enthusiasm and faith of Franz found his heart strangely warmed. Their deep friendship was based on Christian faith and practice. That the germinating of the ideas in *The Cost of Discipleship* began at this time tells us that the faith was there. That book is no cold academic treatise but a record of 'the warmed heart of faith'.

Many a Christian has looked back and said, 'At that time the Lord was working in me and I did not know it'. Perhaps the most perceptive Dietrich saw later what this natural outworking of their faith did not make clear at the time. Christians do 'grow in grace'. Dietrich, to Franz, was an all round Christian who saw Christ at work in all of life. Indeed Franz comments that Dietrich was at times critical of those who only saw God working in the darker days of suffering and persecution. For them both Christ was Lord of life, always, in joy and sorrow, in laughter and tears.

A more difficult question arises with regard to his view on the post-war publication of *Letters and Papers from Prison* and other gathered and edited papers of Bonhoeffer. Eberhard Bethge, who collected the letters and lecture notes and edited them was a former student at Finkenwalde who had become a very dear friend of Dietrich, indeed he had married Dietrich's niece. He and Franz, who could not remember meeting until after the war, became very good friends. Franz expressed the view that he was not completely happy about the publication but promised Eberhard that he would in no way criticize. He could see that Eberhard wanted the ideas of Dietrich, even if not fully thought out and expounded, to be given to the theological public.

Dietrich is trying hard to find the way for the Christian faith in the contemporary world. He talks of 'religionless Christianity', and about a new attitude to God and the church – a reflection on the perils of the attitude which brings God in to solve problems as a 'deus ex machina' and leaves Him out otherwise. But with all his questionings, Dietrich still has Christ in the centre 'In Jesus God has said "Yes" and "Amen" to it all'.

In the Catechism they wrote together, Dietrich and Franz had written 'in the middle of history stands the cross of Christ who died for us all. We fly to Him and pray that He will make certain that His grace is ours until that time when all the world gives glory to God alone'. Knowing that they had hammered out these words together, Franz Hildebrandt was uneasy about the way some people might use Dietrich's explorative thoughts. At times he showed his feelings to his friends as when Bishop John Robinson used Bonhoeffer in his book *Honest to God*. 'He hasn't understood Dietrich', he would say. 'This is not the Dietrich I know.'

He was not alone in this unease. Karl Barth too was unhappy foreseeing possible strange directions. In the USA Professor Paul Lehmann who had known Dietrich since his first visit to America pointed out in the Union Seminary *Quarterly Review* that when

Bonhoeffer's writings were used for 'cultic or atheistic celebrations', it was a grievous distortion of both his thought and his spirit. Lehmann wrote very strongly that Bonhoeffer was not to be regarded as a forerunner of a theology without God.

Dietrich's fiancée, Maria von Wedemeyer, also remained apart from the Bonhoeffer 'schools'. It is recorded that one time someone challenged the fact that she had been Dietrich's fiancée. 'You must be mistaken', he said, stating that Dietrich believed in celibacy. Maria von Wedermeyer records that she did not know this fact and then added that it was easier to live up to Dietrich's expectations than to those of the Bonhoeffer 'schools'. Occasionally she exchanged a letter with Franz after the war.*

Because of the danger of some interpretations by some of the Bonhoeffer 'schools' which he regarded as misinterpretations, Franz would not join any Bonhoeffer groupings or societies. 'Sometimes I can hear Dietrich laughing', he would say. Nor would he make any comment or criticism. 'Dietrich is not there to come back at me and it would not be fair'. He remembered how they had tested ideas, examining and arguing, criticising and defending. He did not deny that Bonhoeffer's work had great value (he could never do that) but he wanted to reach the heart of his ideas. He knew how he would have talked and argued with Dietrich who was, he insisted, an essentially orthodox Lutheran Christian with a sharp probing mind.

Franz had come to friendship with Dietrich as a fellow student, an equal from a slightly different theological position. Arguing with his friend was natural, something they loved, and never found disturbing. Franz would have given Dietrich's ideas minute examination – and would probably not have published the *Letters* as they are because, to him, the ideas were not fully developed. Hence his silence. It is born out of deep respect for his

*Both Dietrich and Franz were attractive eligible young men. Eberhard Bethge recalls in his biography of Dietrich that at one time there was a lady friend with whom from time to time he corresponded. Franz too is said to have had a young lady, who was the daughter of a Confessing Church pastor. In neither case were there lasting developments. It is necessary to note clearly that both young pastors felt a searing call to serve their Lord by opposing the heresy of the Nazis and all its evils. And, like apostles of previous generations, they allowed nothing to divert them from this calling and discipleship. It is interesting that both of them found their true loves when, so to speak, circumstances had withdrawn them from 'the front line of attack'.

friend's scholarship, faith and spirituality. Eberhard Bethge, in editing the *Letters and Papers* has given the world a spiritual classic. Scrupulously honest and completely devoted in his friendship, he has taken meticulous care over the writings. All owe him a great debt: but he did not see *Letters and Papers* in the same way as Franz, and his critique was different. The dynamic of his friendship caused this. Eberhard had come to know Dietrich as a student to his teacher. Their friendship grew from that position. The influence of the teacher must weigh on the pupil. Eberhard also stood near to the theological position of his teacher and had a feeling for what Dietrich was trying to say.

In *Letters and Papers from Prison* there are some passages where Bonhoeffer invites Eberhard Bethge to come back at him. He says he needs his thoughts to be 'clarified' and 'tested'. Eberhard Bethge had been in close touch with Bonhoeffer until his imprisonment and, while he was in prison, both corresponded with him and visited him. To him the ideas which Bonhoeffer expressed in his letters were challenging, forward looking and stimulating. He, better than anyone, knew where Dietrich's thoughts were leading. But the very nature and dynamic of his friendship, his regard and his understanding, prevented him from giving the critique which Dietrich at times seemed to want and which Franz would have given to a living Dietrich. Both Eberhard and Franz honoured Dietrich's scholarship, spirituality and innovative ideas and both honoured his testimony and martyrdom. Some measure of his genius and friendship can be seen in the fact that both men, different and learned, regarded him as a spiritual leader.

The great joy is that Eberhard Bethge and Franz Hildebrandt in post-war years became great friends. Their friendship had developed because of their mutual friendship with Bonhoeffer, although in addition they had both been members and pastors in the Confessing Church and opponents of Hitler and the Nazis. Tribute must be paid to the thoughts and motives of them both. Thanks must be given that Eberhard Bethge collected, edited and published Dietrich's incomplete works.

Martin Niemoeller knew Franz and Dietrich well. He was once asked about Franz's silence (which he understood) and the unease about the developments of the Bonhoeffer 'school'. His reply is memorable. 'Dietrich was a master of that method of teaching which asks questions of students to stimulate discussion and which leaves participants to talk until they come to a stop because they see no solution. Then he would come in, listen to them and show them where and how their thinking should have gone and where it should have led them. But' he paused 'sadly Dietrich never came back from prison and concentration camp.'*

*This in a chat when he was staying with us in May 1968 in Cheadle Hulm. (ASC)

CHAPTER 12

A METHODIST MINISTER IN BRITAIN

On 16 March 1946 Franz Hildebrandt attended the Quarterly Meeting of the Cambridge Methodist circuit and was warmly welcomed as an observer by the Revd John Crowlesmith who was the Superintendent Minister of the circuit. He also attended the next Quarterly Meeting, held on 13 June 1946. In the British Methodist Conference the Quarterly Meeting was the business meeting of the group of Methodist churches gathered together in a circuit. It met, as the name implies, every quarter in September, December, March and June. Here the planning, administration, finances and pastoral care were discussed. Lay appointments were also made and ministerial appointments were recommended. Normally, after invitation and agreement, the ministerial appointments were subject to the overriding decision of the Methodist Conference via its Stationing Committee. It was at the Quarterly Meeting that pastoral arrangements for the churches were discussed with the Superintendent Minister taking final responsibility (Nowadays Methodism works through a Circuit Meeting, constituted in a different way and meeting just twice a year.)

Franz Hildebrandt was already well-known in Cambridge because of his earlier work with the German congregation there, because of his work during the war with the Bible Society and because, as a recognized lecturer in the university, he had given lectures there for some years. Now he believed it was time to make the important decision to join a British church. Britain had given him a place of refuge when he was an exile, had helped him to find work and had, in the person of Nancy, provided him with a wife.

His thinking on this matter was given additional impetus by the effect the post-war situation was having on the German congregation in Cambridge. Later he wrote:

> I could not forbid the younger generations when they desired to attend another denomination where the 'saving and care of souls' was not in question. Herbert Kramm held a differing view. He remained a Lutheran and, in consequence, conducted the Lutheran liturgy in English. Today I often question if he was not in the right.

This, for Franz Hildebrandt, was a major decision. The hand of friendship had been widely offered to him by the denominations, particularly through his work with the British and Foreign Bible Society. These acquaintances and friendships were a good introduction to the variety of denominations and their differences. In the event the decision centred on two denominations: the Church of England and the Methodist Church (although one wonders if, had he been living in Scotland at that time, the Church of Scotland would have been added to the list).

The Church of England was brought to the fore through his friendship over the years with Bishop George Bell of Chichester, coupled with the great help he, Dietrich and the many refugees had received. There were also the personal links with other Anglicans such as Professor Canon Charles Raven and Canon Max Warren. On the other hand the hymns of Charles Wesley, the Lutheran- influenced theology of the Wesleys (we remember John Wesley's words: 'that champion of the Lord of Hosts, Martin Luther') and the open-hearted friendship of the Methodist Church brought Methodism alongside.

The possibility of joining the Church of England foundered on the matter of episcopal ordination. Franz was always aware that he had been ordained as one of the last group – as he used to say – 'to be properly ordained before the Nazi-Aryan anti-Semitic law came into force, before the so-called 'German Christians' moved in'. He remembered that, having a Jewish mother, it would have been impossible for him to have been ordained one day later. This matter went deeply into the heart of his life and testimony. He from a Jewish background, ordained a Christian minister in the Lutheran church, had carried out a ministry with others in opposition to a pagan political rule. Many of his ordained colleagues had died because they had followed their ordination vows. More of them had suffered as he had himself in prison, in exile, in concentration camps and other ways. Yet in the strength of his ordination, believing it to be blessed by the Holy Spirit, he had carried out his ministry. Was Dietrich also not properly ordained? It was a question he often asked.

Both Bishop Bell and Canon Raven explained to him that it was beyond their power to do anything about it. Bell's letter of deep understanding was very sad. Both commended him warmly in his decision to join the Methodist Church.

Canon Max Warren wrote to him after his decision was made:

> We were both so very interested in your news. I think you have chosen well. It never occurred to me that you could ever seriously consider for a moment joining the Church of England. The jump from the Confessional outlook would have been much too abrupt. Your devotion to Wesley would always have suggested to me that the Methodists would provide you with a home. But don't use your influence against Church Union. We in the Church of England desperately need what the Methodists have to give.

Franz was not entirely happy with some aspects of the working of the Methodist ministry. In the 1940s and 1950s the average length of stay in appointment for a Methodist minister was between four and seven years. (As late as the 1970s there was a body of Methodist opinion which thought that five years was long enough). Not only was the appointment too brief in his view but the minister was re-invited (or not) after a short period of time and then for an extension of only one two or, at most, three years. The itinerancy did not appeal to him. Nevertheless he had come to love the Wesleys. He had lectured at Wesley House Cambridge on 'From Luther to Wesley' He said several times 'I came into Methodism because I found in the hymns of Charles Wesley that which previously I had only found in the hymns of Martin Luther.' *Wesley's Hymns* became one of his most loved books and a copy was with him in his closing days. It would probably be safe to say that never before had so fine a 'Wesley' scholar asked Conference permission to become a Methodist minister.

Since 1938 he had been moving slowly towards the realization that in Great Britain the Methodism of the Wesleys was a near counterpart of the Lutheran church into whose ministry he had been ordained. He would have rejected the idea of being a Methodist in Germany. There are good reasons for this view, one being that they do not sing enough Charles Wesley hymns. They sing some – in translation – but certainly not enough for the man who thought that *Hymns and Psalms*, the hymn book published by Methodism in 1983, with 173 (156 from the pen of Charles and seventeen from John, mainly translations) had far too few. So he made application to the Methodist Conference by writing to the Secretary of the Conference, the Revd Edwin Finch, at Westminster. His request and the subsequent interviews and negotiations were handled with such kindness and courtesy that in later years he always spoke highly of the whole experience. To Franz Hildebrandt, Edwin Finch was the exemplar and epitome of Christian bureaucracy. He showed how it should be done.

He duly met the committee of Conference appointed to interview such applicants. In British Methodism the appointed committee is always chaired by the President of the Conference or an ex-President nominated by him. The committee examines the candidate carefully, without rushing, to be sure of the Christian character and sincerity of the applicant. It also considers whether the Methodist Church is indeed the denomination where the applicant will find a spiritual home. In Franz Hildebrandt's case the Revd Dr Wilbert F. Howard chaired the committee. Dr Howard had been President of the Methodist Conference in 1944 and was one of the world's leading New Testament scholars. During the interview in the committee, after Franz had responded well, Dr Howard commented, 'Dr Hildebrandt! You know the ideal Methodism. What will you make of modern Methodism?'

The committee was well satisfied and recommended to the 1946 Conference that Franz Hildebrandt be accepted as a Methodist minister. His year of ordination in Berlin was accepted without demur as official for Methodism. He was notified that this action would be taken so he arranged to attend the business meetings (Quarterly Meetings and Leaders' Meetings) in the Cambridge circuit where he was living in order to familiarize himself with the way things were done in Methodism.

In July 1946 at the Methodist Conference, meeting in London, when the Revd Dr R. Newton Flew, Principal of Wesley House Cambridge was President (Franz having lectured at Wesley

House knew Dr Flew), the Revd Dr Franz Hildebrandt was offi-cially received and became a Methodist minister. 'I was given the right hand of fellowship', he often said with great feeling: 'my ordination in Berlin was accepted without question', and some-times he would add 'as any Christian minister should be welcomed'.

There was the possibility that he might have joined the Methodist Church in Ireland (It is an independent part of the Methodist Church of Britain. They have their own President and Conference structures but the British mainland President presides at their Conference. Surprisingly this works well). He had built up many friendships there which lasted to the end of his life. He received from Alex McCrea this advice: 'It is so small a denomi-nation that you might feel opportunities for the kind of ministry you best render would be very limited.' Ironically his later resig-nation from his chair at Drew University in New Jersey was over what he saw as unjust treatment of an Irish Methodist minister, the Revd Dr Charles Ranson, and when he resigned from Methodism, some Irish ministers gave him great support. But that was all in the future.

On his acceptance by the Methodist Conference Bishop George Bell wrote encouragingly: 'My dear Franz. I am very glad to know that all went so happily at the Methodist Conference … I do hope and pray you will be happy and your ministry blessed.' From the British and Foreign Bible Society came: 'The Methodist Church is fortunate in having drawn such an able recruit' (G. M. Garett) and one postcard (dated 28 July 1946): 'I am so very glad … I expect John and Charles are having a Thanksgiving Service up above'.

Nancy was supportive but had reservations. She would have been happier had he turned to the Presbyterian Church or, in Scotland, the Church of Scotland in which she had grown up but those who knew Franz could not see him, a man who loved the Arminianism* of Charles Wesley, in a church with a Calvinist tradition. Wesley spoke louder in his hymns than did Calvin in his *Institutes*. The fact that some Presbyterians did not observe the Westminster Confession in all its detail made little difference. As later, in discussions concerning the unity scheme with the Church

---

*Arminianism. – The open invitation and welcoming as a believer following the theology of the Dutchman Arminius, summed up by Charles Wesley: 'that *all* may know He died for *all*'.

of England, he took as the norm not the practice of a few but the regulations by which the denomination operated.

Nancy's experience of Methodism had been different from that of Franz. He saw Methodism as a warm, human organization with friendship, cooperation, appreciation and warm acceptance. Nancy, who confessed to being insular, had found it large with a huge impersonal bureaucracy. Her view was that, at university, other denominations tended to join the SCM (Student Christian Movement) together whereas the Methodists kept to their Meth Soc (Methodist Society). This was true in one sense because apart from those of the Church of England there were almost certainly more Methodist students than those of any other Church society and Methodists do tend to gather together. There is in addition also a tendency amongst Methodists, who often are 'activists', to run organizations.

Nancy confesses that she found people in Methodist congregations 'warm' and she made many good Methodist friends but she kept her membership with the Presbyterians. Nevertheless she says that in time 'the hymns of Charles Wesley made their mark' on her. Mildred Cable wrote to Nancy with good words: 'It will be a very great help to Franz in his Methodist connection if you should bring some of the glory and dignity of the Presbyterian.' She also wrote to Franz encouraging him to 'go on in faith'.

Methodist ministers ultimately are 'stationed' in their appointments. The Stationing Committee presents its recommendations to the Conference. The Conference has the right, through any member, to challenge any appointment and take a vote on it. This right is noted but very, very rarely used. Earlier, circuits, through their circuit stewards, have met with ministers, talked about the churches and the work and made invitations which the ministers either accepted or declined. In this way the vast majority of appointments are settled before Stationing Committee and Conference meet. There are inevitably some appointments which are still unsettled for various reasons. Usually they need special care, especially if there has been an unexpected death. Then the Stationing Committee can, does and did move a minister with the minimum of time available, for Methodist ministers are, in the end, the servants of the Conference. In 1946 one of the ministers expecting to go to Cambridge was moved in this way. The vacancy had occurred because Wesley House had reopened to take students after the war and the Revd W. F. Flemington who had served the Cambridge circuit during the war was resuming his position as New Testament Tutor along with the Principal of the college, the Revd Dr R. Newton Flew, who had also served the Cambridge circuit during the war. The Stationing Committee believed that Franz Hildebrandt was ideally qualified to fill this vacancy, caused by moving to another post the Revd Dr A. S. Yates, initially appointed to Cambridge. Not unnaturally Franz was pleased when told of the decision of Conference as he knew Cambridge and for a 'foreigner' he would be learning amongst friends.

On 1 September 1946 he took up his appointment as a Methodist minister in Cambridge and for Saturday 14 September at the Quarterly Meeting held at the Castle Street Methodist Church we read in the Circuit minutes: 'The Revd John Crowlesmith on behalf of the circuit extended a sincere welcome to Dr F. Hildebrandt as a member of the ministerial staff to which Dr Hildebrandt replied'. The circuit staff was: the Revd John Crowlesmith, the Revd A. Kingsley Lloyd, the Revd Ronald V. Spivey, the Revd Hubert J. Martin and now, the Revd Dr Franz Hildebrandt. In the way Methodism often works, he was immediately given an extra task. He became the Circuit Ministerial Secretary in charge of the work of Overseas Missions.

Franz settled into his pastoral and preaching work with a zeal one would expect from one who all his life believed passionately that this was the essential work of a minister. Quarterly Meetings were rarely disturbed by speeches from him. His conscientious work did his speaking. He used the Quarterly Meeting mainly to pass on such information as was needed.

In the March 1947 Quarterly Meeting the minutes record him giving the information that the Circuit Missionary Garden Party would be held at the home of Professor and Mrs Basil Willey (he was soon at work with his new extra duties!). In December 1947 he made an appeal for a Sunday School Superintendent for Romsey Town, one of the churches in his pastoral care. So he was endeavouring to draw on the strength of the circuit to help a weaker cause. At the Quarterly meeting in September 1947 he not only revealed his own initiative but also his love of music. The minute book records that he 'informed the meeting that the Circuit Choir would recommence its activities on the first

Monday in October and that it was hoped to perform Mendelssohn's *Elijah* next spring'. We are reminded that his father and mother once hoped that their Franz would be an orchestral conductor.

His pastoral, preaching and organizational work was obviously very satisfactory. The circuit acknowledged this for, at the appropriate time, at the Quarterly Meeting on 10 March 1949 he was invited to continue his ministry in the Cambridge Circuit 'for a fourth year until 1950 with a tentative invitation to 1951'. At this time the 'norm' was a three year ministry. The further invitation was confirmed at the meeting of 11 March 1950.

Some insight into his pastoral care is given by just one entry in the circuit Quarterly Meeting minute book where it is recorded that he 'reported the sudden death of Mrs J. Arnold (Fen Ditton) and went on to say that the cause 'had suffered a severe loss'. Fen Ditton was one of the smaller churches in his care but to him it was important.

Franz was never at ease with the Methodist expectation that the minister should preach twice at different services on Sundays. It was not the German practice on which he had been nurtured. He found an interesting solution when later he was in Edinburgh at Nicholson Square but in Cambridge the Methodist system of preaching 'round the circuit' helped as he was rarely in the same church for both morning and evening services. This meant that usually he only prepared one sermon each week, preaching it in one circuit church in the morning and in another in the evening in the churches to which the Methodist circuit plan appointed him. Always his themes followed the Christian year.

Generally the Methodist students at the university attended Wesley Church, Cambridge, and they always took special note of the infrequent occasions when 'Hildebrandt' appeared on the plan for their services. He was not in immediate pastoral charge but we knew that his services would be stimulating. The theological students of Wesley House were particularly keen as they knew that they would be challenged by his theology and shown the wonder and majesty of the Christian faith as sung by Charles Wesley. While he was minister in Cambridge, Franz preached systematically through the Gospel of St Luke. It took him four years. Other features of his ministry were a Bible Study group of mixed ages which he held at the manse and an encouraging of his congregations to sing the Wesley hymns, including some new to them. His pastoral visitation was, as always, very important and he liked to visit every family belonging to the church within the first year.

His love of the Wesleys was seen particularly when he organized a trip for the Youth Fellowship of the Romsey Town church to the birthplace and home of John and Charles Wesley at Epworth. It was particularly memorable because on the return journey they drove into a blizzard and for a time wondered if they would manage to complete the journey. They did. It was in the Cambridge circuit that this real 'Wesley-an' had his first experience of the ex-Primitive Methodists. Their non-liturgical background, their freer ideas and practice in worship were something into which he had to grow. Their deep spirituality was not always easy for him to see as it was clouded by other matters. Nancy tells how an 'ex-Prim' leader came to talk to him after the service on one occasion and while talking put his hat on the communion table. She says she saw the shocked look on Franz's face, picked up the hat and put it in a pew! Two vastly different spiritual cultures were meeting and it was not easy for either of them – yet each loved the Lord deeply and Franz came to love them as fellow children of the Father. He also worked hard to heal a division in one of his ex-Primitive Methodist societies and had passable success. Years later in the Anglican-Methodist Conversations debate he learned something of the deep theological strength of the Primitive Methodist ethos.

He maintained his links with the university, various colleges and the different churches in Cambridge and he was invited to preach in many places. In 1950 he was invited to Germany to be a speaker at the *Kirchentag* (Churches Conference). This annual gathering had been initiated by a Christian layman, Herr von Thadden, whom Franz knew. In fact when von Thadden had been arrested by the Gestapo in Nazi times, it was Franz who communicated the fact to von Thadden's wife. When von Thadden was a prisoner in the hands of the Russians, he had vowed that if he survived and returned to Germany, he would start this celebration as a witness to the invincible Church of Jesus Christ. Franz had great difficulty in accepting the invitation. He always had problems with regard to a return to Germany. However, he did accept and went to Essen where it was held.

Ruth, their daughter, was born on 5 November 1947. She was christened by Julius Rieger, their great friend. The service was memorable for the fact that the baby yelled loudly. During this period the German congregation moved from Cambridge to Romsey Town. Franz, keeping his contacts, and Nancy entertained many guests: Martin and Elsa Niemoeller, Pastor Kloppenberg, Bishop Otto Dibelius and Dr Gramme, the Minister for Education in Germany.

Franz loved the pastoral ministry but he was someone who could not be contained within any circuit. His life, testimony and work were well-known and he had an extra calling – to show that there had been strong resistance to Hitler, that the church had been a witness and that, armed with a sound theology, it was possible to stand against and overcome an evil philosophy. At Stuttgart in October 1945 the churches had made a declaration that they had not been strong enough in witness and, on the whole, it was possibly true, but Franz Hildebrandt knew the cost for some of his friends and why they paid the price. He tried to tell how they had kept the faith and that it is possible if one is clothed in the armour of God to withstand the fiery darts of the evil one.

When he entered Methodism Franz Hildebrandt had great hopes, for he saw something of the tremendous possibilities for his 'new' church: the great spirituality springing from the Wesleys, the deep faith and the 'experience' which called Methodism into being. He also saw many ways in which the organization of Methodism could stumble and go wrong. A conversation with him revealed his idealism and his hopes. These hopes for what he would call a 'pure' Methodism never died. Dr Howard's question was, however, apposite. There was that in him which made him an idealist and, to a degree, intolerant of human frailties including his own. The necessary organization must be dominated by the sovereign freedom of the Holy Spirit working through all the members. Often we as members of the Church disappoint the Holy Spirit. Often Franz was disappointed himself in his own service. 'At best I am a poor servant'. He lined up with many of Charles Wesley's hymns.

Nevertheless he believed Methodism could lead God's people towards such a church where the Gospel of the Lord Jesus Christ was supreme in the church and in all her members individually.

The ideal of Christian perfection was, after all, a particular part of the teaching of his beloved John and Charles Wesley.

He often suggested humorously that the ideal church would have:

1) Lutheran Doctrines;
2) Charles Wesley's hymns;
3) The Liturgy of the Anglican Church;
4) The church government of Congregationalism;
5) and (for the pastor) a Presbyterian wife.

This last was an undoubted tribute to Nancy and a very happy marriage.

In 1951 came the invitation to leave the Cambridge circuit to go to Edinburgh to become the minister of the Nicholson Square Methodist Church, a prestigious and renowned church. That this was a major appointment for him was not the important factor as he viewed the invitation. Of course he had a love for Scotland and had a wife who was half Scottish but his paramount thinking was about his sense of the call of God through the voice of the church. Nicholson Square had strong links with the city and with the university. There were significant pastoral and preaching oppor-tunities. He believed he had to use the gifts and the experiences which God had given him. Many wise people felt he was particu-larly suited and equipped for this task. He listened, prayed and agreed to go.

The good folk in Cambridge had come to appreciate and love their minister. They realized that Franz was something special. It so happened that their much loved and appreciated superinten-dent minister, the Revd John Crowlesmith, was retiring at the same time. It is difficult for any circuit when two ministers move at the same time, particularly when they are beloved of the people. The minutes of the Quarterly Meeting of the Cambridge Methodist Circuit must be allowed to speak:

> The same speakers (as had paid tribute to John Crowlesmith) referred to the departure from the circuit of the Revd Franz Hildebrandt and his wife whose long spell in the circuit had been marked by the growth of the work under their guidance. Dr Hildebrandt's scholarship and profound teaching and his devotion to the work of God and his friendship and love to all who knew

him would always be a source of pride to the circuit and members would watch with keen interest his future in the church. The meeting wished him Godspeed in his first superintendency in Edinburgh.

In September 1951 Franz became the superintendent minister of the Nicholson Square Methodist Circuit in Edinburgh with pastoral charge of the Nicholson Square church. His ministry there lasted just two years and came to an end only because he answered a call to another demanding task for which he was particularly suited. While in Edinburgh his work created memories and left influences which were still working in the minds and hearts of people forty years later.

His first and immediate problem, as he was the minister of just one church, was that he had to preach twice on a Sunday, at morning and evening services, to the same congregation. Moreover it was a congregation where there were great expectations from members who carried weight in society. He gave it some thought, trying to decide how he could best use his own gifts and at the same time give a spiritual lead to his congregation. He resolved the problem, as members of his congregation recall, by preaching a sermon at one service, usually the morning one, and using the other for a question and answer session, a discussion time or a period of instruction on the Bible or the Christian faith. He also taught the congregation Wesley hymns they didn't know by having them sung for some weeks successively until the congregation knew them well. Then he would preach on the theme and use the hymn as illustration. Years afterwards these 'special' services were remembered with appreciation both for their style and content, though it has to be recorded that some of those attending hoped that the minister would not direct his questions at them.

His pastoral work was generally regarded as of the highest calibre. He gave himself to his people and they loved him for it. Throughout his ministry in Germany, in the United Kingdom and in the United States he took people to his heart and they responded in like manner. He was basically shy and sometimes gave the impression that he was not aware of the world around him in which life was going on. Some still tell amusing stories of his doing a pastoral visit apparently unaware that furniture was being moved around him and people were coming and going because a move was 'on'. Strangely he gave the impression that he was totally involved in the business of the world and yet at the same time was so 'otherworldly' that he seemed out of touch. In the best sense of the terms he combined a 'heaven' and 'earth' and people recognized this.

Students – and a number passed through in two years – sometimes found his preaching very demanding in terms of concentration. When he decided to preach through one of Paul's letters, some found it hard going, but they were loyal to him because of his love for them. Learned as he was, he could enter into their position and care for them. There was never any problem of understanding or meeting of minds.

The Revd Tom Hall was his junior colleague at this time. He recalls his own evangelical enthusiasm and reckons he must have created some difficulties both for Franz, whose style it was not, and for a reserved Scottish congregation, but 'Franz Hildebrandt was always a consistent and loyal friend, a kindly and supportive superintendent minister and a great encourager'. Sometimes he was sent as Franz's representative to high-powered meetings and trusted completely. When, sadly, his first child died, aged two months, Franz's pastoral care was exceptional. Tom would dare to suggest that 'there has never been a better pastor'. This tribute is multiplied by students and congregation. During his ministry people were 'called' to be preachers and committed church members. He was a minister beloved though he was in Edinburgh for such a short time. Two years is not long to provide lasting evidence of work done but when people still give thanks to God for that ministry some forty years later it is fair to say that it was a good ministry. He was there in joys and sorrows, in the light and in the darkness, and the warmth of the family Hildebrandt remains a fond memory.

Then in 1953 came a pressing invitation to go to be a professor at Drew University, in New Jersey in the United States of America. Some two years previously he had been sounded out about a similar position in Duke University, North Carolina, but it had not developed mainly because satisfactory answers had not been given to some of his questions. At that time the black-white relationships in North Carolina were governed by a strict pattern of segregation deeply imbedded in law and custom. Franz would not consider going. He had experienced divided fellowship in Germany with the anti-Semitic laws. Such division he could not and would not tolerate, for there is no inequality in the love of God.

The same stringent questions were asked of Drew. This time the answers satisfied him. The family were happy in Edinburgh and were not sure it was the right thing to go but – as before – they believed it was the call of God. So they went, leaving their beloved Edinburgh and Nicholson Square and its dear congregation with sadness and great reluctance. But a new door was opening.

CHAPTER 13

A PROFESSOR IN AMERICA

In the decade following World War II, an unprecedented number of men – with some few courageous and hopeful women – studied to qualify for entry into the Christian ministry. The Theological School at Drew University, one of the eleven seminaries of the Methodist Church, was in 1950 approaching an enrolment of 350. Both faculty and facilities strained to meet the demand.

Clarence Tucker Craig, dean since coming from Yale in 1949, had the urgent task of rebuilding a faculty, not only to meet the demands of an increased enrolment, but to replace a number of key professors who were on the verge of retirement. Foremost in his mind was the need for someone in the chair of systematic theology to replace the redoubtable Edwin Lewis, scheduled for retirement in July of 1951. Craig did not limit his search to the USA, but began discreet inquiries abroad as well.

Franz Hildebrandt first came to Dean Craig's attention probably through his colleague, Stanley R. Hopper, who had met Franz on an earlier trip to England. In a letter to Hopper, dated 12 July 1951, Hildebrandt writes appreciatively of their meeting and gives his various summer addresses, 'in case our recent conversation should be followed by a visit from your colleague.' Craig was scheduled to attend the church section meeting of the Faith and Order Commission of the World Council of Churches in August. Before leaving for England on 8 August, Craig wrote to W. F. Howard in Birmingham. Howard was the former president of the British Methodist Conference who had been instrumental in enabling Franz' entry into the Methodist ministry in 1946. Craig's inquiry was specific: 'I wonder if you know him sufficiently well to give me an estimate of his abilities and promise and likewise something about his personal point of view. Is he really committed to the evangelical view of Christianity? Would he make a significant theological contribution in a Methodist seminary? Does he have the personal qualities which would make him a congenial worker in the team of a university faculty?'

From the seat of the Methodist Conference in Bradford (1950), Howard replied in a confidential letter that he knew Hildebrandt 'fairly well'. Responding to Craig's reference to Edwin Lewis' retirement, he wrote, 'Two men more unlike each other, I cannot imagine. Franz Hildebrandt has charm and great personal devotion. But he has not Edwin Lewis' wide grasp of philosophy and all the wider fields of theological study. He is intensely Lutheran and biblical in his approach, with a very keen appreciation of Wesley's special emphasis. If not a Barthian, his sympathies lie in that direction.'

Howard goes on to describe how, when he was President of the Conference, he had at first tried to dissuade Franz from seeking entry into the ministry of the Methodist Church, 'feeling that he would not be at home in our itinerant system but he was so eager that we recommended him to our Conference and he was received.' Howard then expresses his concern for Franz' obligation to the Conference: 'He has been in the Cambridge circuit and next year is due to go to our Edinburgh circuit. It is a long standing invitation and great disappointment would be caused if he failed to keep his pledge.' He then returns to his estimate of Franz as a theology professor. 'I am ... afraid that he might not prove a good member of a team. In charm of character and friendliness he would be all that you could desire. But his outlook and method of work would be quite individual.'

Craig's reply to Howard revealed little about his reaction, 'I thank you more than I can say for your full and frank words about Mr H.'. However, on 1 August, Stanley Hopper wrote Craig from his summer place in New Hampshire: 'I have been reading his (Hildebrandt's) little book in reply to Canon Raven and find it excellent.'* Craig was also interested in the possibility of recruiting J. S. Whale, then professor of theology at Cambridge, but had

*This is the Message, Lutterworth, 1944, in reply to Raven's Good News of God, Harper & Brothers, 1943.

hoped to meet with Hildebrandt first. He reports to Hopper that Franz is 'inaccessible' at the time he had hoped to meet him in Cambridge, but would try to meet with him in London after 12 August. Franz agreed to come to London: '... how glad I shall be to have the opportunity of meeting in London ...' Whether or not this meeting ever took place is unclear. Nancy Hildebrandt, in her diary, *No Winter*, states that Franz and Craig never met. In any event, Franz could not see his way clear to leave Britain for the autumn term of 1951 or even 1952 since he had accepted appointment to the Nicholson Square Methodist Church in Edinburgh, to begin in September, 1951. J. S. Whale was then engaged for a two year visiting professorship at Drew.

Franz Hildebrandt had first considered teaching graduate level theology in the USA in 1949. He had received an invitation to come to Duke Divinity School as a visiting professor with the option to remain as a permanent faculty member. Several factors militated against his going. North Carolina in 1950 was a bastion of racial segregation. Apart from the fact that Franz had known racism first-hand in Germany and wanted no part of it for himself or for his family, the position proffered by Duke was in the field of 'historical theology'. Franz saw himself as a systematic, biblical, perhaps even dogmatic, theologian, but, apart from the Reformation period, not qualified as a church historian. This would again become a knotty issue in his negotiations with Drew. A final factor was the certainty of hot, humid summers in the American South which Franz simply could not tolerate physically. He therefore put himself in the hands of the Methodist Conference Stationing Committee. They concluded it was neither the right time nor the right assignment.

There were a number of factors to be taken into consideration in contemplating a transatlantic move. What provision could be made for the children's education? How would Nancy adjust to the pressures of American culture? Could adequate living arrangements be found? For Franz the deeper question had to do with 'calling'. Before all else he was a pastor. He was called to preach the Word, administer the sacraments and care for the flock of Christ. British Methodism had given him this opportunity without challenging the validity of his Lutheran ordination. He was grateful, although he recognized that the 'real' Methodism into which he was received had come a long way from the preaching of John and the singing of Charles. He was particularly uneasy with the itinerant system in Methodism.

Franz was open to the possibility of an academic position. He enjoyed the stimulation of theological debate. He had already published four books since arriving in England and there were other theological issues which he wished to explore. When, in November of 1952, a firm invitation came from Drew over the signature of Stanley Hopper, Franz was ready to accept. The invitation was for a two year visiting professorship in 'historical theology'. Drew would also provide housing and the cost of passage to the USA. On 3 December, Clarence Tucker Craig, having been in hospital for an operation, wrote to confirm the arrangement. He expressed particular concern for Nancy, assuring Franz that she would not be 'lonesome' in her new surroundings. His concluding sentence turned out to be prophetic: 'There may at first appear to be some difficulties which can be removed if we work on them hard enough'.

Franz, however, still had his doubts. On 5 December he wrote to Stanley Hopper raising three issues. The first was timing. His three years at Nicholson Square would not be completed until 1954. He needed more time to prepare: 'I tremble at the standard which he (J. S. Whale) has set for any successor.' Secondly he was troubled by the fact that the chair was to be designated 'historical theology'. 'Was Dr Lewis' and Dr Whale's chair not really one of systematic theology? . . . my whole approach is systematic . . . What does keenly interest me is . . . the scriptural insights of the two Wesleys.' The two year duration of the appointment was also of concern. Should it not be for one year, allowing for the option of continuation, or for three years, the equivalent of a ministerial term in British Methodism? He closed, expressing the wish that W. F. Howard were still alive to advise him.

On 17 December, Stanley Hopper replied he understood Franz' hesitation, but assured him all the issues could be worked out, but that the one year review of all new faculty teachers was a standard procedure for the seminary. In a letter dated 19 December to Clarence Tucker Craig, Hildebrandt restated the concerns of his 5 December letter to Hopper: 'The parting with my own congregation and my beloved Wesley hymns will be the biggest obstacle for me to overcome.' Craig replied on 30 December, assuring Franz on all points, '. . . we want to think of the invitation as looking forward toward a permanent arrangement.' In a letter of 3 January, 1953, Hopper kept up the pressure: '... American Methodism is in great need of the sort of theological and spiritual deepening that you can bring.'

Franz was moving slowly but steadily towards Drew. There was still one important step – the Conference. On 23 January 1953 he went to London to meet with Conference president Colin Roberts and secretary Eric Baker. Roberts wondered if Franz would be happy in America, suggesting that he was more Methodist than the Methodists. The day after, Franz wrote Craig giving to him the 'green light' he had so long awaited. 'I made it quite clear that I wanted to go as the servant of the British Conference to which I owe allegiance and a great debt of gratitude.' Craig replied with predictable enthusiasm. 'I was overjoyed to receive your letter of 24 January'. On 10 February, Craig wrote Franz again to report that he had heard from Eric Baker who reported the anticipated approval of the Conference, although he intimated that 'there were a few of the brethren who looked askance at 'men seeking positions abroad'. Craig had already written Baker assuring him that 'Dr Hildebrandt did not take the slightest step toward approaching us'. He went on to give a lengthy explanation of the difference between the American and British practice in hiring professors.

The obstacles were cleared; the doubts remained. Franz at the age of 43 was making a significant course change for himself and his family. In a 23 February letter to Craig, dealing mostly with questions of visas, travel arrangements and housing, he closed with these telling words: 'I send this letter and enter upon my new task , very conscious of the honour you have done me and of my own limitations, and relying upon your sympathy with, and prayers for, a very inexperienced newcomer to the academic field'.

Through the spring there was a regular transatlantic correspondence between Hildebrandt and Craig touching on the many details of the Hildebrandt's relocation to Drew. Would Franz preach the opening chapel service? Would he include Drew authors in his course bibliographies? Of more concern to Nancy were the yet unresolved housing arrangements. It was not until 15 June that Craig indicated the availability of the ground floor apartment of Sitterly House. On 27 June Nancy wrote to Craig:

Would it be possible to bring Franz' beloved Bluethner grand piano to the USA? What could be done about the fact that the Sitterly House apartment had only two bedrooms? David and Ruth each needed their own room. There were other decisions to make about what to take to the USA. Was it to be a one year visit or a move that was to be seen as more or less permanent? In the midst of unresolved ambivalence about the whole enterprise, furniture and household items were directed to their Cambridge house which they agreed to keep. A recurring drama in the Hildebrandt household was what to do about the current cat, in this case Tigger. Tigger did not emigrate, but became a permanent fixture in the Edinburgh manse and was adopted by Franz' successor.

There were other concerns; whether to go over on visitors' visas or to emigrate. With the passage of the McCarren Act in 1950, emigration to the USA became a 'byzantine' process that even a theology professor and his family couldn't escape. It was also the summer of the coronation of Queen Elizabeth II and transatlantic bookings were hard to come by. With help from friends on both sides, a passage was finally secured on the Hamburg-America Line's *Italia*.

When the *Italia* steamed into New York harbour on 21 September 1953, there is little doubt that Hildebrandt carried with him a vision of what he wished to accomplish in America. It was a vision akin to that of the early American Methodists, 'to spread scriptural holiness throughout the land.' He would reintroduce John and Charles Wesley to the far-flung denomination. It was a vision he would realize only in part during his time in the United States, a vision fraught with obstacles and frustrations.

Just as the War for American Independence had sundered the political, and to a lesser extent, the cultural and economic ties with Great Britain, the nascent Methodist movement in the United States struck out in its own direction, forming itself into the Methodist Episcopal Church in 1784 under the indefatigable Francis Asbury. Although generally following Wesleyan principles and practice, the exigencies of the expanding frontier created a dynamic ferment in which revivalist innovations in worship, hymnody, theology and order left in its wake the *Book of Common Prayer*, the hymns of Charles and the churchmanship of John. By the time of the Civil War (1861–65), success on the frontier had made Methodists the single largest Protestant body in the USA. With the rapidly expanding industrialization and urbanization that followed the Civil War, Methodism embraced the optimism that fueled the growing wealth and power of the nation. Even the two great wars of the first half of the 20th century could not shake the triumphalism of the American churches. While Europe was still binding up the wounds of the most destructive war in its history, America was experiencing unmatched prosperity. Church membership and attendance was the highest in the nation's history. Yet one was forced to ask, 'Was there anything in the churches , and in Methodism in particular, that distinguished it from the culture at large?'

The enormity of the task soon confronted Franz. Even the relatively minor matter of finding a place for the family to worship was a challenge. At Sunday worship in the local Methodist church one was as likely to hear a passage read from Shakespeare as from the Bible. In meeting his classes for the first time, he made another appalling discovery. Most of the students were unfamiliar with the Bible and didn't have a clue about its content and meaning. Later he was instrumental in introducing a basic exam in biblical literacy which was required for all incoming students.

Anxiety about his new job was further complicated by the confusion that surrounded the unresolved title and scope of his teaching position. Hopper, the acting dean following Dean Craig's death, proposed that Hildebrandt be named Professor of Historical Theology. Franz did not see himself as primarily a historian except for his familiarity with the context of the roles of Luther and the Wesleys. He had understood from Craig that he would be appointed to the Chair of Systematic Theology, but the senior faculty and the new dean, Bernard W. Anderson, were grooming the young and charismatic Carl Michalson for that position. In his July 1955 circular letter to close friends, he complained bitterly about 'the mess in American Methodism,' and the 'uphill struggle it would take against a powerful ecclesiastical system to do anything about it.' In an almost tragic note he wrote, 'I am living under a constant cloud of spying, suspicion and hostility, and have no means of knowing whether I should even be wanted after this third year.' Yet, at the same time he could confide to Nancy, 'I don't really need a chair in theology, a stool would be sufficient.' In any event, in 1956 he was granted tenure as Professor of Christian Theology, perhaps a more fitting title after all. A reconciliation was achieved with Dean Anderson.

Another major factor contributing to his early dissatisfaction at Drew was the administration's reluctance to allow him to serve a pastoral appointment. This was a crucial issue for Franz. Ever since his time with Dietrich he could not understand how one could teach the fundamentals of ministry without having ongoing experience in ministry as a part of one's own vocation. By 1956 the administration relented and Franz was appointed pastor of the Green Village congregation, a small Methodist church in a bucolic setting on the edge of the Great Swamp, a mere three miles from the Drew campus, where he remained pastor until the beginning of his sabbatical year in 1960.

In spite of all the initial doubts and skirmishes, Franz meticulously prepared for his lectures. His course outline for 'Theology of John and Charles Wesley' became the substance for the Rall lectures given at Garrett Theological Seminary at Evanston, Illinois, in the spring of 1954. Nancy accompanied him – it was her first aeroplane ride – and they were house guests of the Harold Bosleys. Dr Bosley was pastor of the First Methodist Church, Evanston. The lectures were delivered under the title of *Christianity According to the Wesleys*, first published by Epworth in 1956 and reprinted by Baker in 1996. Wesley's theology was discussed under four heads: Scriptural, Practical, Missionary and Catholic.

Many Drew seminarians had their first encounter with Dr Hildebrandt in the Wesley course, taught every year, usually in the autumn semester. He strode into the classroom, a curious sight, somewhat intimidating with his thinning white hair, his broad forehead and deep set dark eyes, his Harris tweed sport-coat and the ubiquitous round clerical collar, seldom seen among American Methodists in those days. A further sense of shock rippled through the room when he sat down at the old upright piano in the front of the classroom , called out a number from the British Methodist Hymnbook of 1933 and actually expected his students to *sing* Charles Wesley's theology.

The course however was much more than a hymn singing party. It was a wide ranging, intellectually rigorous survey of the Wesleys' life and thought, grounded in the context of the eighteenth century, looking back to Luther and the Reformation and forward to the last half of the twentieth century. The Wesleys were 'mediators' between the Reformation and the modern era. They were biblical, pragmatic, experimental theologians who lived by what they believed. They could best be understood by a careful reading of the Standard Sermons of John, the hymns of Charles, and John's *Explanatory Notes on the New Testament* (following Bengel). Hildebrandt saw Methodism in the mainstream of Reformation Protestantism. He liked to say Methodism was Anglicanism taken seriously.

The course followed the general outline of the four chapters of *Christianity According to the Wesleys: Scriptural, Practical, Missionary and Catholic*. Wesley had declared himself *homo unius libri*, a man of one book. This did not, however, make him a fundamentalist. Hildebrandt described a fundamentalist as a person of one book, but a *closed* book with no opportunity for the Holy Spirit to shed more light from the *living* word of God. He then went on to classical doctrines of the Faith as seen through the eyes of Wesley. He emphasized, for example, the importance of justification by faith in the face of a uniquely North American liberal theology built on the premise that humankind is basically good and simply needs its attention focused on the supreme moral principles of Jesus the teacher. In contrast, the doctrine of justification begins with the premise that 'all have sinned' and there is no possibility of a redeemed life in God without faith in the atoning death and resurrection of Jesus Christ. Even the required faith is a gift of grace. *Sola gratia, sola fide, propter Christum* is the bedrock of Christian proclamation. Although Hildebrandt adamantly refused any of the then current theological labels, in his interpretation of Wesley he was clearly in the neo-orthodoxy camp of Barth, Brunner and his friend Bonhoeffer. Unless Christians rediscovered the Bible as the *living* word of God and placed it at the centre of their individual lives as well as the church's life, the battle against a rampant materialism would be lost.

Under the rubric of 'practical' Hildebrandt surveyed the organizational and pragmatic genius of early Methodism, including the origin of the circuit system, the formation of the societies, and the ethics and discipline of individual believers. 'Wesley's theology is practical and his practice is theological', was his way of summarizing Wesley's approach. In his discussion of the missionary aspect of Wesley, Hildebrandt begins with the premise that evangelism is the *raison d'etre* of the church. The result of a justified life is a sanctified life. The believer can experience the perfect love of God in this life through worship and service to humankind. The far-flung social programs of the Methodists did not spring from charitable impulse but were the inevitable consequence of an active and joyful acceptance of God's redeeming grace.

On the subject of catholic Christianity, Hildebrandt underscored Wesley's constant desire that the various Christian communions, although they do not think alike, could love alike, irrespective of different opinions. Differing opinions of course included the divisions over the Eucharist and recognition of ministerial orders which were so important to Hildebrandt personally and led him to become a 'dissentient' in the Anglican–Methodist merger talks underway in Britain. In the end, Hildebrandt believed, unity could not be achieved by bringing the churches together on the basis of the lowest common denominator, but only on the basis of scripture rightly read and understood.

Like other senior professors, Hildebrandt taught three courses each semester. Besides 'Theology of the Wesleys', he taught 'Christian Theology', a survey of Christian doctrine required for seniors, the 'Theology of Martin Luther', 'The Person and Work of Christ', 'the Protestant Tradition', and 'The Church Militant and Triumphant'. He also offered seminars on 'Christian Attitudes Toward War and Peace', Bonhoeffer's *Cost of Discipleship*, the 'Doctrine of Perfection', 'Justification' and 'Sanctification', and 'Doctrine of Ministry'. During the early years of his teaching, not all students were happy with his style of close-knit argument backed with innumerable scripture references and quotes from the Wesleys. In the fall of 1954 the president of the student body complained to Dean Anderson. He asserted that the required course in Christian Theology put too much emphasis on the eighteenth century, which created apathy and indifference among the students who viewed the course as a 'grind'. Yet, in the years following their graduation, many of these same students expressed their appreciation for the theological grounding that gave them a solid foundation on which their own theologies could be built. Hildebrandt's growing influence was acknowledged when he was named a representative of the World Methodist Council for Vatican II in Rome.

CHAPTER 14

OBSERVER AT VATICAN II

Among all the Councils of the Roman Catholic Church held in the nearly 2000 years of its history, there were probably no two that were more in contrast than Vatican I and Vatican II. The first Vatican Council held in 1869–70 sought to strengthen the power of Rome and the papacy in particular. Its most famous accomplishment was the promulgation of the doctrine of papal infallibility which declares that when the pope speaks *ex cathedra* on issues of faith and morals he speaks truth without any error whatsoever. During the decades following Vatican I the Church turned inward and shunned relations with the Orthodox churches and other Protestant bodies. All that began to change following World War II. With the elevation of Angelo Roncalli as Pope John XXIII to the Chair of Peter in 1958, the pace of change accelerated dramatically.

Pope John XXIII's purpose in calling the Council can best be described by the term *aggiornamento*, encompassing reforms of Catholic faith and practice throughout the Church. High on his list of priorities was an open and accepting stance toward non-Catholic Christians to whom, in his characteristic generosity of spirit he referred as 'our separated brothers and sons.' In keeping with this new attitude, a Secretariat for Promoting Christian Unity was formed under the capable leadership of Cardinal Bea. One of the important initiatives of the Secretariat was to invite some forty official observers from various Christian communities affiliated with the World Council of Churches who would have full access to the deliberations of the Council which was to convene in October 1962. Franz Hildebrandt was among those invited to represent the World Methodist Council.

He was delighted. Arrangements would have to be made. He insisted Nancy accompany him. She too was delighted. Seven year old Esther would also go. She was thrilled. A leave of absence would have to be secured from Drew for the autumn semester. Drew was willing. Details needed attending to: they would be travelling from Edinburgh. Franz would have preferred to go by train, Nancy by car. In the end there was a compromise of sorts. They would drive their new VW microbus except for going over the Swiss Alps where the bus was then loaded on a train with the Hildebrandt family inside, an adventure which Nancy would just as soon have done without. Before tackling the Alps they had an enjoyable stay in Paris with the Methodist minister Revd E. R. Tribbeck and his wife. In Rome they stayed in an apartment of the Methodist Manse in the Via del Banco di Santo Spirito. Their hosts were the Revd Rex Kissack and his wife Elizabeth who were immensely helpful in getting them settled into the complexities of life in Rome. They had many late nights during the period of the Council. Friends were invited and theology was discussed into the early hours of the morning.

Nancy wrote a lively account of their time in the Eternal City published under the title of *Rome Diary*. She describes her visits to churches and galleries and her experiences in accompanying Franz to various gatherings of the Observers. However, when the Council was in session in St Peter's the deliberations were held in secret. The Observers, who were seated with the highest ranking officials of the Roman Catholic Church, were also pledged to maintain strict secrecy about what was discussed. Franz worried that Nancy, in her enthusiasm, might write about something forbidden. He therefore read her manuscript carefully – too carefully in her opinion – to assure himself she had not transgressed the rule of the Council.

Unlike other Observers who came and went as their other concerns dictated, Franz attended the sessions faithfully, while Nancy was free to explore Rome and its environs. Franz was conscientiously aware that he was participating in an important chapter of the history of the Christian Church in the twentieth century. Pope John declared it was his intention to open the windows of the Vatican and allow fresh air into the Church. As serious and sobering as were the issues before the church fathers, the sessions were not without their lighter moments. There was, for example, the morning when a routine and non-controversial piece of Council business came before the body. When the vote was called, every delegate stood to affirm his assent – except for one elderly cardinal who remained complacently seated. Franz, wondering who this sole nonconformist might be, investigated, and discovered he was soundly asleep! There was the story, the veracity of which cannot be proven, that the Pope was asked by an Observer how many people worked in the Vatican, to which John replied, 'About half'.

To indicate the importance which John assigned to the presence of the Protestant and Orthodox Observers, they were given seats equivalent to Cardinals and high-ranking members of the Curia. Roman Catholic archbishops and bishops were relegated to the nave of the great church of St Peter. The Council's organizers had thoughtfully provided two refreshment stands, affectionately known as Bar Jonah and Bar Abbas. Observers and delegates gathered easily and happily exchanged the gossip of the day. It can be assumed that Franz limited his libations to coffee and tea. (He never drank alcohol, not because of the traditional Methodist stance on temperance, but simply because it upset his stomach.) With characteristic discipline, even to his practice of taking notes in Latin, Franz attended the sessions. While Nancy was taking in the art and history of the city, Esther found her niche. She was enrolled in an English school and subsequently chosen to play the part of – What else? – an English girl in an Italian TV production.

Apart from the importance of doing a first rate job for the Methodists, there was the book on which he was working, uniquely relevant to the work of the Council. In fact, he used all his spare time to work on the manuscript of *I Offered Christ: In Sacrifice and Proclamation*, a major exploration of the difference between the Roman Catholic mass and the Protestant communion. He had begun his research in September 1960 when he went to Dublin on sabbatical. He settled himself in a boarding house and easily made acquaintance with the resident Catholic theologians. He was given access to the libraries of Maynooth College. While there he became acquainted with Father Francis Clark who had just published a book treating the same issue as Franz' projected work, but of course from a Roman Catholic point of view. Franz, in his book, expresses his appreciation to Father Clark for his scholarly and helpful insights.

Franz modestly characterizes *I Offered Christ* as 'no more than a first collection of material for a proper study.' It is hard to imagine the size and depth of a 'proper study'! The book has three divisions. The first is an examination of the ecumenical issues at stake, followed by an exposition of the distinctive Roman Catholic features of the Mass. He then outlines the distinctive Protestant doctrines regarding the role of sacrifice, finally asking if there is any common ground. He concludes, 'Here is the heaviest burden of our division: that in our separate sanctuaries we worship, as Christians, in two completely different ways; the one form of "offering" absolutely excluding the other'. Franz attended the inaugural Mass of Vatican II, but attended none of the daily Masses thereafter. He felt uneasy at any service in which all Christians were not permitted to participate fully. The liturgy of the Mass presented an especially difficult problem. It was a bridge he found too difficult to cross. He simply could not believe that Christ was sacrificed anew each time the Mass was said. Nor was it a matter of adopting the Reformation point of view over and against the Roman Catholic viewpoint. The real question is, 'What does the Bible say?' He quotes the bold words of Luther, 'Why should I worry about the multitudes and magnitude of those who erred? Stronger than all is the truth.'

Part Two consists of a careful and sometimes bold exegesis of the New Testament material, particularly the book of Hebrews. He marshals verse after verse to underline the once-and-for-all character of Christ's death and sacrifice. He also marshals the scriptural arguments against Apostolic Succession which became such a crucial issue for him.in his personal life and would arise again in the 1963 Anglican-Methodist Conversations Report. In his closely-knit argument, Charles Wesley's hymns become powerful corroboration in support of scriptural evidence. Over and over again, he points out that it is not what we do, but what God has done through Jesus Christ that secures our salvation.

The third part, called 'Evangelical Application', calls us to live the faith that is secured by grace. The challenge to the Christian is to live by Word and Sacrament It is the Word made known in Jesus Christ; the Sacrament, instituted by Christ, that calls us to sacrifice our bodies on behalf of the world. Ultimately, the issue is not ecclesiology, but Christology. Christians are, in short, called to 'offer Christ'.

One might get the impression that the book is a polemic against Roman Catholic doctrine but that is not the case. Franz Hildebrandt firmly believed that understanding could come only if both parties would state their positions with full open honesty. Far from making them enemies, such an approach would establish a new level of relationship and could lead to the unity both desired. Franz was often frustrated by those who interpreted a difference of opinion as personal emnity and consequently refused to carry on the dialogue.

It was while he was in Rome that, with Nancy, he visited the German Lutheran Church. For Franz it was a 'might have been', for in 1930 it had been suggested to him that, before he was ordained, he should go to Rome to work with the German Lutherans as a 'curate'. However this did not work out for him. In 1962 the pastor in Rome, to whom the story was told, smiled and promptly invited Franz to be his curate; 'The position is vacant at present: would you like it?'

On their return journey the Hildebrandts called on Pastor Kurt Lang and his wife in Bern. Kurt and Franz had been together in the Confessing Church in pre-war Germany. They had much to talk about after twenty-five years. There was also a call at a Roman Catholic House in Louvain which Franz knew. The professor, a friend, and his wife entertained them and they talked with others who were returning from the Council. After their discussions Franz was asked to close with prayer, which he graciously did.

A brief but significant period of his life had passed. His appointment to attend Vatican II as an Official Observer had coincided with his growing interest in Catholic theology and practice. Back in the USA he would spearhead joint seminars between Drew and St Elizabeth's College and a variety of other ecumenical efforts that would enhance Protestant–Roman Catholic understanding.

CHAPTER 15

CRISIS AT DREW

Franz now believed he had found his place in the Drew scheme of things. His other gifts began to emerge. To a degree far greater than almost any of his faculty colleagues, he viewed the seminary as an expression of the church gathered. In fact, the seminary should be a model of a Christian community in which preaching, worship and sacrament should hold a place equally as important as teaching. For him Christian faith was ultimately a life lived and not a doctrine taught.

As he had first been appalled by the thinness of worship in the Madison area churches, so was he disappointed in the paucity of worship opportunities on campus. The daily morning chapel service with its uneven attendance and smorgasbord of offerings did not provide for the discipline, spiritual depth, and continuity he felt was necessary for future ministers, as well as for himself. Therefore he instituted morning and evening prayers following early Methodist liturgies, based on Cranmer's *Book of Common Prayer*.* In a letter to the Drew Wives Association in 1964, he sought their support:

> I have some notion of, and every sympathy with, your being dead tired at the end of the working day. There are also some to whom the classic Methodist order of service is still unfamiliar ... But let us be frank. Are these not exactly the same excuses you hear from

---

*Two decades later, while serving as a district superintendent, I was worshipping at a church in my New Jersey district. I was deeply moved by the pastor's effective use of the communion liturgy. Knowing his roots were in West Virginia pentecostalism, I asked him where he had learned his mastery of liturgy. 'Attending evening prayer at Drew led by Franz Hildebrandt,' was his reply. (MT)

your parishioners when they avoid church? Must we make apologies for wishing to begin and end the day with common worship in a community of future ministers? Is there the slightest danger on our campus that we will overdo it?

There is little doubt that during his years at Drew Franz contributed significantly to the worship life of the seminary, no small part of which was taken into the field by appreciative students.

Hildebrandt's other unique contribution to Drew during his tenure was his pastoral care of the Theological School community, including students, faculty, staff, adminstration and their families. When appendicitis, pneumonia or some other serious illness struck, he was among the first to visit in hospital. He delighted in welcoming new babies and rejoicing with their parents. He prowled the dorms, searching out those who cut class and counselling those who were struggling with financial problems, domestic crises or spiritual doubts. In the years before and after his Green Village pastorate, he accepted invitations every weekend he was free to visit the churches of student pastors. He would preach, give counsel, accompany them to hospitals and nursing homes in the parish.

Many were instructed and encouraged as they observed him in conversation and prayer with their own parishioners. His warm personal style enhanced his skilful use of scripture and liturgy. He was truly *pastor pastorum*, a pastor to pastors. Max Case recalls the last evening prayer service he attended prior to graduation in 1964: 'I will never forget how Franz went to the back of chapel to say farewell to the graduating seniors and their spouses. He dropped his professional reserve and showed his emotion – clasping our hands, hugging our spouses and dabbing his eyes for all to see.'

Franz Hildebrandt knew that if his vision for an American Methodism reconnected to its Wesleyan roots were to be realized, he would have to reach beyond the Drew campus. A key part of his strategy was in the formation of the Wesley Society with chapters in colleges, universities and seminaries across the country wherever persons could be gathered who had an interest in the Wesleyan renewal of the church. The Wesley Society was born at a meeting called by Franz in New York City on 31 January 1955.

Ministers, students and teachers gathered. They formulated a statement of purpose for the Society 'to hold conferences and retreats, do research and publishing that will foster further interest in the Wesleys.' The various chapters formed a loose connection held together by Franz's determination and a newsletter that was published sixteen times between 1955 and 1965.

The first retreat took place at Kirkridge, a well known retreat centre in eastern Pennsylvania in the autumn of 1955. Franz spoke on the topic, 'Methodist Worship Today'. Nancy, in order to keep expenses down, cooked the meals. Richard Cameron of Boston and David Shipley of Garrett also presented papers.

The Society meeting at Drew in the autumn of of 1956 drew seventy persons. Franz was able to recruit to the Advisory Council such distinguished professors as Robert Cushman of Duke, and Albert Outler, of Perkins (Southern Methodist). At the height of its activity, the Society had twenty-nine chapters. However, with Hildebrandt's departure for his sabbatical in Scotland in 1966 the Society's work at the national level quickly faded. It simply could not maintain its momentum without the strong leadership of its founder.

Another attempt to stir the heart of the somnolent American Methodist Church was the publication of the *Wesley Hymnbook* in 1958. Shortly after his arrival at Drew Franz had prepared a collection of 111 Wesley hymns, the *Asbury Supplement*, for use in Craig Chapel. Now this larger collection of 154 hymns was published by Epworth. Hildebrandt wrote in the editor's Foreword: 'Our purpose is in no way antiquarian, but severely practical, it is to make our present day parishes know, love and sing Wesley.' Although it went to a second printing, the little book did not find wide use among the churches. Even though Franz had been careful to give alternate tunes familiar to American congregations, many of them were of British origin, not familiar to American ears, and were therefore cause for complaint. It is probably also true that the larger number of Wesley hymns in the 1964 edition of the *Methodist Hymnal* in America was influenced by Hildebrandt's work.

In the spring of 1960 Robert Cushman, dean of the Divinity School at Duke University, wrote Franz asking him to meet with a small group of Methodist scholars 'concerning the production and publication of a critical edition of the works of John Wesley, together with the poetical works of John and Charles Wesley.' Along with Dr Albert Outler, Franz was asked to present the case for the project to a larger group of scholars meeting in Denver in May. With the support of five major Methodist-related universities, the work went ahead. It was hoped that the project could be completed in ten years, a hope that proved to be overly optimistic. Franz was elected secretary of the Editorial Board, a position which he held until 1968. Of course his real interest was in volume 7, to be entitled *A Collection of Hymns for Use of the People Called Methodist* (known as the 1780 book), of which he was to be editor along with Oliver Beckerlegge. The significance of his work on the collection is difficult to overestimate.

During his fourteen years in the United States, Franz Hildebrandt made an important contribution to American Methodism in general and to Drew in particular. He motivated several generations of Drew students to examine the biblical and theological roots of their faith. He initiated and sharpened the ecumenical dialogue, particularly with Roman Catholics. He modelled ministry by his diligent pastoral care for the campus community and during his years as pastor of the Green Village Methodist Church. His insistence on the discipline of worship, his courage of conviction in controversy that sometimes made him enemies as well as friends, were all part of his American legacy.

In spite of these considerable achievements, he remained ambivalent about continuing to teach at Drew, particularly after he and Nancy decided their children should continue their education in Great Britain. Nor did Franz take well to prolonged separations from Nancy who felt it necessary to stay in Britain in order to be available for the children. He also nurtured the hope that he might find a suitable circuit assignment within British Methodism – even though the itinerant system was not to his liking. However, by the time he went to Edinburgh on sabbatical in 1966, events were transpiring that would force his decision sooner than he might have liked.

It was a troubled Franz Hildebrandt who returned to Drew from his sabbatical year in September of 1967. He arrived on a campus torn asunder by suspicion, anger and confusion over the dismissal in the previous December of the Theological School's respected dean, Charles Wesley Ranson, by the university president, Robert Oxnam. Oxnam was the son of the well known liberal bishop, G. Bromley Oxnam, who had figured prominently in the McCarthy hearings of the 1950s. Bishop Oxnam was well represented in these hearings by Methodist layman and attorney Charles Parlin. Robert Oxnam was named president of Drew in 1960. Early on he announced his intention to integrate more closely the three parts of the university: the College of Liberal Arts (Brothers College, founded by the Baldwin brothers in 1929); the Graduate School, founded in 1955; and the Theological School, which was supposed to be celebrating its centennial year. Probably the most sensitive aspect of the planned integration was the diversion of endowment funds, originally bequeathed for the support of the seminary, to the general university budget. It was perhaps with this battle looming on the horizon that Bernard Anderson, an effective dean for the previous nine years, sought to relinquish the office and devote full-time to teaching and research.

Charles Wesley Ranson – his name alone might have been enough to win Franz's approval – was a son of Irish Methodism, and a leading figure in the world mission and ecumenical circles. He was appointed full-time Professor of Ecumenical Theology in 1962. He was respected by the entire faculty and Anderson naturally turned to him when he surveyed the field for a successor. Ranson was installed as dean in December of 1964. The Theological School faculty, having long enjoyed depth in the biblical and theological fields, now had added breadth in ecclesiastical and ecumenical studies. One of Ranson's initiatives was to begin an exchange programme between students from Drew and New College, Edinburgh. This programme was important because, in his words, 'The Church of Scotland recruited most of its theological school teachers from the ranks of parish ministry, thus demonstrating that the working minister was capable of maintaining high standards of scholarship and ensuring prospective ministers were taught by those who had direct experience of the work of ministry in the parish.' This was something for which Franz Hildebrandt had fought since he first arrived at Drew in 1953.

Although Ranson had taken a clear position in favour of the seminary regarding the use of endowment funds, the issue remained unresolved. The flashpoint of the crisis had its beginning with the tragic and untimely death of Carl Michalson in a plane crash in November 1965. Professor of Systematic Theology, 'Mike' was well loved by students and colleagues alike. He was at once playful and profound, at home in all the obscure corners of Bible and tradition, yet always ready to explore new ground on which his students were invited to follow if they had the courage. It was clear that no one could take Mike's place, nevertheless his position had to be filled. Ranson approached Robert Cushman, dean of Duke Divinity School, who had expressed the wish to step out of his administrative post and devote full time to teaching and research.

Keeping Oxnam informed at each step, Ranson extended the invitation to Cushman to fill the chair of Systematic Theology, but when Ranson requested a salary of $20,000, the same as Cushman was receiving at Duke, Oxnam balked. The top faculty salary paid at Drew was $16,000. Ranson was left with the unenviable task of disinviting Cushman. The faculty was furious. On 8 December, all but one of the twenty-four full time members signed a letter to the Board of Trustees 'respectfully asking for an early opportunity for an exchange of views' between the trustees and faculty. Although a copy of the letter was hand-delivered to Oxnam's office, he steadfastly maintained he had not been informed of the faculty's action. On 12 December Ranson was summoned to the president's office and asked to submit his resignation, ostensibly for going directly to the trustees and bypassing the president's office.

A second request was made a few days later and again Ranson refused, asking that the president's request be put in writing. On 8 January 1967, Ranson was informed that the trustees had voted to dismiss him as dean of the Theological School. No reasons were stated and no opportunity was granted him to hear charges or to make any statement on his own behalf. A student reporter for the *Circuit Rider*, the seminary newspaper, asked Professor Will Herberg if ' dismissal like this happens anywhere else?' Herberg replied, 'Never, never, not only now but for centuries. The formality of process has always been followed.'

Reaction to the dismissal was swift and wide-ranging. On hearing of the trustees' action, nearly 150 students attended an 11 p.m. Student Council meeting to listen and plan strategy. There were marches, vigils, press releases, letters, telegrams, all reflecting anger at the injustice of the trustees' action and showing confidence in the leadership and character of the dean. In the face of a unified faculty and an aroused student body, President Oxnam retreated to his office behind the walls of Mead Hall and waited for Charles Parlin to come to the rescue as he had for his father a decade earlier. Parlin headed a trustee committee instructed to investigate the dismissal of Ranson, hardly an impartial committee, Parlin himself having made the original motion.* Nevertheless, he was on campus numerous times during the spring of 1967 trying to mend the hopelessly broken bridge between administration and seminary.

By the time Hildebrandt returned to Drew in the fall of 1967, the opportunity for decisive action had passed. A study panel known as the Wicke Commission, named for its leader, Dr Myron Wicke, under the auspices of the University Senate of the Methodist Church had made seventeen recommendations to resolve the situation at Drew. Although touching upon several issues of mutual concern, many of the key grievances were not addressed. Hildebrandt, in a letter to Charles Parlin dated 20 October, spelled out the unresolved issues. His concluding remarks were vintage Hildebrandtian eloquence:

> Now we are all asking, Is it too late to call a halt to this fatal course, to avert the threatening exodus of students and faculty to other institutions? Must Drew's centennial turn into its requiem? We have waited for many years; we have agonized for the last ten or twelve months. Let me plead with you in Cromwell's word, 'I beseech you, in the bowels of Christ, think it possible you may be mistaken!'

It was too late. On 27 October, Franz Hildebrandt submitted his resignation:

> To President Oxnam, stating, in part, 'I wonder whether you and they (the Trustees) are aware of the irreparable damage done to Drew both at home and abroad, of the unspeakable disgrace brought upon the name of Methodism among our fellow Christians.

He was the first of twelve senior professors to do so over the next

---

*When the papers of Charles Parlin were bequeathed to the Methodist Archives, there was nothing on this subject to be found. All relevant papers had disappeared.

several weeks. He was the only one who had resigned without a new position already secured.

Writing to Nancy on 8 December, Franz lamented the pall that had fallen over the Theological School, '... the pathetic thing is that the faculty (most of them) do not see how step by step they have been driven to accept the enemy's position.' Franz knew the battle had been lost. Meticulously, with the help of sympathetic students, he packed his twenty-five boxes of books, the remaining household items and prepared to cross the Atlantic for what he thought would be the last time.

As word of Hildebrandt's resignation travelled around he received many messages of support, sympathy and offers of help, but there was little anyone could do. A former colleague on the Drew faculty, Professor William 'Bill' Farmer, wrote from Perkins School of Theology in Texas: 'I quite understand your decision to resign and hope that you will let me know at any time that I can be of help to you ... I shall never forget how much your loyalty to me meant in those difficult days when I left Drew'. Professor Robert Nelson wrote from Boston: 'I feel a mixture of sympathy for you and angry resentment towards the men who have caused this debacle.'

The response from former students voiced anger as well as sympathy. The Revd Stan Wiley, a minister on the staff of First Methodist Church in Bridgeport, Connecticut, wrote that he and eleven others had drafted an appeal to the Drew Trustees urging them to take immediate action, including the removal of Robert Oxnam as President of the University. 'Such an expression', he wrote, 'will surely fall on deaf ears and insensitive hearts. But the uncanny, almost demonic, activity of the President and Trustees lowering the boom on the life of Drew Theological Seminary cannot go unchallenged. You deserve high praise for your courage'. The Revd Ira Zepp, Dean of the Chapel at Western Maryland College wrote: 'What you have done for and been to us all is not yet fully known and will never be completely measured.'

Perhaps the Revd Larry Snow said it best : 'The printed page (Snow had read *From Luther to Wesley* before Franz had arrived at Drew) and the Wesleys introduced me to you quite before I had any notion that C. T. Craig and Drew would be inviting you to our beloved campus. My thoughts go back to those moments with profound gratitude – and how peculiarly fitting that one of the

Wesley quotations should bespeak the wonder of incarnation as we stand on the threshold of Advent 1967. It was as though you had become my Pastor – 'curing my soul' before crossing the Atlantic. And so you have been to countless others'. He goes on to make an apt comment about Franz's influence on the new American Hymnal: 'Some of us know, every time we open the new *Methodist Hymnal* that an 'editor' not listed in the Preface stands in the shadow simply because you 'Aim at pleasing Him more than yourself, or any other creature.' Franz Hildebrandt had made his mark on American Methodism, but in a way that not even he had fully understood.

CHAPTER 16

THE ANGLICAN–METHODIST CONVERSATIONS

At the Methodist Conference of 1955 in Manchester twelve representatives were appointed to meet with twelve appointed by the Church of England to hold 'conversations' (later the word gained a specific meaning in Methodism) with a view to having closer relationships between the two churches.

Ever since William Temple, in his sermon at his enthronement as Archbishop in Canterbury Cathedral in 1942, had referred to the ecumenical movement as 'the great new fact of our time', many in the churches had been reflecting on his words. Then in 1946 Geoffrey Fisher, his successor as Archbishop of Canterbury, preaching in Cambridge, invited the Free Churches to consider 'taking episcopacy into their system' in an attempt to bring about intercommunion. The Church of South India had been created in 1947, embracing Presbyterians, Congregationalists, Methodists and Anglicans, and the idea of 'churches together' was very much 'in the air'.

However, there were those who noted that in fact the Church of England had not moved at all. The proposal was that the Free Churches should take the Anglican episcopacy into their systems. Thus it seemed to many that it was not just a question of church order but a deep theological criticism of Free Church ordinations. Otherwise it would have been possible to call Moderators, General Superintendents and Chairmen of Methodist Districts by the name 'Bishop' (Assuredly some would have found problems in the very word because of past associations but, with some grace, problems of language and tradition could have been overcome.) But the question was not simply 'Can you make your leaders into bishops?' but *Can you make your leaders into bishops who are consecrated as ours are?* This means effectively becoming Anglican Bishops'.

Other Free Churches pondered but did not feel ready to move on the matter. The Methodists were ready, and so the Methodist twelve met with the Anglican twelve. In 1958 an 'Interim Report' was published by the whole team jointly.* It dealt with background matters. There were no particular resolutions other than that the document should be discussed by both churches.

In the United States Franz Hildebrandt, Professor of Christian Theology at Drew University analyzed the document in an edition of the *Drew Gateway* in 1959. His critique was a searching examination. He continued this examination in a paper 'Wanted: a Methodist Doctrine of Ministry' in which he argued against the necessity of episcopal succession in a united church and he stated that he remained 'unconvinced that re-union without reformation can ever be the will of God for his church'. He always held and stated *ecclesia semper reformanda*. (The Church always needs reforming.) Whether because he was in the USA his words did not reach the panel or because being in the USA he was thought to be away from the action or because his comments were so analytically sharp that they went against the tenor of the time is hard to say. That there were members of the panel who raised such issues is clear (from the Dissentient View in the Final Report). For whatever reasons his critique seems to have had little effect on the end result. His questions were not answered.

The final 'Report on the Conversations' was published early in 1963 and the unease which many had felt earlier was in no way allayed. This unease had been captured and expounded by the 'Dissentient Report' with which the document concluded, signed by four representatives of the Methodist twelve. They were men of great and sound scholarship, men of integrity who could not and would not give their signed consent to a document with which they did not agree. They were the Revd Professor C.

*I was at that time minister in a Midlands circuit and had excellent relationships with my two nearest Anglican colleagues. I was, however, uneasy. Without laying claim to any special theological, scholastic or ecumenical acumen on ecclesiastical matters, I was appointed, as a very junior member of a group in my own Synod, to formulate a series of questions for discussion. (ASC)

Kingsley Barrett, Professor Thomas E. Jessop, Principal the Revd Thomas D. Meadley and the Revd Professor Norman H. Snaith. The other eight Methodists felt that they could with integrity sign the propositions in the Report. This group also included competent scholars and men and women of good standing. The division in the Methodist 'twelve' was also seen in the Methodist Church herself.

At the Methodist Conference in Preston in 1963 the Revd Dr Harold Roberts who had led 'the Methodist twelve' and was himself in favour, proposed a resolution that the document should be referred to the synods and circuits for discussion and debate. This resolution was seconded by Professor Barrett. It was agreed by both sides that on a matter so important there should be full consultation. After voting in the circuits and District Synods and with their comments and votes to hand, a clear decision would be taken in 1965 at the Conference meeting in Plymouth. To go forward it was agreed that there should be at least 75 per cent of the Conference voting in favour of the propositions.

In both the Church of England and the Methodist Church the debate waxed fast and furious. Various arguments were advanced on both sides. There was a welter of publications and leaflets. In all the religious journals of both churches articles were written and letters published.* Men and women of great scholarship and personal integrity stood on either side. Different arguments were used and weighted differently. Ordinary folk followed the arguments and asked questions which were answered in the main, but the phrase 'liberty of interpretation' fogged some points made. In addition to this there was no common way of assessing the arguments, for one would see one factor as crucial only to find it relegated to a subordinate point by another.

Undoubtedly there was ambiguity in the document. It was openly acknowledged by some to be the only way in which various differing positions and interpretations could be held together *within* the proposed new church. Others believed that

*At that time I was editor of a weekly paper published by Cliff College which had a circulation of 10,000. I published in alternate weeks articles 'for' and 'against', mostly from invited writers. My postbag was full, with more letters on this subject than on any other: it was a fascinating debate. (ASC)

only a clear concise statement precisely outlining the different problems and positions could aid the future of the churches. Total honesty and truthfulness, they said, *whatever problems arise*, is the only way forward. Emotional arguments entered into the matter – such as personal relationships with other churches. Non-theological issues – if there are any such – were raised like the question: 'Can we in this present age dare to carry on without uniting?' One has to say that there were those in both churches who regarded that argument as defeatist. The major line of argument of the 'Dissentients' had been voiced clearly at the Preston Conference by Professor Barrett. He held his copy of the Report and said clearly, 'This is the document. We must debate the text in front of us.'

In the USA Franz Hildebrandt, teaching theology, saw, heard and followed the debate. He was by now a true 'Wesley' Methodist. He studied the Final Report, worried over it and wrote a second article in the *Drew Gateway* giving his views. This article, together with his earlier one was published in 1964 by Epworth Press in Britain as *Critique of Two Reports*. As in all his work his arguments were backed by a deep knowledge and understanding of both scripture and church history. The second article contained strong objective criticism. In the same year he also had a briefer booklet published by Epworth Press entitled *Re-union and Reformation* in a 'popular' series of booklets on the Report. Shortly after this he wrote an article for a publication in the USA which he sent to Charles Parlin en route. Parlin was perhaps the leading layman in the Methodist Church in the USA. Taken together with his 'Wanted: a Methodist Doctrine of Ministry', he provided what is probably the most devastating critique of the Report, raising arguments which are still valid in today's climate.

It is difficult to appraise his comments on the Report without having the document and his critique side by side. Nevertheless without producing the detailed precision of his arrows hitting their targets it is possible to show the main lines of his criticism. First he sets aside any idea of accepting vagueness. 'Liberty of interpretation' in a document of this nature is not a valid concept. The way of the Kingdom of God is not advanced by loose and imprecise language even if it is prompted by kindness, goodwill and a wish not to be obstructive. Any document on which joint action is to be based must be as clear as human minds can make it – otherwise the action will be a cause of problems in the future. How can anyone make a decision on anything when different people understand sentences to mean different things, sometimes things in direct conflict, e.g. was the Service of Reconciliation ordination or was it not? Such a document can only be unreliable. He said in conversation many times: 'Our God makes order out of chaos, He does not make chaos out of order. He is a God of order.' So he asked 'What does the Report actually say? Can we see that clearly?'

Franz was quite clear in his own mind what the Report actually said. He was sure that the carefully worded service and the phrase 'liberty of interpretation' was an attempt to allow those ministers who had grave queries about 're-ordination' to put their consciences to rest. For him the whole report was dominated by the concept of episcopacy as held in the Church of England. The Revd Dr Norman Snaith, in correspondence with him, felt he dwelt too much on this and not enough on 'the priesthood of all believers', the equality of laity and ministry working together. While Franz admitted the validity of Snaith's point in the total picture he was quite sure that 'episcopal ordination' was the key to the whole.

It is interesting to note the apparent influence of Adolf von Harnack here. In his great book *What is Christianity?* (*Das Wesen des Christentums*) published in 1900, Harnack exploded the theory of episcopacy as a blessing and the priesthood as a necessary means of grace. His words about the development of the power of forms becoming regulations and these regulations then being 'insensibly regarded as though they contained within them the very substance of religion' are a continual reminder to all who hold office and create rules. Franz Hildebrandt as always was influenced by Harnack. Snaith was essentially a good Protestant and Nonconformist. They were doughty comrades-in-arms.

The crux was the 'Service of Reconciliation' in which all ministers would take part. The service had the objective of uniting and unifying the ministries of the two churches. Methodists laid hands on Anglican heads and Anglicans (bishops) laid hands on Methodist heads. But Methodists had no doctrine of 'digital contact' or 'tactile succession' or the creating of an order of priests set apart (this is where Snaith and Hildebrandt were at one). Nevertheless the 'digital contact' in succession (the Apostolic succession) was of such importance to some sections of the Church of England that this service had to shadow the rite of Anglican ordination. Indeed one of the contentions of some in the Church of England was that Methodist ministers were not properly ordained and this must be put right (at one point Franz comments that this was how the Roman Catholics viewed Anglicans and Pope Leo XIII had said so unambiguously in 1896)

Methodist ministers had never made a similar accusation against Anglican orders so there was little point in using a cover of words to suggest putting right what was lacking in this ordination. Methodists were satisfied that Anglicans were ordained in a way *accepted and treasured by their own church* just as Methodist ministers – from various origins – had been ordained in a way approved and treasured by the Methodist church. Each denomination had developed its own ministry. Traditionally Methodists welcoming ministers from other denominations into Methodism had given, after a rigorous examination, 'the right hand of fellowship'. This was how Franz Hildebrandt himself had been welcomed into Methodism and he treasured the memory, for it accepted his Berlin ordination as of the Holy Spirit.

Various unofficial comments only confirmed that the object of the 'Service of Reconciliation ' was to make Methodist ministers into priests in the Church of England succession. Archbishop Michael Ramsey was reported to him as saying that after this service 'they will be priests'. (Perhaps Norman Snaith was right). And this would only come about by Anglican bishops laying hands on their heads. For Franz the basis of thought, faith and therefore opposition was the cry of the Reformation: *sola scriptura, solo Christo, sola gratia* – judge only by scripture, faith only in Christ, salvation only by grace. Here Norman Snaith and all the 'dissentients' stood. Our unity, as Christians, said Franz could only come by proclaiming the Gospel. If we fail in this whether we are episcopal or not, we have failed, for by this we are judged. Snaith once wrote saying: 'This scheme denies the openness of the Gospel'. 'By faith alone, through grace alone.'

Hildebrandt's critique then was directed at the insistence of the Church of England that *their* type of bishop was essential. Even so some Anglicans were hoping that an infusion of Methodists would change their episcopacy into something perhaps more pastoral. It was not laid down in scripture that the church must have bishops, said Hildebrandt. 'Is episcopacy necessary for the full blessings of the New Covenant in Christ as circumcision was the essential channel for the old Covenant in Moses? My friends in the Anglican body do not like me to ask that question in those terms because, asked in those terms it answers itself.'

His language was clear and fair. Those who know him well remembered his background – Luther in his studies, Hitler in his early ministry – and saw in him something of the spirit of Luther before the Diet of Worms and the Confessing Church before Hitler. For him it was of the essence of his life and being, that the grace of God should in no way be conditional. Sometimes people said to him 'It isn't much to do' and he said over and over again 'it wasn't much for the Christians in the early church to put a pinch of incense on the fire of the imperial altar and say 'Caesar is Lord' but they died rather than do it'. To understand Franz Hildebrandt one needs to understand that.

The document also meant that; (a) Methodist ministers were invalidly ordained, therefore; (b) Methodist members were invalidly confirmed; and (c) Methodist sacraments had no validity. This is a remorseless logic but nevertheless has to be faced. He admitted that the nouns 'bishop' 'priest/presbyter', and 'deacon' were used in the New Testament but their meaning in the Church of England in 1960 was not the same as their meaning in the early years of the Christian church. And he argued this from the scriptures. In his letter to Charles Parlin, who was not unsympathetic, he states quite clearly his position with regard to bishops by quoting John Wesley: 'I still believe the episcopal form of church government to be both scriptural and apostolical, I mean well agreeing with the practice and writings of the Apostles. *But that it is prescribed in Scripture I do not believe'* (Letters III.82).

He held that the Methodist, non-episcopal, form of order was equally blessed by the Holy Spirit as were those of other denominations. Any church which prescribed a totalitarian approach was denying the freedom of the Holy Spirit and, in doing this, was contradicting sound theology and the teaching of the New Teatament. By their insistence on episcopal ordination the Church of England was behaving like a totalitarian dictator. He also remembered that the Church of England bishops had not always emphasized the freedom of the Holy Spirit and had sometimes been restrictive in interpreting the call of Christ. After all, John

Wesley's clash with episcopal authority had produced one of his most memorable sayings: 'I look upon the world as my parish'. It follows that he did not regard the church as 'impeccable' nor the traditions as invariably acceptable. Even in the book of Revelation in the New Testament the church was criticized as failing. So the church 'always needing reform' always stands to be judged at the bar of scripture – as do we all.

He became angry when some said they would go through this form of service to receive 'any *extra* blessing which could be given'. 'Is the grace of God freely given not enough?' he would ask. 'What extra can the Church of England bishops or anyone else give which comes on top of God's grace, full and free?' He always said that the whole church needed to look carefully at what ordination was and did. So we see that in his view by going through the Service of Reconciliation Methodists would be climbing over a fence into the Church of England camp (and into a ministry and episcopacy still not recognized by Rome). They would not in fact be removing a barrier but supporting it. They would also be denying the validity of their own orders as inspired by the Holy Spirit and proved by history and they would be limiting the grace of God. And, as he read the documents, it would mean closing the Lord's Table to other Christians with whom there was an 'open table'.

Yet while he made a hard attack on the scheme he also had many positive thoughts. Unity comes not from organizations but from motive and work. He points to Wesley's picture of the character of a Methodist and its consequences. Wesley desires to be a Christian and to save souls. He distinguishes himself from the *unbelieving* world 'but from real Christians *of whatsoever denomination they may be*, we earnestly desire not to be distinguished at all'.

This not only raises the question as to who are the 'real' Christians but, as Franz points out, widens 'universally through the grace which is free for all and in all and the means of grace – emphatically including the Open Table – by which the Spirit renews the church'. The Lord's Table, open to all Christians, is a vital concept. He quotes Wesley: 'Experience shows the gross falsehood of that assertion that the Lord's Table is not a converting ordinance'. (Letters II.202). He also makes the point that while Wesley exercised a strict discipline with members of his societies, yet he records in his Journal (30 September 1749) severe self-rebuke for having refused Communion to a saintly man who had not been baptized by an episcopally ordained minister.*

It is possible, Hildebrandt allows, that Methodism might be accused of being schismatic and divisive, but this he counters by saying that Methodism's aim is not to divide Christians from Christians. There is no need for anyone to enforce his or her views on any other person or to apologize for one's own. He points out that Methodism is episcopal in America and in Europe, but not in Great Britain and Australia. He reminds us that Wesley's answer to the question: 'Why is it that there is no determinate plan of church government appointed in scripture?' is 'without doubt because the wisdom of God had a regard to the necessary variety'. Church order has no other purpose than to bring souls to God, according to Wesley, and to build them up in fear and love. The test is 'efficacy', never 'ancestry'. Therefore the principles of the Reformation are at stake. The argument has been made by German scholars that Luther retained bishops not for any inherent virtue (or lack of it) but because it enabled him to retain some structure and order. Wesley's test regarding 'evangelical' or 'Catholic' is the Holy Scriptures and 'sufficient, sovereign, saving grace'. 'This is shown in the Lord's Supper from which no Christian believer may be excluded under whatever canonical rubrics.'

So, as her contribution to ecumenical dialogue, Methodism must learn afresh and then testify 'that church order by its very nature is flexible and open to regional and pragmatic variations'. Our duty is not to form a new church but to reform the nation. 'The way to unity' he writes 'does not lead through the yoke which Anglicanism everywhere tries to force on Christendom, the

---

*Wesley, in the course of his ministry, appears to have taken three varying positions regarding the Lord's Table. In summary:

First: is the one just described – somewhat rigid. He repented of this.

Second: the 'Open Table' is used as a welcoming, converting ordinance for all.

Third: the Table is open to all members of any church who are in good standing and to anyone wishing to approach who has the consent of the presiding minister. (We do not know any reference that this permission when requested was refused.)

Franz Hildebrandt seems, like Wesley, to hover between positions two and three. He certainly wished the Lord's Table to be open to all 'who love the Lord Jesus' and, to all who were seeking to know Jesus as Lord.

'regularization' of Methodist ministries by 'the inoculation of Asbury's successors into the Seabury pedigree', and especially not when the proposed ceremony of re-ordination is camouflaged as a 'Service of Reconciliation'.

He follows a suggestion picked up from Karl Barth of differing 'orders' in the whole church, working together, respecting the different ways of working and accepting one another: 'a genuine recognition of brothers in Christ giving and receiving the right hand of fellowship' (Gal. 2:9); and he suggests that the oft-quoted words can be properly used: 'If thine heart is as my heart, if thou lovest God and all mankind, I ask no more: Give me thine hand.'

For Franz church unity is the product of a united witness. The vision of Methodism born out of John Wesley's sermon on 'The Catholic Spirit' and controlled by his sermon 'A Caution against Bigotry' is not in the past. It must not be lost in regional or local churches. The world is our parish. Unity of structure does not necessarily mean strength. Assuredly it does not come through ambiguity. Unity is working and living within the Holy Spirit, each accepting the other as a full partner. Maybe he could be accused of desiring a church with minimal order, but this is not so. Nevertheless he knew how order could be manipulated. Even the Confessing Church in Germany needed constant reformation and care. Anyone who knew him well, knew how much he cared that 'the Bride of Christ on Earth' should be open, loving and full of saving grace.

At the Methodist Conference of 1965 held at Plymouth the vote was a little over the 75 per cent in favour, which had been the agreed figure. There had been much confusion in the voting 'lower down' at the circuit level. Some circuits voted 'No unless ...' and stipulated alternatives: others voted 'Yes, if ...' and also with stipulations. In fact there was no way that any alteration could be made. However as the majority of voting was like this, the panel tried to explain in its report to the Conference and said that *as a rule of thumb* votes beginning 'No' were regarded as basically against, whereas votes beginning 'Yes' were basically in favour. A proposition was made in committee that only unequivical 'Yes' votes be counted 'Yes' but this was thought not to be fair either. It never went to a vote and made little difference. Members of Conference appeared to have their minds fixed and the debate in Conference mattered little. The vote of Conference was clear.

A new joint committee was appointed to prepare the next step and various opinions and ideas were to be hammered out. This in fact justified the supporters of 'Yes if ...' resolutions to some degree. The Methodists decided not to put a 'dissentient' as one of their representatives. This caused hurt to about half of Methodism though it is quite understandable that when a committee to implement a decision is appointed they would not desire a member who was against that decision. It was a matter of wisdom against practicality – of including a known 'dissentient' to show fairness to the opponents of the scheme against that of having a built-in negative vote and therefore not being unanimous.

Soon after Conference there was a coming together of representatives of various dissenting groups. They met under the cumbersome but accurate title of 'The National Liaison Committee'. It was on this committee that I as a young member came to know Franz Hildebrandt so much better, for he attended whenever he was in the UK at a time we were meeting. The Chairman was Professor Barrett: the secretary was the Revd Kenneth Mackenzie. Franz, as a welcomed member, brought an input from a wider background. He was in touch with a broader Methodism within which he was a well-respected figure. His considerable correspondence shows not only his wide area of contacts but a wider unease abroad about what was happening in the UK. This unease was not openly expressed, for others overseas did not wish to appear as 'meddlers' in the British scene.

Nevertheless the Methodist leaders in different countries with whom he had contact had suggested to him that if the 'Dissentients' were compelled 'for conscience sake' to leave the British Conference, doors would be opened to welcome them. Because of his own standing and reputation, he gained opportunities to speak at meetings from which he might have been excluded because he was an opponent of the scheme. Increasingly he felt more and more alienated from 'official' Methodism in Britain. He wrote to the World Methodist Council asking that those who could not assent to this scheme might be assured of 'caring' by World Methodism.

One must say that while not all 'Dissentients' felt isolated there were some who did. Not all those 'in favour' practised this isolation on opponents but some did. Snaith and Jessop both expressed a feeling of 'the cold shoulder' from some quarters in Methodism. So it was not just that Franz was too sensitive. His philosophy had always been to argue strongly, but never to break friendship.

He was also very upset as he travelled in the USA and contacted various people of influence to find that *official* British Methodism gave to outsiders the impression that there was minimal dissent. Letters to his friend Kingsley Barrett and to the Secretary of the NLC (Kenneth Mackenzie) were regular and informative. Always his arguments were both theological and practical. He was passionate, for to him – as for most 'dissentients' – it was not a busi-ness of an ecumenical or ecclesiastical joining into a new organization but a decision dealing with the heart of the Christian faith. As he came to NLC meetings and knowledge of him grew, all came to realize that even the Anglican-Methodist Conversations debate with all its deep challenges regarding the faith, came secondary to the proclamation of the Gospel of the grace of the Lord Jesus Christ. Nothing could ever come before that to him.

During this period he experienced a 'cooling off' towards Methodism's brilliant Luther scholar the Revd Professor Gordon Rupp, who had advocated the scheme from the beginning. Rupp used his razor sharp wit against his opponents like a whiplash, sometimes not realizing how much it hurt. It did not always win friends and sometimes turned friends into enemies. *Ad Hominem* (attacking the person) is always the weakest of arguments, often the most hurtful.

Franz had not Rupp's charisma – but he had a deep love for Luther and was also a comparable expert. He saw Wesley as a true successor to Luther. For a 'Luther expert' and professed admirer to betray the principles for which Luther had fought (so he saw the 'scheme') and also to betray the whole attitude of John Wesley to church order and thus to diminish the Gospel of Jesus Christ was too much for him. When this was accompanied by sharp witticisms which neither argued nor answered questions but were calculated to create belittling laughs, it threw him into the opposite camp. It seemed to him to disregard scholarship and things he loved and he said more than once that it would be diffi-cult to remain in a Methodist Church which elected Gordon Rupp as its President. As it happened, it was at the ministerial session of the Conference of 1968 that we heard of the resignation of

Franz Hildebrandt. Gordon Rupp was inducted as President three days later.

Periodically at NLC meetings Franz would suggest that we prepare for an 'exodus'. He believed a *fait accompli* would gain support from the World Methodist Council and American Methodists. For this man, who at the Steglitz Synod in Berlin in 1935 was prepared to lead an exodus even from the Confessing Church in Germany if it did not live according to the sovereign free grace of Christ *for all*, it was not difficult to speak strongly. We sensed the agony in his heart.

Just as Niemoeller in the 1930s had said: 'when a burglar enters your house, you get rid of him. You do not give him the house,' so there were those who said: 'This is *our* Methodist Church. We must stay in and fight for it in spite of an adverse vote.' As always with Franz, an honestly held viewpoint was honoured. The crunch question was 'Could the essence of Methodism be saved?' There was little to allay his losing faith in the leaders of Methodism who, to him, were selling out their heritage and proclaiming a poorer restricted gospel. He felt that, at bottom, there was a lack of faith in God, judging by comments of some leaders. He saw this attitude as defeatist. This he could not accept. The victory lay in the proclamation of the Gospel of the Lord Jesus. The key to this victory lay not in a church organization but in a church of dedicated members, dedicated to the Gospel of Jesus Christ. Proponents of the scheme may have been upset by the passion with which he prosecuted his case. They may have felt that because of his sharpness and remarkable memory he regarded them as inferior. This was not so. If anyone had an argument Franz would allow him to state it and to state it strongly. If in the end neither he nor his opponent were persuaded he would not wish it to destroy a friendship – but when it was a matter of defending the Gospel ...

Some were afraid of meeting him in debate. There is evidence that when he was in the USA, some British Methodist leaders would not meet him on the same platform. He could be a fearsome opponent; so that when he returned to Britain after the Drew upheaval and applied for permission to serve for a short time in a Church of Scotland parish as a locum,* he was not

*In the Church of Scotland when a minister has moved from one parish to another, a 'locum', might be engaged for a time until a formal successor is officially appointed.

entirely surprised when that permission was refused.

Looking back we must reflect on his arguments, historically and theologically. His mastery of Luther and the Wesleys, allied to his cool logic and precise knowledge, asked vital questions still to be answered. His thesis 'if it is not logically sound and of good sense, it is not good theology' is surely right. Woolliness in thinking is not the work of the Word become flesh. It is wrong to think he did not love the Church of England, this man who used Cranmer's Prayer Book until the day he died. How could a man who had counted William Temple as a friend and George Bell as a 'father in God', who held Max Warren and Charles Raven as friends, be an enemy of the church to which they belonged? He was simply against a 'bad scheme'. For them episcopal ordination was right and valid. They were correctly ordained, 'So are we. As we do not deny that God the Holy Spirit has used you and your ordination, so must you not deny us in turn that which the Holy Spirit has evidenced that He has given us'.

He also reflected on his own life. There was for him special poignancy in the fact that he was the last to be 'properly ordained' in Germany as a Lutheran pastor before Hitler and his anti-Semitism took over. Then after the war when he felt he could not return to Germany and pondered joining the Church of England or Methodism, he had received a letter from Bishop George Bell, full of apology and sadness, explaining that if he wished to join the Church of England he would have to be ordained by their episcopal hands. This could not be sidestepped.

To Franz this meant that he was regarded as 'not ordained'. Nor, therefore, were others he had known: Paul Schneider, who stood against the Nazis and died in Buchenwald; Ludwig Steil in Dachau; his dearest friend Dietrich in Flossenberg. Martin Niemoeller had been a prisoner for eight years. He himself and many others had been imprisoned. He could not deny the ordinations of these people. 'Are their ordinations invalid?' he said once. 'Dare I deny *their* ordinations by having episcopal hands laid on *my* head?' When he turned towards Methodism he had found men like the great scholar Dr W. F. Howard and the great preacher Dr W. R. Maltby who offered him a welcome and the right hand of fellowship. Surely their ordination and their recognition of his own was not invalid?

From this background he pressed his case. It gave a special

urgency to his argument. Increasingly he wondered about his own place in Methodism. He remembered the words of Dr Howard uttered in 1946 when he was interested in becoming a Methodist minister. Maybe he saw the 'ideal' Methodism. Certainly he was not happy with what 1960s Methodism was saying and doing. He felt he must either leave her or be cast out by her. When he suggested a walkout, a breakaway, people said, 'Wait! The time is not yet.' To him these had always been the words of the devil to prevent any action.

Some people who were dissentients were drifting away to other Churches. Dissentient ministers were resigning – admittedly only a small number, and often to somewhat narrow Biblical groupings. It was a sad comment that a scheme designed to unite churches began to divide Methodism. In 1968, in addition to his questions about the unity scheme where he saw a 'for all' gospel being narrowed to the 'circumcision' of Anglican Episcopal ordination, there were two other occassions where, to him, the gospel was being compromised. And so, not out of pique but as a step of faith, he resigned from the ministry of the beloved Methodist Church.

CHAPTER 17

RESIGNATION

Franz Hildebrandt's decision to resign from the ministry of the Methodist Church was brought about by three crises coming within a short space of time. Together they produced a greater pressure than he could bear. Perhaps another man would have reacted differently. Perhaps had they come with a larger interval of time between, he would have ridden them out. Being the man he was, they tore him apart. It was possibly the least important of these crises that precipitated his drastic action.

Over the years Franz had grown to love the Wesleys. He saw them to be in the direct line of succession from his beloved Martin Luther and he felt completely at home with them. John's direct 'no nonsense' writing and preaching and his careful logic spoke to his own heart. To the day of his death the hymns of Charles Wesley were a source of strength and a voice of comfort. Moreover when he asked to join the Methodist ministry he had been accepted by Methodism, the church of the Wesleys, *as he was*, a Lutheran minister, ordained in Berlin. He needed no further validation. Thus Methodism had both honoured his past ministry and also opened for him new doors of service as pastor, preacher and teacher.

When he became a Methodist minister he had accepted the appointment he was given. Care had been taken in his appointment though he had never asked for special consideration. Later his professorship at Drew had come about through negotiations initiated by others in the church. His talents, gifts and graces were always at the service of the gospel through the church. For himself he wished nothing more than to be a minister of the gospel of the Lord Jesus Christ. Like many he had his criticisms of modern Methodism (he never did fathom the itinerancy of the Methodist ministry). Nonetheless he accepted Methodism as it was. In the eyes of those who knew him well, his was a skilled, loyal, devoted ministry. He had become well 'ingrafted' into Methodism.

Yet early in 1968 Methodism in her official robes showed towards him a strange lack of understanding, almost as though his past had never happened. The sympathy and perception shown in the 1940s by men like Dr W. F. Howard and Edwin Finch when he was welcomed into Methodism, now seemed to be absent. Franz himself would never have claimed anything because of his past. He was too good a Lutheran to rely on 'works' of any kind, but he had been shaped by that past which clearly revealed the qualities which 'made him tick'. These seemed, to many, to have been forgotten by those in leadership. Sadly, sometimes, even greatly caring people can lose the threads of compassion and understanding. The two committees in whose hands lay the vital decisions did not grasp the agony he was suffering nor the turmoil in his heart and mind. So he came – inevitably – to a decision which churned within him for the rest of his life.

The factors which those responsible in Methodism had to consider included the following: he had resigned from Drew on an issue of principle; he had returned to British Methodism; he was unhappy about the Unity Scheme and the way he saw Methodism was being led; and, certainly to be considered, he needed some work and income. When the offer came of a 'locum' position for about a year in a Church of Scotland parish, it seemed to be a solution to his problems. The parish was in Edinburgh – a city he loved – and he could live at home with his family. It could be described as an 'ecumenical' appointment. He could also continue his labours on *Wesley's Works*. To accept this offer he needed the approval of the Methodist Conference committee appointed to consider matters such as serving outside normal Methodism. He talked with his District Chairman* who warned him that permission was unlikely to be given. Nevertheless, he

*'District Chairman' is the name given in British Methodism to the minister with pastoral care over the Methodists in a fairly large geographical area. Sometimes he or she is spoken of as 'parallel to an Anglican bishop'. In this case the area is 'The Methodist Church in Scotland'.

applied for permission to serve an 'outside organization', i.e. an organization not under the direct control of the Conference. Such permission had been granted when he went to Drew in 1953 and had been renewed annually on his request while he was there.

Presumably his Chairman had made some prior 'soundings' and, as forecast, when Franz made application his request was not granted. One of the reasons given was that Nicholson Street Church of Scotland parish was not far from Nicholson Square Methodist Church where he had been minister. However, that ministry had been fifteen years earlier and the committee members should have realized that he was a man of integrity whose word was his bond. He would not allow the two to conflict. Nor did those consulted seem to remember that in 1946 he had been 'stationed' in the Cambridge Methodist circuit within whose area only a few months before he had been minister to the Lutheran congregation. This had been the decision not of Franz but of the Methodist Stationing Committee.

He also believed that his stance at Drew and his attacks on the Unity scheme counted against his receiving permission. 'Had I asked to serve in an Anglican parish, I would have been sure of every official blessing as an ecumenical pioneer', he wrote in the letter of resignation which he sent to his Chairman on hearing the decision. He once wrote to a friend; 'I realize that, not being born in Methodism, I have always lacked that sense of 'connection' and pride in it which is peculiar to Methodists.' He was never happy with officialdom but on request did withhold his resignation temporarily in hope of a change of mind. However, the final decision of the committee was confirmed. Permission to serve the Church of Scotland congregation would not be given. 'Here for me the story ends; I am not making any further appeal. As I have been denied the breathing space and the ecumenical opportunity for which I asked, my original letter to the President of Conference takes final effect ... I must wait and work from outside for another day of Methodism.'

Sadly when on enquiry we looked for the records of these events in the Methodist Conference office, they could not be found. An astute and sensitive committee should have seen his tensions and his needs. It must have been possible to find some place in the area of Edinburgh Methodism where, if he were thought to be not completely right in the decisions he had taken, he could have been given time to reflect and serve. They should have recognized the calibre of work done and the calibre of the man who had done it who now found that private and understandable emotions had invaded his normally cool logic.

It was not to be. Never one to turn away from what he saw as yet another venture of faith, it was with a heavy heart that he resigned. He had burned his boats in Germany, at Drew and, now, with British Methodism. In each case, as he viewed it, he was fighting for the truth of the Gospel and its application. As it happened things did not turn out as he thought they would. Sadly the 'locum' situation in the Church of Scotland proved to be a great disappointment. It was not as it had been pictured to him. In 1969 the Church of England rejected the Unity Scheme. The 'dissentients' had now to work with the 'proponents' within Methodism. Franz Hildebrandt, one of their clearest thinkers and theologians, was not with them to give his help. In later years at Drew there were those who felt sadness over the events and saw that Franz had presented a case there which deserved very careful consideration. Those who had known him were very disappointed at his resignation for this was no matter of discipline but a case of the burning heart.

After the notice of resignation had been given to the Ministerial Session of the Conference of 1968 along with other resignations, a brother minister said: 'Do you realize that this morning we accepted without comment the resignation of Franz Hildebrandt?' and he paused and then added, 'one of our great men'. Though the hurt had gone very deeply into his being, his love for Methodism and the Wesleys remained. He gave encouragement to those who sought him out to 'talk Methodism'. Though serving as a 'locum' or assistant minister in the Church of Scotland he preached Methodist doctrines! Whenever he was able, he used the hymns of Charles Wesley.*

He continued his work on the *Collection of Hymns for the Use of The People Called Methodists*, (Wesley Works, Vol. 7) along with Oliver Beckerlegge and James Dale. Before he died his older

---

*When I became President of the Methodist Conference in 1983 I received a heart-warming letter from him: The Conference service had been broadcast by BBC radio and he had made a point of listening to it. Not only did he compliment me on my sermon but he added 'I miss the hymns of Charles Wesley more than I can say'. (ASC)

daughter Ruth had married James Grayson an American Methodist minister and together they were serving in Korea. In 1984 his younger daughter, Esther, was commissioned as a Methodist missionary lay teacher to New Guinea and his friend, the retiring President of Conference, conducted the commissioning service. She later married a Methodist minister, the Revd Chris Shreeve. It seemed that the wounds were beginning to heal.*

The many warm letters and words of appreciation which he recived on his resignation and the friendships which continued reminded him that there were many who held him to be a true follower of Jesus Christ in the path of Luther and the Wesleys. He would not have wished for any other tribute.

---

*In 1983–84 as President of the Methodist Conference, I asked him to allow me to open the door for his return to his beloved Methodism. But sixteen years was too long an interval and he was in poor health. Sending copies of some of his correspondence he said, 'it is too late now'. The fact that his health continued to decline and his death came all to soon proved him right. The emotional stress would have been too great. (ASC)

CHAPTER 18

STEADFASTLY BY FAITH

Towards the end of his life Franz Hildebrandt was persuaded by the editor of *Der Londoner Bote* – a newsletter for German-speaking Christians in London – to give an account of his life. It is very summary and simply factual (one can hear him saying 'This is so unnecessary') but in its last sentences the account reveals the heart and mind of his calling:

> Preaching and parochial work have always meant more to me than lecturing and administrative work and since 1969 I have remained actively involved with the congregation in Slateford-Longstone Church where I first of all acted as locum and later shared the pastoral work with Roy Manson, the Parish Minister.

When he returned to Edinburgh after his resignation from Drew University Franz was happy to be with his family again. Nancy had never been completely at home in the USA. He confessed: 'Scotland became and remained my homeland. America could, naturally, only be a guest country.' Nancy and the family had returned to live in Edinburgh in 1963. There had been visits both ways, but Edinburgh was 'home'.

His resignation from the Methodist ministry in Great Britain had been prompted by the refusal of the Methodist Church to give him permission to serve as 'locum' in a vacancy in a Church of Scotland parish, Nicholson Street church in Edinburgh, which had seemed to him at the time to answer his need for an occupation. Otherwise he was a minister 'without pastoral charge'.

His friend Eberhard Bethge, once minister in the post-war years of the Bonhoeffer Memorial Church in Sydenham, suggested again that he might consider being minister there but he rejected that idea – understandably so, for the memories of Dietrich were too poignant. He accepted the 'locum' invitation to the Nicholson Street Church of Scotland church. In retrospect it was a mistake. He needed some kind of position with pastoral and preaching duties but he was unhappy in this one. He did not find the warmth he had known in Methodism. He found the worship 'barren' and discovered he was minister of a church preoccupied with raising money.

This depressed his spirits and at times he wondered if he had done the right thing when he entered the ministry. He thought perhaps his father was right. He should have listened and become a professional musician. He missed the beloved hymns of Charles Wesley. The few used in the Church of Scotland often had an altered text. His feelings of dissatisfaction made it difficult to pray extempore. He did his best.

His situation was not helped when Nancy had to go into hospital for a hysterectomy and he had to take up the additional duties of cooking and looking after the house. In May 1969 he decided it would be best if he and the Nicholson Street church parted company. (Not long afterwards it was joined with another church). Fortunately, he was then invited to be a 'locum' at Slateford-Longstone Church of Scotland. Then began a happy relationship which lasted until he died. It was a complete contrast to the previous church. The congregation was open-minded and willing to listen to his suggestions. The one area where his success was limited was the choir – but choirs often have a special character of their own and sometimes find changes difficult to accept. Nancy, now recovered in health, was working part-time as a social worker for two hospitals. She realized the need for a chaplain to the geriatric hospitals and wards. Generally the pastoral care of patients was in the hands of ministers who were also very busy in their parishes. Some of them had spoken to her over the years and confessed that they could not do the task as they would have wished because their parish work was so demanding.

In addition, there were special needs involving the elderly and the disabled. They needed more care than could be given by a busy pastor dropping in with a cheery word and quick greeting. Some patients had no regular visitors. Some had no family visitors at all and felt there was no place in life for them any more. They felt they were just waiting to be taken by death. Then they would no longer be 'in the way'. Such persons needed special spiritual care. Investigations discovered that at that time there were 936 people in various hospitals who had such needs and the problem was growing.

Nancy sounded out some of the officials in the hospitals she knew and found that opinion was divided. Opinion was also divided amongst the ministers. One minister who visited 240 patients in one hospital on Friday afternoons saw no need. He said that, though there were five geriatric units in Edinburgh, a full-time chaplain for them would be encroaching on his duties. Others were very much in favour of such a chaplain.

Soundings were made and a Nuffield grant from the National Corporation for the Care of Old People in London was being favourably negotiated for a three year experimental period, the chaplaincy to be ecumenical and rotating round the churches. The Edinburgh Chaplains' Committee were opposed to the idea. A letter was received from London containing this sentence: 'I understand that there can be differences of opinion over such a proposal but I wonder whether we could all put our hands on our hearts and say that the spiritual needs of old people in hospital are fully cared for'. Franz Hildebrandt's friend, the Revd Professor James Stewart, was keen on the idea as were many others including the Revd Professor Hugh Anderson of New College and the Revd Dr Lewis Cameron. Dr Cameron did write that without unanimity from the church no scheme would succeed – and here it fell down.

On 21 July 1970 *The Scotsman* carried the headline 'No geriatric chaplain for the Kirk' and Tam Dalyall, the MP for West Lothian took up the fact that these folk had no visitors; but the idea was effectively defeated by ordinary parish ministers. Doubtless some saw Franz, who did much of the preparatory work to set it up, as a rival for the position. One actually spoke about 'a minister outside the Church of Scotland trying to manipulate things'. In fact the idea had first been put forward while Franz was teaching in the United States and was therefore in no position to be involved. During these years and even later Nancy fought battles over the care of the patients. It was the first time since her marriage to Franz that she was living and working in the world outside the church. Also with a home to keep and a family living in Edinburgh the extra money from her part-time employment was very helpful. Franz's 'locum' appointment at Slateford-Longstone church gave him a working centre three miles west from where they lived. Nancy's hospitals were three miles east and as the bus service was not very convenient they decided that a second car was necessary. This meant extra expense. They also employed someone to give help in the house. Their income was just adequate, the net gain being small, but both were happy.

However, over the preceding few years Franz had been under great strain: his arguments and – as he put it – defence of the faith in the Anglican–Methodist Conversations, the crisis at Drew which to him was essentially a matter of Christian ethics and his resignation from the ministry of the Methodist Church. In a deeper sense he had broken his links with the heritage of the Wesleys, the church which had given him a welcoming 'home' after Germany. These struggles had sapped his energies. They had involved major decisions. He was spiritually and physically exhausted and his health was failing.

He consulted his doctor who sent him to the Northern General Hospital for tests. This was to take a whole day; however, a telephone call came to Nancy during the day to tell her that while in hospital Franz had suffered a stroke and was probably dying. He was unconscious. Nancy rushed to him. He was restless all night and did not respond to her voice. The next day in the afternoon she tried to use the German which he had taught her and she noted a flicker of response. She telephoned Pastor Schwesig of the German-speaking congregation in Edinburgh (Franz had always kept a link with them and preached for them from time to time). He came immediately, read from the Bible in German and said the *Vater Unser* (Lord's Prayer) in German. Franz responded with 'Amen'. The next day he sat up in his bed and demanded to know what had happened to his last three days!

The stroke might have been caused because of a lapse on the part of the hospital staff. He had been given an angiogram without asking for his consent. He had not been told that he must not sit up immediately afterwards. He sat up and collapsed. Nancy was angered that they had not been consulted. She would have asked for a second opinion. Their own doctor asked them if they wished to sue for damages but Nancy felt it was against Franz's Christian belief and practice. Instead she did have what she described as 'a straight talk' with the neurologist. The hospital also discovered at this time that Franz needed a prostatectomy. In the following weeks his blood pressure stayed 'obstinately high'. Nancy tried to foresee and avoid situations which would cause extra strain and stress for him. From that time they counted each day as a special gift from God.

The minister of the Fairmilehead church found that he just could not do all the work of his parish and care for the folk at the Marie Curie Nursing Home; he asked Franz if he could possibly take on the chaplaincy there. Now Franz entered a new world. He discovered that terminal illness did not necessarily make the patient interested in spiritual matters. On the other hand he never found a patient whose Christian faith had been diminished by the cancer. He used to talk to Nancy about the great need for counselling both before and after bereavement. He discovered a number of tragic cases. On the lighter side, he found that his lack of knowledge of football and especially of football pools and the way they worked was something of a handicap when talking to the men.

Both Franz and Nancy had been supporting the movement for establishing a hospice in Edinburgh ever since it had been first mooted. Now they could pinpoint specific services which were needed. Meanwhile, as soon as he was fit, Franz had returned to the Slateford-Longstone work knowing that the congregation was looking for a permanent minister. After the usual deliberations the Revd Roy Manson was invited to be Parish Minister.

Nancy and Franz went to the induction service and to the reception afterwards. Franz in his natural way wanted to slip away quietly. He had done the job of 'locum' and the new minister had arrived ... but let Roy Manson tell the story himself:

In May 1968, with my wife Noreen and our four Primary School children I had come back from India where I was a Presbyter of the Church of South India in the Diocese of Madras. After some preliminary employments and looking around for a change I was duly called to be minister of Slateford-Longstone Church (originally two villages, Slateford and Longstone on the western outskirts of Edinburgh now swallowed by new housing and becoming part of the commuter city). I was inducted into the Church by the Presbytery of Edinburgh in January 1970 and there was a 'welcome' social.

At this social, quite well on in the evening, a distinguished minister came across to the newly inducted minister. I must have been introduced to him briefly before because I seemed to know that he had been the locum. 'I guess this is where I bow out' he said. 'Why?' I replied in a tone that I suppose implied that I could see no reason why he should do so.

He turned on his heel and walked away. And that was it. We never sat down and worked out any division of labour or plan of action or what we should do. He and his wife, Nancy, just kept coming to church every Sunday morning for the next 16 years. I somehow got into the habit of going across to see Franz every Monday morning or otherwise telephoning him to talk over plans for pastoral work and he covered some and I covered some. Franz built up his own pastoral lists and you can imagine what an enriching of that congregation's life it was to have so senior and so wise a pastor sharing in its life. Franz was incredibly thorough in everything he did. He never forgot an anniversary. Birthdays, weddings, bereavements – all were marked and remembered.

In the meantime some of Franz's friends in Germany had taken up his cause. Although he was not eligible for state compensation, the church in Germany decided that as his career had been cut off at its beginning he was eligible for church compensation. This was paid to him until his death. It made life much easier for the family and meant that he no longer had to look around for 'locum' appointments. He was indeed free to accept Roy Manson's invitation to continue as his colleague. Due to this fortuitous circumstance, he entered a period of his life which was tremendously happy. He was working with a capable, warm-hearted colleague. They had great respect for each other. At this time Ruth completed her degree at St Andrews University. She decided to take a post graduate course in London to train as an archivist. She managed to find a place to stay in a hostel for overseas students.

Franz's links with the German Congregation in Edinburgh meant that when Pastor Schwesig was moved back to Germany to join the staff of the Cathedral at Ulm he hoped Franz would succeed him. Franz, who met and knew the congregation did not feel it was right for him. Indeed he wondered if his record in the Confessing Church and his outspokenness in the Church struggle had disturbed some members whose parents perhaps had been acquiescent towards the Nazis. The Edinburgh congregation was small and was linked with a German congregation in Aberdeen which Franz also visited. He was happy with them but was not persuaded that this was the way for him to go.

He continued to receive invitations to preach and lecture. Very often on the anniversary of Dietrich Bonhoeffer's death he would be invited to share in a special service. He took part, along with Bishop George Bell, in the dedication of the Dietrich Bonhoeffer Memorial Church in Sydenham, London. One of his invitations was to Dublin and he took Nancy with him. Her impressions, she remembers, were of Roman Catholic churches well attended. This was not true for the Church of Ireland. She also remembered the problem of ageing priests who had no official retirement age and consequently they stayed on and on and on ...

When Roy Manson and Noreen went back to India for a three month visit in 1980, as well as at other times when they were away on vacation, Roy was quite happy to hand over the pastoral and preaching care of the church to Franz. The congregation was also happy with this arrangement. When Roy was appointed a chaplain to Edinburgh Prison he had to take his turn in conducting worship. Franz therefore had a fairly regular opportunity to preach in Slateford-Longstone. It was then, Roy confesses, that he learned that preaching was Franz's life-blood and that the congregation really appreciated his sermons. Occasionally Roy would ask Franz to stand in for him at the prison. Franz was pleased to have the opportunity of taking the Gospel to prisoners and much enjoyed telling them that the person in the pulpit preaching to them had himself done time in prison! Doubtless he told them why.

One day while Roy and Franz were discussing the work of the church the suggestion arose that they might preach through the Letters of Paul to the Thessalonians. This proposal stemmed from the fact that many in the congregation were apathetic about Bible study. They worked through several New Testament books in this way as well as holding two Bible study groups.

Later Roy Manson said that his greatest sorrow was that he did not 'more consciously appreciate the great privilege we had in having Franz Hildebrandt with us'. Franz was invited to serve on the Kirk Session and gave it one try. Thereafter he declined to attend. Throughout this period of his life he was invited to preach on various special occasions. Pastor Schwesig who had been his friend in Edinburgh and was now on the staff of the Cathedral in Ulm, invited him to preach in Ulm in 1974. It was the 40th anniversary of the declaration of 1934 at which Franz was present, to which he had been a signatory. That gave him great satisfaction. Holy Week special services were an area where his biblical preaching had a ready acceptance and he was invited across the denominations to conduct these. In Rosyth in 1976 he preached every evening in a Holy Week series where the united congregations included Roman Catholics too. This stayed in his memory because he had to cross the Forth Road Bridge and its height always bothered him so much that he had to close his eyes when crossing. Fortunately Nancy was available to drive – and did. In Holy Week 1977 there was another 'united series' of services at Hope Congregational church where other congregations within the district joined together. He was always pleased when congregations were united to hear the Gospel.

A special occasion for the Hildebrandts occurred on 23 April 1978 when their friend Ella Wardrop was commissioned as a Methodist Local Preacher. This was at Nicholson Square, the church where, when she was young, Franz Hildebrandt had been her minister. She asked the then resident minister if Franz could preach the sermon at the special service since he had instructed her in the faith and she wished to express her deep gratitude to him. To this he readily agreed. Fortunately among his papers is a copy of the short sermon he gave on this occasion (see Appendix 3). His text was Ps. 71.16: 'I will go in the strength of the Lord: I will make mention of thy righteousness, even thine only.'

His yearning for spiritual food and his sadness that both Methodism and the Church of Scotland had lost their high standard of preaching pours out in his opening sentences. He expounds the need for good and faithful preachers who know Christ. He concludes with the collect for St George's day, which he had some difficulty locating, not so surprizing when one considers that St George is the patron saint of England and he was preaching in Edinburgh, the capital of Scotland. He had at the back of his mind the memory of a lovely collect for that day and he was determined to find it.

So he began to hunt. New College Library and the Episcopal College yielded nothing but in his German encyclopaedia he discovered a reference to the fact that John Wordsworth, a century before, had written some prayers for the dedication of St George's Chapel in Jerusalem. He went to the National Library and was confused by the microfilm unit. His search was made more difficult because of the material linked with the poet, William Wordsworth, and his sister Dorothy. However after searching through the index he discovered two prayers by John Wordsworth. One of these was the one he wanted. He sent a copy to the Episcopal College. Ella Wardrop was thrilled that the preacher who had helped her so much had given such a challenging address.

Franz always felt that pastors did not take time to prepare adequately for their preaching. When he could and when his retired friend was preaching he would go to hear the Revd Professor James S Stewart who was living in Edinburgh and was probably the finest preacher of his day. James Stewart, he knew, would present the faith clearly and expound the Bible faithfully. Franz's great worry was that exposition of the Word of God was lacking in preaching. His own experience had been that the Word always matched the situation. Anyone who endeavoured to preach by expounding the scripture received encouragement from him. He had also developed a link with the Thistle Foundation which cared for the disabled and their families. Here he regularly conducted worship and services of Holy Communion which gave him satisfaction.

In May 1977 Nancy and Franz visited the General Assembly of the Church of Scotland to give support to Roy Manson who was pleading for the male diaconate. On their return journey they had a long discussion about the merits of an established church. Nancy's whole background had been in the Presbyterian Church of England which was Nonconformist. The church in Germany in Franz's youth would come under the heading of 'established' since it was linked to the state. They discussed Hitler's surprise that this apparently 'dead' established church in Germany could produce such resistance. Franz ventured the belief that those who were spiritually alive would always be so and would always be ready to act, established or nonconformist The implication of this thought is clear.

Nancy and Franz tried to take a regular vacation. One year they visited Norway on a cruise and in Bergen they met a former student from Drew who took them to his home. Not many of their fellow-passengers had the good fortune to be invited into a Norwegian family home. On another vacation in Galloway they were joined by former colleagues from Drew, Dr B. W. 'Barney' Anderson and his wife, Joyce. Barney explored the 'standing stones' and their meaning while for Joyce there was the fascination of coming to an understanding of the words 'o'er moor and fen'. She had sung the words of John Henry Newman so often.*

Another place where they vacationed was Bamburgh, a town very near to Holy Island or Lindesfarne where St Cuthbert had spent time. One tiny island, known as St Cuthbert's Island, is where his monk's cell was located. It was while on this vacation that he put down on paper many of his reminiscences about Dietrich Bonhoeffer. He wrote several letters containing them to Marianne Leibholtz, the daughter of Dietrich's twin sister Sabine. She persuaded her 'Onkel Franz' to record, in letters to her, experiences about which normally he would not speak. But he could not refuse an 'adoptive niece' whom he loved.

While in Bamburgh one Sunday they drove to Seahouses and as it was time for morning worship they decided they would attend church there. They noted three churches. The Anglican, they discovered, used the Alternative Service Book and for Franz, who loved Cranmer's *Book of Common Prayer*, that was 'out'. Then he persuaded Nancy to peep inside the Methodist church to see what hymns were denoted on the hymn board. There was not a Charles Wesley hymn amongst them so they went to worship in the United Reformed Church. His argument was that he didn't expect Wesley to loom large there but a Methodist Church service without a Charles Wesley hymn meant he was deprived of *expected* sustenance.

On another vacation in Galloway they had come across 'Preaching stones' and were full of admiration for the Covenanters, earlier nonconformists, people after Franz's own heart. They enjoyed learning about these lively Christians from Elizabeth Whitley who was an authority on their beliefs and ways.

As time passed Nancy found it more and more difficult to persuade Franz to take a vacation. The house in Edinburgh had an

*The hymn is *Lead Kindly Light*.

extension and he was always comfortable with the cats and used to quote (according to him) a Boston lady: 'Travel? Why should I travel? I am already here!'

In 1980 an invitation came from the pastor of Morrow Memorial United Methodist Church in Maplewood, New Jersey, to serve as Theologian-in-Residence during Holy Week of 1981. The assignment would have called for preaching and leading groups on different aspects of the Wesleyan heritage. He wrote, '... there is the nagging doubt that I am simply not up to major adventures such as the transatlantic journey and the Holy Week with you. I know that you will believe me that there is nobody in the USA whose company we relish more than that of the two of you; but the physical limitations are just too evident ...'

During this period David, their son, gained his nursing qualification and eventually found an appointment in Edinburgh. He loves music, particularly the organ which he plays regularly He also loves trains. He enjoys a vacation with a rail 'runabout' ticket so that he can travel where he will. Gradually he turned the basement of their home into an extensive model railway layout. His parents were happy to have him near. Ruth worked on her Ph.D. thesis and obtained her degree. She also did a research task and then taught history at Heriot-Watt University. At Nicholson Square Methodist church she met James Grayson, an American Methodist minister who was in Edinburgh working on his own Ph.D. They became engaged. James was the son of the organist at the Madison Methodist Church in New Jersey. After completing his degree he went to teach in Korea.

In July 1980 they were married in Nicholson Square and Franz shared in the service at the invitation of the local minister. James' father played the organ for the service. Ruth then joined her husband in Korea and while there they adopted two Korean boys, Andrew and Christopher. Esther also gained her initial degree and subsequently became a teacher. She earned a Ph.D from Durham University and eventually went out under the auspices of the Methodist Church to teach in Rarongo, Papua New Guinea. Esther, while at Durham, stayed at the home of Kingsley and Margaret Barrett. Kingsley and Franz, on the same side in the 'Conversations' debate, had a mutual respect and deep friendship. With their wives they met regularly – at least once a year – and in his last days the Barretts visited Franz in Edinburgh.

Franz was secretly amused that his two daughters were missionaries. The Lutheran Church in Germany in which he grew up was not a keen missionary church. Their missionaries tended to be pietistic and fundamentalist. Nancy, however, had herself intended to serve overseas until she met and married Franz. Her sister, Margaret, worked for a period in China. In 1982 Nancy visited Ruth in Korea and saw something of the Christian church there. Franz stayed in Edinburgh.

While training at Selly Oak, the Missionary Training college for Methodism, Esther met the Revd Chris Shreeve who was due to go to Sierra Leone. The romance blossomed, developing in spite of the fact that they were going to destinations so far apart, where the postal services were erratic. Franz was very pleased that the Commissioning Service for Esther in June 1984 was conducted by his friend, the retiring President of the Methodist Conference.* In 1981 Franz took a train to Kings Cross station, London. He had always rather enjoyed the journey from Edinburgh to London. It gave him time to think and read. This time his old friend Julius Rieger was passing through accompanied by his daughter. Rieger was now blind and frail. They lunched together at the railway station and then straight way Franz returned home, glad to have made the effort.

In December 1981 Franz travelled to Cambridge for a celebration of the German congregation formally established in 1941. Unfortunately his train was delayed and a connecting train did not wait. Feverish telephone calls between Cambridge, Edinburgh, Doncaster (where he picked up the train after visiting Esther in Lincolnshire) and Peterborough meant that the Station Master secured a taxi and he arrived just in time to preach the sermon. This was his last long journey by himself. He found that he was losing his sense of balance on steps. Escalators became a problem. When, a little later, he wanted to visit his friend Werner Simonson in London who was some years older, Esther accompanied him.

---

*In our occasional correspondence during my busy Presidential year Franz had not mentioned that Esther was offering to serve overseas. When, before the Commissioning Service, I was introduced to the group of missionaries to be commissioned (I had already seen the names) I looked at Esther and said, 'Is it? ...' She replied with a lovely smile, 'Yes it is. Daddy is not well. He sends his love and he said to me, 'If Amos is doing it, it will be properly done!' I hope it was. (ASC)

He continued to work with Roy Manson and was very happy. Roy had introduced some 'healing' services. Franz was never at ease with 'the laying on of hands'. He was not sure that the 'apostolic power' was intended to be inherited by the succeeding Christian church, but he supported Roy and attended, playing the piano for the hymns. Many testified to the fact that his pastoral visits gave them strength. Before he left after a visit he would always say a prayer and shake hands. The Revd Dr Henry Sefton pays a heartfelt tribute to Franz's pastoral care at a time when his wife was terminally ill. 'Franz seemed to know just when to drop in and how long to stay. Sometimes it was a very short visit, sometimes longer especially when we celebrated the Sacrament.' In this way he took Christ's 'healing' to the people.

The senior staff changed at the Nursing Home where he was a chaplain. With this change came what he sensed as a change of atmosphere and with his own ageing, he felt it time to lay down his task. He was not strong. He gained comfort from the word *VIVIT* – 'He lives' – which Luther had written in chalk on his desk when he was low in spirits.

On New Years Day 1984 his dear friend Julius Rieger died in Berlin. The one who had given him refuge when his exile began, who had baptized both David and Ruth, had departed this life. Then in March 1984 his battle companion Martin Niemoeller died. In 1983 on the 50th anniversary of Franz's ordination, Roy Manson had arranged for Martin Niemoeller to make a greetings call. Later in the year, in October, Franz spoke to him again and noted that Niemoeller's voice was weak and understood he could neither stand nor walk anymore. Martin had visited them in 1978. He, who had been a close friend and fellow soldier in Christ for nearly fifty years, at last suggested that they should use the intimate German form of address 'du' instead of the more formal 'Sie'. Franz, ever courteous, always held that the suggestion must come from the senior of the two – so he had waited.

Early in 1984 Franz received 'out of the blue' an invitation to Seattle in the USA to give a lecture on the Barmen Declaration in celebration of the 50th anniversary of its signing. Franz was hesitant about accepting. He had noticed some slight hesitation in his speech and he also knew he was deaf in one ear and his eyesight was deteriorating. Indeed he had wondered if he should cease preaching. Nancy had persuaded him that when the time came for him to give up, God would make it plain. However when he heard of the death of Martin Niemoeller he realized that there were fewer and fewer of the Confessing Church warriors left. Indeed he said that, as far as he could ascertain, there were only two, of whom he was one, who had been involved in the discussions at Barmen. There was an extra magnet to draw him. It was possible that Ruth and James could come across from Korea and meet both Nancy and Franz as well as James's parents. So he agreed. He would give the lecture: 'Barmen: what to learn and what not to learn'.

Amongst others who were to give lectures were Heinrich Vogel who with Franz had taught in an 'underground' college run by the Confessing Church, Eberhard Bethge, Wolf-Dieter Zimmerman, and Paul Lehmann, Dietrich's great friends. The lectures given were later published in the *Toronto Studies in Theology*, Volume 26. It is a book which demands serious attention. At this time Franz was not well himself. Everyone was anxious and he was persuaded to travel in a wheelchair. Seats were booked 'Executive class'. Dr Herbert Locke, the Director and Senior Fellow of the William O. Douglas Institute in Seattle, who had arranged the Symposium, realized that he had invited three elderly men, none of whom was robust, to travel over 6,000 miles to the meeting to deliver lectures. He went out of his way to help. This help included bringing Ruth and James to the airport to meet them when they landed.

The Symposium went well. The lectures are fascinating. Franz concluded his in a way he would never have done in 1934, by quoting two verses of Charles Wesley. In his address he had already twice quoted John Wesley. We also see the principles on which his life and thought had been based. It is full of relevant study and experience. He spoke of the challenge to Hitler from Barmen. Then he centred on Jesus Christ revealed in the Word. Churches must return to preaching the Word of God 'the Word, the whole Word and nothing but the Word'; of the need for ecumenism to recognize the forces of Antichrist and make a clear break with them; of the priority of faith and doctrine over church order: 'there is no room for hierarchy in the church of Christ'. He challenged the Anglican communion to allow others (Lutherans, Methodists, etc.) to perform the act of consecration of the elements even when their bishops (or archbishops) are present.

He spoke of the need for a witness for peace, of the fact that the church is in the world but does not 'belong' to it. Nevertheless she has the duty to call the world 'unto God's marvellous light'. It is a carefully, logically argued statement of the faith encapsulated in the Barmen Declaration and is a worthy memorial of one who all his life had been Mr Valiant-for-Truth.

After saying 'goodbye' to Ruth and James, Nancy and Franz went to the plane for their return journey to find it had been over-booked – so, wheelchair and all, they were put into the First Class section and travelled in comfort. He continued to work with Roy Manson as he could.

1983–4 saw the publication of the 1780 Wesley's Hymns, with Biblical references, edited by Franz Hildebrandt, Oliver Beckerlegge and James Dale in the series of Wesley's Works. It contains as an Introduction, various essays, the first being one by Franz Hildebrandt on the theology of the Hymn Book. In the minds of many it should be reprinted as a separate booklet to be more readily available.* His love for the theology of the Wesleys shines through the book and, although the notes are not credited to particular people, some recognize Franz Hildebrandt's voice in certain expositions which previously had been used as outlines for his sermons.

Christmas 1984 was quiet. Esther on her way to New Guinea had gone to Seoul in South Korea to spend Christmas with Ruth and James. Only David was in Edinburgh. They attended church on Christmas Day and later entertained some friends but Franz caught a chill and was in bed for almost two weeks. In February he was better and enjoyed a walk in the Pentland Hills. Then they took a vacation in the spring at Seahouses in Northumberland and visited Holy Island again, though Franz had to take a rest everyday.

He recognized his health limitations. In April 1985, he was invited to Exeter to address a two day meeting of the Methodist District Synod. He telephoned his immediate enthusiastic agreement, then later that day made another telephone call: 'I've been for a short walk and now feel so weak. Please forgive me. I must say 'No' – and I'd already chosen a text for my sermon!'

During the summer Nancy and Franz discussed and spent time

---

*A précis is appended in Appendix 4.

preparing for the marriage of Chris and Esther. Summer 1986 seemed to be the best date. However in Autumn 1985 Franz had a severe stroke. Esther, who often argued profoundly with her father but loved him dearly, came home on extended leave. Ruth came for three weeks leaving behind in Korea a six-month-old baby.

Franz battled on. Friends sent good wishes and lifted up him and his family in prayer. Chris came home on furlough. Roy and Chris gave him regular communion. Roy says that he realized that Franz was no longer going to be able to play such an active part in the work and so he felt the time had come for him to move too. Chris had to return to Sierra Leone. He and Esther hoped that Franz would recover enough to share in their wedding service even if from a wheelchair. While they were together they had visited the circuit in Hawes, Yorkshire, and Franz was happy to know that after their marriage they would be settled in the United Kingdom. He had been due to preach on the Sunday after his stroke. He had chosen the text from Ps. 119.11: 'Uphold me according to Thy promise that I may live and let me not be put to shame in my hope.' He always asked for the Psalm and the collect for the day to be read to him. With *The Book of Common Prayer* he held also the King James Bible and Wesleys Hymns with him at his bedside. He was moved from the Royal Hospital to the Rehabilitation Hospital and with Roy the family planned an Advent service to be held at his bedside conducted by Roy with two of Wesley's Advent hymns.

But he fell victim to a chest infection. Nancy writes: 'We knew that he was dying. Esther and I stayed beside him, sometimes together, sometimes separately. I was alone with him in the early afternoon of Monday, 25 November. He had been watching me as I sat there. Then I saw he was looking away from me. I know that to some people at the moment of death a vision is given. I don't know whether many wives are given the privilege of sharing that vision. I was. I could see it in his eyes and spoke it out loud: "Darling, you can see Jesus on His throne: He is coming towards you now – and it will be advent for you for ever and ever." I didn't realise then, until 26 December that we had shared the vision of Stephen.'

Roy Manson earlier that day had visited Franz. He writes thus: 'I left his bedside where Nancy was keeping watch over a Franz who was terminally ill. I was interviewed and appointed for the post of Assistant Chaplain to the Royal Edinburgh Hospital that same afternoon. Immediately I returned to the hospital to find Nancy and Esther just coming out ... Franz had slipped away. Our part in the ministry of Slateford-Longstone had come to its appointed end. It was the end of a time when he had served as he believed a pastor should. While always ready for consultation on academic subjects, he had been caring for the souls and bodies of the family of Jesus.'

For him there was no greater task.

The funeral service was held privately at the crematorium on 28 November. It was conducted by his friend and colleague Roy Manson, all as he wished. On 4 January 1986 a Service of Thanksgiving was held in Slateford-Longstone Parish Church. The order of service had been drawn up by Nancy and Franz together. According to his wishes there was to be no eulogy. Four of the six hymns were by Charles Wesley, one by George Herbert and the last a Scottish paraphrase of 1 Pet. 1.3–4, a classic selection. Prayers and scripture lessons were read by those who were friends, colleagues and students during the various periods of his life : Roy Manson, his partner in ministry during his last years; Eberhard Bethge, representing the Evangelical Church in Germany and the Evangelical Church in Berlin-Brandenburg; C. Kingsley Barrett representing the Methodist Church in the United Kingdom and Maxwell Tow representing Drew and the United Methodist Church in the USA. The final hymn of the service ended with this verse:

> Saints by the power of God are kept
> Till the salvation come
> We walk by faith as strangers here
> But Christ shall call us home

Franz's wishes were not followed entirely. At the conclusion of the service the congregation gathered in the Church Hall for tea and one after another rose to speak of their love and appreciation for this great and humble saint.

CHAPTER 19

MR VALIANT-FOR-TRUTH

The twentieth-century was among the most violent known to the human race. Many millions lost their lives. Many more bore the 'marks and scars' of the century's conflicts. Many succumbed to guilt, despair, bitterness and grief stemming from the human predeliction to destroy or enslave its perceived enemies. Franz Hildebrandt's life spanned nearly all that century. He did not escape injury although his wounds were more spiritual than physical.

During World War I he saw his father's health destroyed by the foolishness of the military system. Young Franz could well have become a part of the 'lost generation' that came to maturity after the Great War. He might also have embraced Communism which would have appealed to his idealism and concern for the poor and others unjustly treated. He could have become a nihilist, drifting into a life of cynicism and self-indulgence like so many of his contemporaries. He was not captivated by any secular ideology. It was on the pilgrim path to the heart of the Christian gospel that he received his marks and scars. He bore them with dignity and courage. He used his considerable gifts to urge others into the way of Christ.

The depth and breadth of his scholarship is undoubted. In what is probably his best book, *From Luther to Wesley*, Franz Hildebrandt shows that Wesley is the logical successor to Luther. His approach is to delineate the various subjects from the 'righteousness of faith' to the 'nature of Lutheranism' and in twelve chapters to show the links in thought. Then follow two critical sections, 'the Revival of the Reformation' and the 'Reformation of the Revival,' each divided into three parts. He then concludes with a brief chapter called 'Harmony' which is a commentary on the theology, the verse and music of hymns. For many Christians, hymns are viewed as being something peripheral to worship, the icing on the cake. We cannot understand Franz Hildebrandt unless we understand that the hymns are at the heart of the faith-poetry and music combined – inviting us to meet God.

He agrees completely with John Wesley in the area of hymnology. He knows what tunes he likes. He is sharply critical of the hymns of the Victorian Age. Only the very best are good enough for the worship of God. Sometimes one feels he forgets that when Wesley sings, 'I hold thee with a trembling hand,' he may well be describing the faith of those who sing the Victorian verses of 'Sankey-Moody-Bliss.' Not everyone can readily sing the Luther–Gerhardt–Bach hymns.

His knowledge of the Bible was awesome, but he never allowed higher criticism on one hand or fundamentalism on the other, to cloud what for him was the essential word of truth. When he discerned the truth of a passage, he clung to it tenaciously regardless of what others thought. Sometimes Franz had difficulty in discussion because his mind leapt ahead and it was easy for him to leave his listener behind. He tried to guard against this tendency, for he had genuine consideration for his listeners.

His systematic way of thinking made him a capable organizer as well. When he was given a task that needed doing, whether it was treasurer of the Pastors' Emergency League, Camp Leader of the German internees in Britain or organizing the Wesley Societies on American campuses, he moved to accomplish the work with skill and efficiency. He had little patience with bureaucracies and committees.

Franz Hildebrandt's disciplined and extraordinary mind was balanced with warm human qualities that included compassion, camaraderie and openness to friendship. His innate shyness led some to think he was haughty and aloof, but those who allowed themselves to get to know him found him a winsome companion. He had a rich sense of humour that included a standard repertoire of anecdotes as well as the ability to recognize the amusing incongruities of the actions of persons around him, especially of those in authority. He viewed the world with an eye focused on the folly and pretence of all human activity, knowing that, ultimately, it was all subject to the judgement and grace of God.

Mahlon 'Skip' Smith, writes about his experience while a student at Drew:

> I found him to be the greatest inspiration to me. I took every course he gave and still have volumes of notes on Wesley and Luther. I acted as a faithful scribe seeking to preserve every gem that fell from the lips of my teacher. During 1963–64 when Nancy was with the children in the UK 'Papa Franz' was senior member of the Davis House community that included me, John Peterson, Luther Sturdivant and Rich Matthews. We all have many warm and sometimes humourous memories of this very earthly saint.

His incisive criticism of the institutional aspects of the churches rang true. Not even the Confessing Church during the days he was at the centre of its life escaped his lucid, critical insights. His ecumenism was practical, but also theologically grounded. He had no patience with the shallow 'togetherness' espoused by some church leaders. All doctrine and schemes of church order were subject to the correction and guidance of the Word of God in scripture, and what could not be shown as true must be rejected. It is a telling irony that at the end of his life, this lover of the Church was not listed on the ministerial role of any of the denominations he had served so well.

Yet he embraced individual Christians who sought to follow Jesus regardless of denomination. The road to the Kingdom was one on which all Christians could walk together – and that included his family. He also rejoiced in the many friends – in Germany, England, the United States and Scotland – who walked with him in the pilgrim way. His joy was tempered by the fact that so many of his friends preceded him in death. One wonders if he ever recovered fully from his grief over the death of Dietrich Bonhoeffer. Why was it that Dietrich had died and his own life been spared? Should he not have died with him?

He survived. And it was his task to bear witness to the Gospel in which he believed. This required courage. If courage is the ability to face adversaries without fear of personal consequences, Franz had it in abundance. Perhaps it was the monstrous character of Nazi evil that brought out the best qualities of Franz and his Confessing Church comrades. In any event, that same courage was evident in the later Anglican-Methodist union controversy and in his response to the crisis at Drew. In each of these situations his courage was forged from his opposition to what he believed was the misuse of power by authorities who would take the course of expediency against what Franz Hildebrandt believed to be just and true.

This is not to say that Franz was without fears and doubts as he faced these issues. Indeed, shortly before his death in a telephone conversation with a friend he said, 'I sometimes wonder what I have done . . .' and was surprised and heartened to have been told, 'You have opened up the faith to me and to many through Wesley's hymns.'

In the end he relied on faith to sustain him. His was not a facile, sentimental wishfulness, but rather an objective, reasonable, supportive faith, grounded in the word of God. It was a faith sustained by worship, prayer and love for his brothers and sisters in Christ. The Lord of history, whose will can be known, brings about His purposes through the obedience of His servants. Obedience calls for courage. In a letter to Nancy, written at the height of the crisis at Drew, he wrote that he felt 'upheld'. This was not a word he used lightly. It echoed the confidence of the Psalmist. It signified that God could be trusted in the most difficult circumstances. Therein lay the source of his courage. He was Mr Valiant-for-Truth.

> Ready for all Thy perfect will
> My acts of faith and love repeat
> Till death Thy endless mercies seal
> And make the sacrifice complete.
> – Charles Wesley

APPENDIX 1

ONLY BELIEVE – AND YOU'RE THERE

an attempt at a Lutheran Catechism
by Dietrich Bonhoeffer and Franz Hildebrandt,

translated by William Benson and Amos Cresswell.

Foreword

This Catechism is intended for Confirmation candidates but not only for them. It meets their needs as it seeks to formulate what the Lutheran faith says today. Questions and answers are aimed at careful, focused reading. Amplifications and clarifications are left for the one conducting the class.

What is the Gospel?

The message of God's salvation which is revealed in Jesus Christ and is transmitted to us through His Spirit. The message of the Kingdom of God which is challenged in the world and is intended for those whom He has justified. The message of the purposes of God who is speaking today and deciding over life and death.

Who is evangelical?

He who rejoices in the grace of God, confesses the name of Christ and asks for the Holy Spirit. He who is ready for the rule of God, is not afraid of the power of others and is sure of the final end of all things. He who hears God speaking through the preaching of the Word, who loves God's church and lives by God's forgiveness.

'The fact that God has given Himself completely to us with everything He is and has' (Luther), the Evangelical creed confesses in these words:

I believe in God, that He is my Creator, in Jesus Christ, that He is my Lord, in the Holy Spirit that He is my Sanctifier. God has created me and has given me life, soul, body and all things. Christ has brought me into His Lordship through His body and the Holy Spirit sanctifies me through His Word and the Sacraments which are in the church and He will make us fully perfect on the Last Day. 'The Christian faith is this: to know what you should do and what is given to you' (Luther W.A. 30.1.94).

ABOUT THE TRUE GOD

How do I know about God?

From your Baptism, for, before you even asked, God spoke to you. From your Church, for when you searched for God, you already belonged to the Church. From your Bible, for it is from the power of its preaching that your Church lives.

Why then is God here?

He alone is the Lord. He can speak of Himself wherever He wishes. But it is through His compassion that He meets us in earthly form and that we are able to know where He is to be found. That is His revelation in Christ and His church.

Is that then the only God?

In every other case you are praying to the God of your own wishes. There is only One who Himself comes to you so that you can no more avoid Him. His Word alone calls the whole world into life and also calls you into His own possession.

ABOUT FAITH

How can I be certain of this?

Only through the faith which grasps the joyful message with both hands. No other way is given to us for if we could see God we should be in eternal life. That is why faith dares to trust in God.

Where does proof of that lie?

A god who could be proved by us would be an idol. The Lord, in whom we trust, binds us so firmly to Himself that we are freed from superstition and the desire for miracles. To him to whom God has granted faith, God gives faith whatever happens to him.

Is God really interested in me?

Whoever in his piety thinks that he is so insignificant before God is not thinking in God's terms but in those of mankind. For the glory of God is seen in the fact that He comes down to us in Christ to lift us up to Himself in the Spirit. He is the 'three-in-one' God.

THAT GOD BELONGS TO US AND WE BELONG TO HIM WE DECLARE IN OUR BELIEF IN THE FATHER: I BELIEVE IN GOD AND THAT HE IS MY CREATOR.

May we call God our Father?

It is the only name which can reveal His mystery to us. He cannot forget what He has created. How should we forget that we are His children?

Does not the Creation story contradict science?

To research and to believe are two different kinds of thing. Science has its own rightful claim. Every child knows that the earth was not created in six days; but not every one knows that God created the world through His own Spirit and created mankind in His own image.

Why don't people see that?

It sounds really strange to us. The demons of the world, money, power, sex rob us of God's light so that we must die. God's laws are destroyed. Our lack of faith does that and misuses our freedom against God making us slaves of our own idols.

How can a just God allow so much evil?

The catastrophes of nature and mankind silence our wisdom. Where God's gracious mind is completely hidden from us, our mind cannot comprehend His ways. We do know, however, that to those who love God, all things work together for good.

What, then, am I to do in the world?

That task which your job in life gives you to do. God has called everyone of us in his own time to his own particular task – that is His law. And we must obey Him until He calls us from it.

Is there then nothing wrong in earning a living?

To be sure everyone today who is earning a living is taking his bread from another. Work becomes a curse where our power over things becomes changed to the power of things over us. Whoever knows this will become humbled and request God that He will make him happy again in his work.

How may the Christian have possessions?

I suppose he would be truly happy if he had none. He recognizes the power and deceit of money, but he tries to use it for others. In this way he is to possess all things as though he did not have them.

Is the instinct for self-preservation really sinful?

In it the natural and the unnatural are completely interwoven. As Christians we believe that our body belongs to God. Where the instincts of hunger and sex are torn away from their original purpose, they err blindly.

Are there no rules for our sexual relationships?

Wantonly to destroy health means to harm one's soul and what belongs to God. Marriage is given to us from God as the fulfilment of the union of body and soul. He who is given open eyes to see the wonder of each birth is afraid of violating the life of another and asks God to forgive him wherever he has sinned through pride or weakness.

But must we not destroy life in war?

For that very reason the church knows nothing of a just war. In war the struggle for existence is conducted with inhuman means. The church which prays the Lord's Prayer calls on God only for peace.

Is that not unpatriotic?

God has created from one blood all nations of mankind who live on the whole face of the earth (Acts 17.26). Therefore a nationalistic pride in one's own flesh and blood line is a sin against the Holy Spirit. The blind fervour, which is only self-assertive, itself is controlled within the state. God has so instituted His scheme of things that we as Christians serve the state.

How should a Christian stand politically?

Even if he would prefer to distance himself from the political battle, yet the law of love forces him to be involved even here on behalf of his neighbour. Whether for him the commands of the state may lead him to act against his conscience, his own faith and love must decide. In each decision he experiences the irreconcilable division between the peace of Christ and the hatred of the world.

Have Christians no other solution?

We recognize the error of our thoughts and deeds. That is why the whole world hopes restlessly for the appearance of the Saviour and His righteousness. We ask God not to judge us, but to make us really ready to do His work.

THAT GOD STEPS IN FOR US AND WE FOR HIM WE
DECLARE BY OUR FAITH IN THE SON: I BELIEVE IN JESUS
CHRIST, THAT HE IS MY LORD.

Did Jesus live?

Whoever knows the Bible and the pagan writings about Jesus sees
in its diversity and paradoxes the proof of His life. Not even the
Jews have denied that fact. Texts like: Matt. 11.19, 21.31; Mark
10.18, 15.34; Luke 14.26; and pictures like Matt. 15.21ff; Mark
10.13ff, 14.32ff; Luke 7.36ff; 15.1ff cannot be made up. All
attempts to do away with His church by the disavowal of Jesus
collapse on the experience of His inescapable presence.

How does Jesus of Nazareth help me today?

To know about Jesus is not the same as believing in Him. Mere
intellectual acceptance is certainly dead. Faith does not depend
on the dead letter, but on the living Lord who, beyond any doubt-
ing in the Bible and its stories, stands before us in His
commanding presence.

Why is He then the Lord?

He is the answer to all the questions of mankind. He is the healing
for all the pain of the world. He is the victor over all our sins. In
Him you have God Himself in His power and mankind in all his
weakness.

How can a man be God?

In no other way than that God humbles Himself wonderfully and
shares all things with us. The man Jesus, born of the mother Mary,
through His temptation and suffering even unto death on the
cross is God's miracle and His Word. That He says Himself and
with this authority He acts. 'Thou art to point to this man and say:
'That is God' (Luther).

Why do so few accept this?

Even if He should work miracles today we would remain unconverted. We want a prouder God than One who has become our brother in the manger and on the cross. However, God wraps Himself for our sakes in sin and death so that faith alone may see what to the whole world remains incomprehensible.

Why did Jesus have to go to the cross?

That remains God's secret. We can only say this about it: what happens here is not human heroism. Here God Himself is at work. The Holy One goes into a world estranged from God in order to bring sinners back home. He must suffer both abandonment by God and death just as we do. It is His own sacrifice for us which deals with and overcomes our sins and opens for us the door to the Father's house.

And in that way is evil really removed from the world?

Christ is risen. He has taken power away from the Devil. But no one sees that, and in the world Christ and Antichrist are still fighting. Only to His church does He appear as the conqueror; only to the members of His body does He appear as the head. He shapes the church into His body and in the church He makes manifest His life.

Does the church then do the will of Christ?

The church knows today more than ever how little she obeys the Sermon on the Mount. But the greater the dissension in the world becomes, all the more Christ wants to have proclaimed the peace of God which rules in His kingdom. Still the church stands daily in prayer for the return of her heavenly Lord and He lays His hand on her until He brings her to her fulfilment.

THAT GOD GLORIFIES US AND WE HIM WE DECLARE BY
OUR FAITH IN THE HOLY SPIRIT: I BELIEVE IN THE HOLY
SPIRIT THAT HE IS MY SANCTIFIER.

Who is the Holy Spirit?

No worldly spirit but the Spirit of God and of Christ, who is
present in the church. Without Him we would know nothing of
Christ just as without Christ we would know nothing of God. In
Him the Godhead is brought to perfection on earth for 'if you had
no church then you would not be God' (Luther).

Is God only in the Christian church?

In all peoples at all times the Spirit of hope has spoken. But the
Holy Spirit is the Spirit of fulfilment by which every other spirit
is judged. Where apart from Christ fear or delusion determine the
religion of mankind, the Spirit leads His Christendom to grace
and truth.

Why then are there so many churches?

We ought really to be one church. From our incomprehensible
disunity we press towards a new fellowship of all Christians. To
have it is possible for us men and women in no other way than in
our patient expectation and in the faith which is the hallmark of
His church.

Where is the true church?

It is where the preaching stands and falls with the pure Gospel of
a gracious God against all human self-justification; where the
Sacraments depend on the Word of Christ without magic; where
the fellowship of the Spirit stands in service and not in domination.

Do I need the church?

If you knew what the church is and why she needs you, you
would not ask but you would rejoice. The joyous Gospel would

allow you no rest so long as you can hold on to it. You would seek the fellowship where one person intercedes for another, confesses all things to him and forgives him all things, and where the promise that here 'one may become Christ to the other' (Luther) becomes a reality.

Does one become another creation through the church?

Here God rouses you from sleep to a balanced life, from the narrow to the broad place, from slavery to freedom. Here you surrender yourself every day and become in your discipleship of Christ master of all things. That is the faith and the new life. But as long as the church is in the world, no one can decide whom God has chosen for eternal life.

Who is chosen?

At the beginning and the end of all life stands the mystery of the divine Spirit who pardons and rejects whomever He wills, and silences all questions and claims. At the centre of history stands the cross of Christ who died for all. To Him we fly and pray that He guarantees His mercy until all the world gives glory to God alone.

What do we know about eternal life?

Whether we will or not, as certain as there is a God, our life rests under His judgement and is raised up by His hand. Not flesh and blood, but spirit, soul and body shall rise from the dead. We do not know when the hour will come but the church looks forward with all creation to a new earth and a new heaven.

THAT, THEN, IS THE CHRISTIAN FAITH: TO KNOW WHAT YOU ARE TO DO AND WHAT IS GIVEN TO YOU.

CONFIRMATION

You are to thank God that your church has the Gospel. You shall ask God that your faith stays loyal to Him. You are to give praise to God for the fact that you venture your life on His Word.

COMMUNION

You have the first communion which Christ Himself gives to you. You have the Holy Communion which is the daily bread of the church and comfort in all sorrow. You have the eternal communion in the blessedness of the Kingdom of the Father.

APPENDIX 2

DIETRICH BONHOEFFER

Sermon at the Memorial Service in Holy Trinity Church,
Kingsway, London
27 July 1945

Neither know we what to do; but our eyes are upon Thee.
2 Chron. 20.12

In May 1932, a few months before Hitler came to power, Dietrich Bonhoeffer stood in the pulpit of the *Dreifaltigkeitskirche* in Berlin and preached from this text. He was then chaplain to the students of the *Technische Hochschule*, alongside with his *Privatdozentur* in the University. This text was on his mind a long time before and a long time since; today we may use it as a kind of inscription to the life which we remember. To enter into biographical detail on this occasion would be a disservice to our friend and brother; but let personal recollection serve as illustration of the Word that was the centre of his thought and in whose service he was consumed.

He came from an academic home and seemed destined for the academic life. He was unashamed of the scholars' tradition of his ancestors, the culture of his family; he never shared the theological fashion of contempt for the humanities. He knew his classics in art, music, literature before he criticized; he knew how to read and listen before voicing his opinion. And when he voiced it publically for the first time, in the dissertations on *Sanctorum Communio* and *Act and Being*, he did it with a measure of maturity and a power of concentration which made it almost incredible to think that the author was just 21 or 24 years old. They might well be proud of him in his home in the *Wangenheimstrasse*, proud of him as of his older brothers, one of whom has shared his lot, one was killed young in the First World War, and only one survives, at this moment still ignorant of Dietrich's fate ...

'We know not what to do'. The young theologian faced the problem of Christian life and action. He would not be content with provisional and conventional answers. With socratic thoroughness he would go on questioning where others stopped; and his questioning would be taken up by his students. Soon it became clear that he was a born educator. His confirmation class in North Berlin with whom he lived for three months in closest proximity was the prelude to the plans later realized in the seminary of Finkenwalde. The intervening period could have opened for him a brilliant and secure academic career – if he had cared to choose it.

But instead he went to London. This was not his first post abroad; he had been as curate in Barcelona and as exchange student and teacher at Union Seminary in New York. Important ecumenical contacts had been made. But the departure from Berlin in October 1933, had special programmatic significance. It marked his clear break with the church of the Third Reich. When he refused to conceal his stand in his dealings with the London congregation, one of the new Berlin pundits remarked: 'what a complicated sort of man you are!'. Little did he know Dietrich Bonhoeffer. His complexity was not such as to allow for any doubt between right and wrong. To probe the problem of ethics was not to indulge in the game of 'dialectical' theology. The search had to lead to the goal, the quest demanded an answer.

His eighteen months in London finally clarified his course. Others will have to tell of his work as Pastor at St Paul's, Aldgate, and in Sydenham;[1] his parishioners who are amongst us here today all know the impact of his brief ministry upon their own history, and none of us who lived as his guest in Forest Hill can ever forget that time. I vividly remember his sermon on Remembrance Sunday 1933; the text (Wisdom of Solomon 3:4, about the righteous) was 'but they are in peace', and he related the story of a patient, given up by the doctors, losing consciousness, hanging between life and death, looking, as it were, across the border and exclaiming: 'My God, this is beautiful!'. In many conversations of those days he remarked that to reach the age of 36 or 37 was quite enough for a Christian.

Yet he had still ten years left. And still he felt the burden of the word: 'we know not what to do'. 'I shall always remember him,' wrote the landlady of the boarding-house next door to his manse, 'pacing up and down our lounge, trying to decide whether to remain here or to give up his church here and return to the persecuted church in Germany; longing to visit Gandhi in India and feeling a premonition that unless he seized that moment he would never go. I knew, being himself, how he must eventually decide.' The decision repeated itself when shortly before the outbreak of the second war American friends invited him and tried to persuade him to stay. A brief visit ended with his final return to Germany. His place was by the side of his hard-pressed brethren and disciples in the ministry and with his own family which was increasingly drawn into the battle between Christ and Antichrist.

'We know not what to do; but our eyes are upon Thee.' The unrest of the quest ends in the discipleship of Christ, the theme of his last book,[2] now carried into practice in his own life. Law and Gospel, command and promise point to the one clear certain way which he had sought: 'only the believer is obedient, and only he who obeys believes'. From the 'life together' of which his brochure treats and which finds expression in the brotherhood of his seminary it becomes clear why the text says in the plural: 'we know not ... our eyes ...' For only within the communion of the church can the call of the Lord be heard and followed. But we speak, of course, of the one holy catholic church; and loyalty to his own confession never made Dietrich Bonhoeffer uncritical of the faults even in the Confessional Church, never unmindful of what he had learnt and received from other traditions and witnessed in his writings.

So he remains ecumenical in his attitude and more so, perhaps, than any other German theologian of his generation; so he refuses to enter the Second World War as an active combatant and renews the link with the British brethren, even after the frontiers have been closed, and travels into neutral countries become more dangerous than ever. He sees the growing dilemma of German Christians in their isolation; as in the Samson story one man's hand threatens to bring down the whole house; and there is, but for the very rarest exceptions, no understanding voice and no helping hand from without. Political action becomes inevitable. 'Why,' Dietrich said on his last visit here, 'should it always have to be the bad people who make the revolutions?'

He risked everything in this battle, as did his brother, his brothers-in-law, his friends. The outcome was at least uncertain, not only for the men, but for the cause. Bishop Bell has spoken of the apocalyptic undertones of his last conversation with him in Stockholm; the impending doom of Germany, even of Europe, appeared to have become certain in his mind. But even now and precisely now the word remained in force: 'We know not what to do, but our eyes are upon Thee.' Even the last two years in prison with their unexpected pastoral opportunities and the last two months after he and Klaus had been sentenced to death[3] were to him but a new, higher stage of discipleship. He had written of the grace of martyrdom. And the text of his first sermon had been: 'Likewise ye, when ye shall have done all those things which are commanded you say, We are unprofitable servants: we have done that which was our duty to do.'[4]

It is, perhaps, significant that we have few good pictures of him; he was averse to the photographers; the best shots show him in the family circle, with those to whom he belonged most closely and who escorted him to the end: the parents to the trial, two brothers-in-law to concentration camps and one brother to death. One of the happiest, freest, bravest homes in Germany has been bereft of its children – this is where the real victims of this war are to be found. Speech and hope fail us; we know not what to do. But let us not stop here, but follow the text: our eyes are upon Thee. In this turn from the agonizing quest to the confident discipleship lies the secret of Dietrich Bonhoeffer and his legacy for us. One can study it from the development of his style; from the earliest abstract analyses to the last pages of the *Cost of Discipleship* it grows more and more simple and unburdened. A reviewer of *Creation and Fall* writes: 'there is more in these hundred pages than in many a theological tome; every word is weighed and every sentence fits.' It was not different with his life. The yoke he took was easy, and the burden of his Master light; the vision cleared as he looked to Jesus, away from himself, and what years ago he had written of the Christian's hope, was now fulfilled: 'he becomes what he was – or rather, never was – a child.'[5]

We know not what to do. After these anxious weeks of uncertainty through which we have lived with you, dear Sabine and Gert,[6] and with your parents, we know less than ever how to carry on without the counsel of our brother on whom we could lean and who was so desperately needed by the Church at this time. Today we understand what Harnack said when Holl had died: 'with him a piece of my own life is carried to the grave'. Yet: our eyes are upon Thee. We believe in the communion of saints, the forgiveness of sins, the resurrection of the body and the life everlasting. We give thanks to God for the life, the suffering, the witness of our brother whose friends we were privileged to be. We pray God to lead us, too, through His discipleship from this world into His heavenly kingdom; to fulfil in us that other word with which Dietrich concluded his obituary of Harnack: *'non potest non laetari qui sperat in Dominum'*[7] – 'while in God confiding I cannot but rejoice'.

Notes

1. Both churches were destroyed by German bombs in the Second World War; St Paul's is now amalgamated with St George's Lutheran Church in Aldgate, and Sydenham rebuilt and named Dietrich Bonhoeffer Kirche.
2. *Ethics* and *Letters from Prison* were, of course, not available in 1945.
3. This information proved incorrect. There was, so far as we know now, no sentence of death before 8 April 1945, the night before his execution.
4. In August 1958, by strange coincidence, this was the text of Bishop Bell's last sermon in Nyborg, Denmark.
5. The concluding sentence in *Act and Being*.
6. Professor Gert Leibholz, and his wife, Dietrich's twin sister Sabine, lived as refugees in England during the war.
7. Possibly a quotation from Augustine.

APPENDIX 3

NICHOLSON SQUARE, EDINBURGH

Sermon given at Nicholson Square Methodist Church,
Edinburgh on the occasion when Ella Wardrop was received as
a 'Local Preacher', 23 April 1978

> I will go in the strength of the Lord;
> I will make mention of thy righteousness,
> even thine only.
>
> Psalm 71:16

They say: the day of preaching is gone. But it is not true. It may be
nearer the truth that we cannot preach, we have nothing to say,
and then no wonder that nobody is listening to the church. But if
one reads the signs of the times aright, there is in all sorts of places
and quarters a hunger for the Word, like the one of which Amos
speaks: 'a famine in the land, not a famine of bread, nor a thirst
for water, but of hearing the words of the Lord' (Amos 8:11). It
certainly was so in Wesley's day; and when so many ministers
failed to feed the flock, he had to invent Local Preachers.

Not only the people's hunger has to be stilled, but there is
another side to it: it is in the nature of the Word itself that it must
break out and be proclaimed: 'our God shall come, and shall not
keep silence' (Ps. 50:3). In spite of the prophets' reluctance and the
apostles' timidity, the Word must break through and be preached.

Who is sufficient for these things? (2 Cor. 2:16) It seems an
impossible undertaking. The young Karl Barth described graphi-
cally his predicament – note that this term comes from the same

stem as *praedicare*, preaching – when as a Pastor in a Swiss village he was faced with the open Bible and forced to break the Word to his people. 'I will go in the strength of the Lord': only thus it is made possible. For it is not our opinions, our pet notions, our 'singularities', in Wesley's phrase, that we have to proclaim; but 'as the Lord liveth, what the Lord saith unto me, that will I speak' (1 Kings 22:14). That distinguishes Micaiah, the true prophet, from the false prophets who tell the King what he wants to hear.

'I will go in the strength of the Lord'. So it is no empty phrase, when the Local Preacher makes his vows and faces his task 'with God's help, I will'. Johann Sebastian Bach wrote over each new cantata or composition 'JESU JUVA, Jesus help'. It is not so far away from the story of David confronting Goliath: 'Thou comest to me with a sword, and with a spear, and with a shield; but I come to thee in the name of the Lord of hosts' (1 Sam. 17:45).

'I will go in the strength of the Lord; I will make mention of thy righteousness'. Out of the abundance of the heart the mouth speaketh (Mt. 12:34). 'My heart is full of Christ and longs its glorious matter to declare' (MHB 270). Note how in this seventy-first Psalm the words 'daily', 'continually', 'all the day long' are repeated (e.g. vs. 6, 8, 14, 24). But at this point caution is needed – lest we mistake the Gospel for the pious phrase and make the costly grace cheap. It is, after all, God's Word and never simply at our disposal. When the Psalmist prays: 'O Lord, open Thou my lips' (Ps. 51:15), there is a perceptible pause before he continues: 'and my mouth shall show forth Thy praise'. Russell Maltby has spoken of what he called a preacher's damnation: 'He spoke of great things and made them small; of holy things and made them common; of God, and made Him of no account'. I will make mention of thy righteousness – this word 'mention' in the Hebrew language is a profound and extensive word; it includes weigh, ponder, remember, glorify, 'read mark, learn and inwardly digest'.

'I will make mention of Thy righteousness': here is the preacher's theme, the Gospel summed up in one word. For it is by grace that we are saved, by grace we live, by grace we are upheld in all our doings. Karl Barth again: 'a Christian is a man who does not live by his works but by the fact that his works are forgiven.'

> Just and holy is Thy name,
> I am all unrighteousness;
> False and full of sin I am,
> Thou art full of truth and grace (MHB 110).

'I will make mention of Thy righteousness, even Thine alone'. And in that little word 'alone' is the whole secret of the Protestant Reformation: by grace alone – not by any merit of our own; by scripture alone – not by the statutes and traditions of men (Mt. 15:3, 9); by Christ alone – not by any other mediator between God and man (1 Tim. 2:5). John Wesley said it in a famous letter 'On Preaching Christ':

> God loves you; therefore, love and obey him. Christ died for you; therefore, die to sin. Christ is risen; therefore, rise in the image of God. Christ liveth evermore; therefore live to God, till you live with Him in glory. So we preached, and so you believed. This is the scriptural way, the Methodist way, the true way. God grant we may never turn therefrom, to the right hand or to the left!

23 April is St George's Day. There are many legends about the dragon-killer, many pictures of the saint, many religious orders and societies called after his name. What is certain is that he died as a martyr and confessor in the fourth century. I will go in the strength of the Lord; I will make mention of Thy righteousness, even Thine only. And it seems to me that the Collect for St George's Day sums up exactly what this text has to say to us:

> O Lord God of hosts who didst give grace to Thy servant George to lay aside the fear of man and to confess Thee even unto death, grant, we pray Thee, that we and all our countrymen who bear office in the world, may think lightly of earthly place and honour and rather seek to please the Captain of our salvation who hath chosen us to be His soldiers, to whom with Thee and the Holy Ghost be thanks and praise from all the armies of Thy saints, now and for evermore. Amen.

APPENDIX 4

WESLEY'S HYMNS

At the beginning of their work on this biography Amos Cresswell wrote a summary of the essay by Franz Hildebrandt for the Introduction of Volume 7 of Wesley's works *A collection of Hymns for the Use of The People called Methodists*. He sent it to his friend Max Tow to be used as a possible reference point for Franz Hildebrandt's final thinking.

As the biography was being written Max felt this précis should be included – and so it was decided to put it as an appendix.

Late in 1983 Oxford University Press in conjunction with the Abingdon Press in Nashville, USA, published Volume 7 of the Works of John Wesley. It was a special volume for many folk because it was the 1780 collection of Wesley's Hymns, that definitive edition which to many Methodists is *the* great hymn book, ranking, according to the Congregational scholar Bernard Manning 'in Christian literature with the Psalms, *The Book of Common Prayer*, the Canon of the Mass'.

The difference was that this time it was edited by Franz Hildebrandt and Oliver Beckerlegge assisted by James Dale and it had Biblical references for the hymns and an introduction of seventy pages along with many other useful pieces in footnotes and especially in appendices.

Amongst the essays which form the Introduction, the first is by Franz Hildebrandt on the words of John Wesley used to describe that 1780 Hymn Book: 'a little body of experimental and practical divinity'.

Before this essay was written he had laid out carefully his

ground plan for following the theology of the Wesleys. He tends to treat John and Charles together as John edited so very much of the work of Charles. In his book *From Luther to Wesley* he shows that 'Wesley' is in the tradition of the Reformation. But his best introduction to his thinking about 'Wesley' is in this essay, even though it is his last official publication on that theme.

One of the traditions of the Reformation on to which the Wesleys latched was the teaching of the faith through the singing of hymns. When Franz Hildebrandt came to the Wesleys he picked up the hymns and, added to his own love of music and singing, it made him one with Charles. Both the theology contained within the hymns and the expression of that theology gripped him and, as one of his means of spiritual sustenance, he lived with Wesley's hymns. Towards the end of his life he used to say that his three great books were: *The King James Bible*; *The Book of Common Prayer* and *Wesley's Hymns*.

In this introductory article his love for Charles and John speaks through every line.

Hildebrandt begins by stating that whereas other traditions refer to Articles and Confessions of Faith, Methodists, while accepting the historic creeds, find their doctrines expressed in three sets of Biblical expositions: Wesley's Sermons, Notes on the New Testament and Hymns. 'It is doubtful if without the hymns there could have been a Methodist Revival.'

The main purpose of the 1780 Hymn Book edited and published by John with most hymns by Charles, was as a primer of theology for the Methodist people and a manual for public worship and private devotion. Franz Hildebrandt admits that at times one needs to look outside the '1780 Book' for expressions of the faith on some themes.

The complex Wesley relationship means that John stands *behind* Charles authorizing the publication, here and there editing and changing, occasionally leaving and not quite accepting his brother's words, sometimes underlining a truth with a 'yes' or a difference with a 'no'. Charles receives the limelight. In the Preface to the 1780 Book, John places on record his opinion of Charles' poetic genius and gives the book his theological imprimatur as a 'distinct and full account of scriptural Chaistianity, a declaration of the heights and depths of religion, speculative and practical'.

The hymns sing of the attributes of God, the heights and depths of the love of Christ, and they attack many plausible errors but their purpose is 'perfecting holiness in the fear of God', scriptural Christianity. 'The Bible, the whole Bible, nothing but the Bible – this is the theme of John Wesley's preaching and the glory of Charles' hymns.' Experience is not a second source of authority but, in John's own words, 'Experience is sufficient to *confirm* a doctrine which is grounded on scripture'.

The table of contents represents this experience and shows the stages in which the Gospel is appropriated: 'For believers rejoicing, fighting, praying etc: for the Society meeting giving thanks, parting. One man's experience and inspiration becomes the voice of the whole church. Charles had a new song in his mouth. He had been caught by Luther's commentary on Galatians 2.20. He needs no concordance. The Bible and the *Book of Common Prayer* lie behind it all. When puzzled about a line the rule is 'if in doubt, it is scriptural'.

Hildebrandt suggests that Charles Wesley uses the Bible better than Watts or the German writers whom John translated. He offers a summary of key texts which outline Charles' theology (in footnote 4, p. 5). Yet Charles is no 'fundamentalist' but holds to the broad meaning of scripture. Then he suggests some main themes.

He cites the fact that Charles dwells 'on the name of Jesus'. His name is the secret of His nature. 'Wrestling Jacob' is a good example of this:

> Wrestling I will not let Thee go
> Till I thy name, thy nature know
>
> Thy mercies never shall remove
> Thy nature and thy name is love

Many hymns outline this theme: 'Jesus is his name'; 'Thy new best name of love'; 'I dare believe in Jesu's name'; 'Thy mighty name salvation is' ... and so on. We use it in battle shouting 'our Deliverer's name' – for the Church Militant is the New Israel and Jesus is 'Captain of Israel's host '... militant here on earth, triumphant in heaven: 'One church above, beneath ...' 'One army of the living God' ... 'Deliverer' is the favourite name for the Saviour.

Hildebrandt's understanding of Wesley's hymns would bring the Wesleys completely in accord with those who rightly see the

Old Testament not as a Jewish book of faith but clearly as the preliminary and necessary part of *Christian* scriptures without which we cannot rightly understand Christ. 'As Wesley rhymes his way through the books of the Old Testament the Christological interpretation is basic and compelling.'

But, says Hildebrandt, when turning to the New Testament Wesley opens the book at its title page and asks the all-important question

> And can it be that I should gain
> An interest in the Saviour's blood?

What that interest is, is spelt out 'in a few verses that admit no possible abbreviation. From the mystery of godliness (the Immortal dies) to the *kenosis* (empties himself of all but love) to the liberation of the captive (my chains fell off, my heart was free) to the boldness of imputed and imparted righteousness:

> Alive in him, my living head,
> And clothed in righteousness divine.
> Bold I approach the eternal throne,
> And claim the crown, through Christ, my own.

The wonder that it should happen 'to me' never left Wesley as it never left St Paul. It is 'the glory not to be expressed, the joy unspeakable'. As with Paul, the word 'unspeakable' is indispensable in Wesley's vocabulary. And the Aldersgate discovery issues in mission

> 'I long to know and to make known
> The heights and depths of love divine'

Hildebrandt points out that we find it difficult if we are described as 'guilty brethren' but it is an idea central to Wesley and to the Bible. Then with a telling quotation from his friend Dietrich Bonhoeffer (*Life Together*) he underlines the point.

The misery and sin which is the essence of man turns into the song about the Person and Work of Christ. 'He breaks the power of cancelled sin'; 'Thou, O Christ, art all I want.' This theme alone needs a separate treatise and many great hymns on the incarnation, sufferings and glory are omitted from the 1780 Collection;

but there are enough to make the point.

If any one hymn could summarize Wesley's thought it would be 'With glorious clouds encompassed round'. Here is the waiting with bated breath for the revelation of the mystery, 'the wonderful design 'where' the Man of grief and love' comes and is 'the pardoning God I know' who redeems and lifts the sinners to 'the heights and depths of grace'.

Wesley knows the 'weight ' of the Gospel which captivates his every thought. He also knows 'the pursuing grace'. He does not wish for the freedom which makes him want to move away from God whose only wish is that we ask for more love. This means praying for the Holy Spirit to move within us. He is the seal of our redemption. We need the Spirit to be revealed in us more and more so that we know and feel the assurance that God has pardoned us. The secret of Wesley's 'experimental' divinity is the Johannine (I John 4.13) 'hereby we know' though sometimes we need to wait patiently 'to prove that Jesus is thy healing name'.

The *raison d'être* of Methodism is the move to holiness. Charles wrote many hymns specifically on this theme though his other hymns are shot through with the subject. The 'chief of sinners' of I Timothy reaches the triumphal confession of II Timothy 'I have fought the good fight':

> Kept by the power of grace divine
> I have the faith maintained

and:

> Ready for all thy perfect will
> My acts of faith and love repeat
> Till death thy endless mercies seal
> And make the sacrifice complete.

The mountain of sin which stands in the way can be removed, for:

> All things are possible to God
> To Christ the power of God in man
> To me when I am all renewed
> When I, in Christ, am formed again
> And witness, from all sin set free,
> All things are possible to me.

John and Charles were not always in accord on the theme of perfection. Charles claimed it was 'by degrees insensible' but John added the footnote 'both suddenly and gradually'. Both taught the Second Blessing (which cannot be proved to be scriptural) and Charles was very critical of the 'professors of perfection'.

There are prayers for 'a blessing to make the first complete' ' to take away my inbred sin', 'to redeem from all iniquity'. There are hymns for believers groaning for full redemption but the crucial fact is that they are *believers*, who are rejoicing, fighting, praying, watching, groaning for full redemption, etc.

The second blessing can be greeted with the unexpected warning:

> When e'er thou dost thy grace bestow
> Lest *proudly* I the blessing *show*
> A second grace impart
> 'Tell it to none' – with vain delight
> 'Tell it to none' – in mercy write
> Upon my broken heart

Such was and is indeed the goal but there is no set time table. Prayer is the heart of the matter. It takes the place of self-reflection:

> Do with me, Lord, as seems thee meet
> But let me always pray.

The question 'when?' is answered when the servant of the Lord has ceased from his own works and left 'the deed, the time, the manner' to God, knowing that He does all things right. 'The passive clay' bears 'the stamp' of the Lord.

Hildebrandt concludes with a few comments on the fact that there are thirteen hymns describing heaven in the *Collection* though countless more look in the same direction. Heaven, for John, means to see God, to know God and to love God and to receive more and more of the love. For Charles the end is 'all the heights of holiness ... all the depths of humble love' and 'all the silent heaven of love'. Silence concludes his picture of the beatific vision:

That great mysterious Diety
We soon with open face shall see;
   The beatific sight
Shall fill heaven's sounding courts with praise
And wide diffuse the golden blaze
   Of everlasting light.

The Father shining on his Throne
The glorious, co-eternal Son
   The Spirit, one and seven,
Conspire our rapture to complete
And lo! we fall before his foot
   And silence heightens heaven.

And this, as Hildebrandt points out, is written 'for believers suffering'. On our march to the new Jerusalem 'that palace of the glorious King – we find it nearer while we sing'.

'Antepast of heaven' is a key phrase and the first hymn in the *Collection* bids us:

Anticipate your heaven below
And own that love is heaven

But there is no *theologia gloriae* (theology of glory) without *theologia crucis* (theology of the cross): 'always to Jesus look' and then 'feel that Christ is all and all'. 'Pardon and holiness and heaven' is but a revised version of St Paul's theology:

This is a new song which none but the redeemed can sing:

Come Jesus and loose the stammer's tongue
And teach even us the spiritual song.

This point was always dear to the heart of Franz Hildebrandt. Singing about heaven is something for which our world and, maybe, our church has little time today – to our loss. We are so eager to be contemporary, 'with it,' that we have lost our perspective and so lose out on the gospel.

The words of Peter Boehler to John Wesley 'Preach faith till you have it and then, because you have it, you will preach faith' can be adapted to the singing of the faith also, though Hildebrandt reminds us in an age when Charles Wesley's Bible – the King James Version – has been largely rejected, there is a tendency to lose hymns based on it. We cannot afford to set aside 'an incomparable witness to an indispensable truth.' We do well to remember that our priceless gift to the universal church is the faith as sung in the hymns of the Wesleys. And as the church uses this treasure we trust they will honour John Wesley's plea – even if his own followers have not always been so careful – and leave the hymns as they are without alteration and mutilation.

In this essay one can capture the tremendous enthusiasm allied to the vast knowledge of one who knows the Wesleys so well that their words become an expression of his own faith. There is joy also in the fact that the heights and depths of that faith are explained so that the ordinary person can grasp it. The wonder of Wesley to Franz Hildebrandt is that the farm hand and the miner can sing with the professors and scholars in unison and neither finds measure nor end in that expression.

Working on the '1780 Book' was a service of love, albeit at times painful, for he had severed his official link with Methodism in distressing circumstances. Franz knew his Bible (King James) and Prayer Book and he knew the riches which the Wesleys had drawn from Germany. He himself had followed the same route. But in the end coming before God and the Lord Jesus Christ through the power of the Holy Spirit is what matters most. To this end he was dedicated and in a remarkable journey he opens up the treasury of the Kingdom of God.

Probably the essay on Wesley's Hymns is his greatest spiritual gift to us all.

APPENDIX 5

HIS LAST SERMON AT SLATEFORD-LONGSTONE C.S. CHURCH

Let the words of my mouth and the meditations of my heart be now and always acceptable in Thy sight, O Lord, my Strength and my Redeemer. Amen.

Our text, read in the second lesson, is taken from Acts chapter 8, verse 39. 'And when they came up out of the water, the spirit of the Lord caught up Philip and the eunuch saw him no more. And he went on his way rejoicing.'

This probably is my favourite story in the Bible. I've preached on it more often than any other text. My records tell me that it is ten years since I preached it from this pulpit. So I return to it today not because of Ethiopia* – though Heaven knows a lot could be said about this – and not because it was a eunuch, which meant that the man did not qualify for a place in the congregation of Israel and in all probability he may have been a Gentile and out of the chosen flock altogether, and not even because he had come to Jerusalem to worship – imagine the length of the journey – and the clear purpose of going to the temple to worship (great lessons could be learned from all this): No! it is because of the last sentence 'the Spirit of the Lord caught up Philip and the eunuch saw him now more. And he went on his way rejoicing.'

What are the reasons for this rejoicing? First of all because he

*There was a famine in Ethiopia at the time this sermon was preached.

had a Bible – to be exact he had one scroll of it, the prophet Isaiah – for no volume in complete form existed as yet, but there he is sitting in his chariot on the return journey reading the prophet Isaiah. How many of us bother, I wonder, to look up the Bible when it has been preached here?

The passage that he reads is: Isaiah 53, the story of the crucified Messiah. And when Philip is told by the spirit to join himself to the chariot Philip of course asks 'Do you understand what you are reading?' and the eunuch replies 'How can I unless someone guides me?' Philip then joins the chariot and expounds Isaiah 53.

We are infinitely more fortunate than the eunuch. We know of whom the prophet is speaking for we with the Old Testament have the New and that means we have the clue that opens those pages. We know that in Jesus Christ all the promises of God are fulfilled. We have, in short, the Gospel and plenty of people to guide us, old and new commentators, notes of the Bible Reading Fellowship, classes in which the Bible can be studied open to us all. We are indeed blessed if we see, blessed if we hear. And let us not exaggerate the role of the commentators. It is quite an erroneous notion to hold that the Bible is an obscure book. In this way the Roman Church has always claimed that the church has to be the Master over the Word and without it, the church cannot be understood. The Bible, said the Reformers, is a plain, clear, open book to all and it is not in doubt what its comfortable words say. If you want it in three words, it is 'the grace of our Lord Jesus Christ and the love of God and the fellowship of the Holy Spirit.' So that it is safe to leave a man alone with his Bible and to be guided by Him who really opens the book.

> Come Holy Ghost, for moved by Thee
> The prophets wrote and spoke
> Unlock the truth, Thyself the key
> Unseal the sacred Book

So Philip began from this passage and preached to him Jesus. And this is the function of preaching anytime anyone stands in this pulpit. To preach Jesus, to restore the book to its original oral form so that the word of God speaks to us today and always and we listen.

The Revised Standard Version paraphrases this by saying 'He preached to him the good news of Jesus'. That is what 'gospel' means. That is what preaching does. It's the good news. Never on any account go for that dreadful hymn 'Tell me the old, old story ...' It's nothing of the kind. It's a *new* living powerful word of God. It is Jesus Christ preached by prophets in the Old Testament and apostles in the New Testament and the church is but a servant and handmaid of the all important 'Word'. That is why he went on his way rejoicing.

And then the second reason is that he is baptized, by immersion of course, when they come to water. And Philip baptizes him 'in the name of Jesus'. It is not Philip anymore that matters but Jesus – and the name that is given to me indicates whose property I am. There is a famous question and answer in the old Heidelberg Catechism going back to the sixteenth century. This is how it opens:

> What is Thy only comfort in life and death?
> This, that I, body and soul, living or dying, am not my own but my
> dear Lord Jesus Christ's who has redeemed me.

That is the foundation stone of our faith and that is important enough for Luther, for example, in hours of temptation or depression to write in front of himself the Latin words 'I am baptized' so as to make it quite clear to the devil that he belonged to Jesus. He is baptized on confession of faith. 'If thou believest with all thy heart, thou mayest ...' But these words are not contained in all handwritings (manuscripts). They are put here at the bottom of the page and perhaps this is a useful reminder that what matters supremely is not that we believe but that we are baptized.

People talk glibly and again quite wrongly about 'the time when I accepted Christ'. This is quite unscriptural and unimportant. What matters is that He accepted me and that I am His and He is mine. As a friend of mine decades ago put it at a valedictory missionary service, he said 'As I'm going out my grip of Him is very shaky, but His grip of me is very strong'. Precisely! That is what matters. The grace of our baptism; the love from which nothing can separate us; the Word and Sacrament that stand forever. That is why he went on his way rejoicing.

And, lastly, the reason for this joy is that he has found company. He is in the company of Philip and he is, by implication, a member of the church. In the phrase of the English Prayer

Book 'incorporate members of thy mystical body which is the blessed company of all faithful people'. That is the best definition I know of the church 'the blessed company of all faithful people'. And that takes us beyond the boundaries of space and time. It links us here in the church militant with those who fight for their faith and the church triumphant in heaven with those that on another shore sing his praise.

And you note that this rejoicing takes place when the Spirit has removed Philip and 'the eunuch saw him no more'. I think of three pictures, that hang over my bed, of friends of mine that counted for a great deal and they are all in the church triumphant. And the story of the travel of this eunuch to Jerusalem and back becomes a reminder of the travel in which we are all engaged, the travel to the world to come, to the life everlasting. It is a thousand pities that the latest hymn book has removed the section which was headed in the old one 'Pilgrimage and Guidance' (and Perseverance) for that is an essential part of our faith.

'And he went on his way rejoicing.' It doesn't mean that you are artificially grinning all the time. That type of Christian has never appealed to me. I'm even doubtful if you can talk glibly as people do about a 'radiant faith'. The source of rejoicing is in no one else but the Holy Spirit. 'I will see you again' says Jesus 'and your hearts will rejoice and your joy no man taketh from you.' It is the Spirit of the Lord that is at work; the One that tells Philip to join himself to this Chariot, the One that opens the Bible and points to Christ, the One that is effective in the baptism of the believer and the One that points us on our way to heaven.

> Then let us rejoice
> In heart and in voice
> Our Leader pursue
> And shout as we travel the wilderness through.
> With the Spirit above
> To Zion we move
> Triumphant arise
> And walk with our Lord until we fly to the skies.
>   Amen.

FURTHER READING

Many books have been written about the rise of Hitler. In my view three stand out. They are William Shirer's *Rise and Fall of the Third Reich* and two by Alan Bullock: *Hitler – a Study in Tyranny* and *Parallel Lives – Hitler and Stalin*. Sadly their weakness is that they almost totally ignore the Church Struggle – a mistake Hitler did not make!

Thus the best book in English is Eberhard Bethge's magnificent biography: *Dietrich Bonhoeffer* (Collins. Fount). Also a first class historical novel, extremely carefully researched is *The Cup of Wrath* by Mary Glazener (Gracewing, 1996). Usually people say 'I just couldn't put it down.'

The major work, unfortunately only published in German, is by Wilhelm Niemoeller, Martin's brother, *Kampf und Zeugnis der Bekennenden Kirche* (Bielefeld, 1946), a book recommended to me by Franz Hildebrandt himself. There are other volumes: *Kirche in der Krise* and *Um Verkuendigung und Ordnung der Kirche* which contain various documents. (I am indebted to my friend Pastor Eberhard Strecker for obtaining these and other books for me.) A slim volume, in English, by E. H. Robertson, *Christians Against Hitler*, makes a starting point.

There are many good books in English about Martin Niemoeller (those by Dietmar Schmidt and James Bentley are recommended) and Dietrich Bonhoeffer (Keith Clements, Otto Dudzus, Edwin Robertson and Renate Wind are just some of the many writers on his life and thought). One should always read Bonhoeffer's *Cost of Discipleship* and *Letters and Papers from Prison*. I would bracket with these the collection of letters and testimonies gathered under the title *Dying We Live* (Collins. Fount), surely due for another reprint. It is also a spiritual classic. See also *A Spy for God* by Pierre Joffroy (Fount).

Perhaps one day Dr Holger Roggelin's published thesis *Franz Hildebrandt – ein lutherischer Dissenter in Kirchenkampf und Exil* will be translated and published in the UK. He has travelled in the same way as Mary Glazener and we have done through the Hildebrandt letters, books and papers, but he has delved more deeply into the early years in Germany.

Hildebrandt's various books are mentioned in the text, but *From Luther to Wesley* (Luttherworth, 1951) is the place to start. He wrote a great deal and in his thesis Dr Holger Roggelin has five pages listing Hildebrandt's many writings.

A.S.C.

INDEX

Franz Hildebrandt's early ministry began and developed under the shadow of the swastika in Hitler's Nazi Germany. His close, deep friendship and pastoral colleagueship with Dietrich Bonhoeffer in fighting that evil power marked them both as true witnesses for Jesus Christ.

His subsequent exile to England (1937) – his mother was Jewish – his work as a pastor to refugees, as a Methodist minister, as a professor of theology in the USA and finally as assistant pastor in the Church of Scotland reveal him as a man who was fearless for the Gospel and who was also a loving, caring friend practising the faith both in words and life. His faithful witness led him at times to face difficult and painful decisions.

On his pilgrimage of faith he was captured by the vibrant hymns of Charles Wesley, Cranmer's *Book of Common Prayer* and the 'King James Bible'.

Two of his friends, Amos Cresswell and Max Tow tell the story of this Mr Valiant-for-Truth.

'Without the existence of this spirited, upright and consistent friend of Bonhoeffer in especially important years one cannot have and know Dietrich Bonhoeffer . . .'
Eberhard Bethge

'I have been extraordinarily pleased to hear that you have written a biography of Franz Hildebrandt. My parents would also have been very happy about it.'
Marianne Leibholtz, daughter of Dietrich Bonhoeffer's twin sister Sabine

---

Amos Cresswell was born and brought up in the West Midlands of England. He graduated from the Universities of Durham and Cambridge and spent a year in a seminary in Germany. After a time teaching, he entered the Methodist Ministry in 1949 and served in England in the Clitheroe, Darlaston, Bramhall and Welwyn circuits as well as teaching in Richmond and Cliff Colleges. In 1976 he became Chairman of the Plymouth and Exeter District of the Methodist Church where he served for fifteen years. In 1983 he was elected President of the Methodist Conference of the United Kingdom. He has preached widely and is now retired in North Devon where he lives with his wife Evelyn.

Maxwell Tow is a retired United Methodist Minister who lives with his wife Geri in Deposit, New York. A native of Cedar Rapids, Iowa, he received his BA degree from Iowa University and his M.Div from the Theological School of Drew University. He has served churches in Paterson and Maplewood, New Jersey and Windsor, New York. He also served as Director of Urban Ministries in Paterson and District Superintendent in the Northern New Jersey Conference.

GRACEWING